Feminisms Matter

Feminisms Matter

DEBATES, THEORIES, ACTIVISM

VICTORIA L. BROMLEY

UNIVERSITY OF TORONTO PRESS

Library and Archives Canada Cataloguing in Publication

Bromley, Victoria L., 1959–
    Feminisms matter : debates, theories, activism / Victoria L. Bromley.

Includes bibliographical references and index.
ISBN 978-1-4426-0500-8

    1. Feminism.   2. Anti-feminism.   3. Feminist theory.   4. Women political
activists.   I. Title.

HQ1154.B85 2012   305.42   C2012-905269-8

We welcome comments and suggestions regarding any aspect of our publications—
please feel free to contact us at news@utphighereducation.com or visit our Internet
site at www.utppublishing.com.

North America
5201 Dufferin Street
North York, Ontario
Canada, M3H 5T8

2250 Military Road
Tonawanda, New York
USA, 14150

ORDERS PHONE: 1-800-565-9523
ORDERS FAX: 1-800-221-9985
ORDERS E-MAIL: utpbooks@utpress.utoronto.ca

UK, Ireland, and continental Europe
NBN International
Estover Road, Plymouth, PL6 7PY, UK
ORDERS PHONE: 44 (0) 1752 202301
ORDERS FAX: 44 (0) 1752 202333
ORDERS E-MAIL: enquiries@nbninternational.com

Every effort has been made to contact copyright holders; in the event of an error or
omission, please notify the publisher.

This book is printed on paper containing 100% post-consumer fibre.

The University of Toronto Press acknowledges the financial support for its publishing
activities of the Government of Canada through the Canada Book Fund.

Cover design: Michel Vrana. Image composited with photos from Shutterstock: wall,
donatas1205; figure, Warren Goldswain.
Text design: Zack Taylor, Metapolis.

Printed in Canada

RECYCLED
Paper made from
recycled material
FSC
www.fsc.org   FSC® C103567

For my family James, Yvonne, Tekie, and Kuwor.

CONTENTS

ACKNOWLEDGEMENTS

I would like to begin by thanking my students over many years who have given me the opportunity to teach and learn alongside them. You have helped to create a space for us to explore feminisms from diverse perspectives, to travel together through feminist debates, and to engage in feminist activism. I would also like to thank my many dedicated teaching assistants who have enriched my teaching experience, provided insights into student perceptions, and helped me to develop my feminist pedagogy.

I would like to thank my friends and colleagues for their unwavering support throughout the process. To Aalya Ahmad, my friend and colleague: you have been both my academic sounding board and intellectual cheerleader. You were always ready to listen to my ideas, help me over the stumbling blocks, and edit my work before I would let anyone else read it. You made it possible for me to write this book. To Beth Hughes, my friend and colleague, you made the often-lonely task of writing this book tolerable. You suffered through my almost daily updates. Allowing me to talk about my progress and difficulties was more important than you will ever know. The endless coffee shop excursions to talk about not just the book but about life made this book possible. Your comments on drafts were invaluable to the end product but your friendship extends far beyond this publication. To Virginia Caputo, who is my friend, mentor and colleague, you have taught me what it means to be a feminist. Your generosity of spirit on every level offers a model for teaching and living life to its fullest. Your enduring support and confidence in me has given me the strength to continue the fight for justice. To Pamela Walker, my friend, trusted advisor and colleague, your comments on this book were excellent and made it a better product. Your sense of humour, even under difficult circumstances, is always appreciated. To Karen March, my friend and colleague, thank you for sharing your vast intellectual insights regarding qualitative methodologies. You were incredibly generous with your time in offering critical commentary, and your record for fastest turnaround on chapter drafts remains unchallenged. I want to thank André Turcotte for carefully reading a book about which you knew nothing and yet still provided great insights! To Andrew Asare, thank you for creating diagrams that allowed some of my concepts to be visually interpreted by readers. Mark Slater, our telephone collaborations on the illustrations for the text were an enriching experience. Your ability to interpret my sense of humour graphically has made this a very different kind of feminist book.

I wish to thank the fantastic team at the University of Toronto Press, especially my editor Tracey Arndt who believed in the need for a feminist text of this type and my ability to deliver it. Thanks also to Beth McAuley and her team for pushing me to make this book better.

Finally, I would like to thank my family. To my daughters, Tekie and Kuwor, you have made my life complete by allowing me to be your "other" mom. I appreciate deeply the loving care you gave my mom when I was diverted by writing and unable to do so. My love and appreciation for you both is immeasurable. To my mother, Yvonne, who will never read this book because of her ongoing struggle with Alzheimer's disease, you have always given me the unconditional love that has made me believe that a better world is possible. And lastly, to my husband James, you have been my constant support and inspiration. Your unconditional love, unfailing trust, and constant belief in me has made my life complete.

INTRODUCTION

As you sit on the bus, in the library, at home in the living room, or in a commons on campus, you might find people looking over your shoulder and asking you what you're reading. When you respond, "I'm reading *Feminisms Matter: Debates, Theories, Activism*," they might ask you why. Why indeed? Perhaps it's because you're interested in feminisms or because the book has been assigned as part of a course you're taking. The word on the street, on the other hand, is that feminism is dead, so what could possibly be important about feminism? The short answer is, "Everything!" The longer answer is that feminisms help us to understand ourselves and the world in which we live. Feminisms help us to redress oppressions and bring about social change. Most people, if they don't quickly change the subject to something more neutral like the weather, roll their eyes and dismiss these statements as naïve or just plain crazy. But then there are the people who are genuinely interested in how we can go about envisioning and making social change. These are the folks who may not think of themselves as feminists but who still want to know more. So be prepared: the questions will soon follow, and not just from other people—you may have some interesting ones, too. Because once you get feminisms, you will look at things differently.

This book is a reader-friendly guide to thinking through the multiplicities of feminisms: their various conceptualizations; the diverse issues they address; the critical dialogues among feminisms, feminists, and activists; the struggles and achievements of women's movement; and strategies for social change. The book incorporates exercises, questions, illustrations, and case studies as learning tools to assist in the process of thinking through feminisms. Readers are invited to learn not only about feminisms but also to think about how feminist theories can help us understand the world in which we live and even frame social change.

As a way of opening the door to new ways of seeing the world, this book confronts the major reasons that people offer for not being feminists. This book challenges negative stereotypes, unravels myths, and confronts assumptions about feminisms, and goes beyond the response, "I'm not a feminist but..." *Feminisms Matter: Debates, Theories, Activism* encourages readers to engage in processes of critical thinking about feminisms that move beyond popular anti-feminist rhetoric.

As you read, you will become familiar with the basic concepts and definitions commonly used by feminists while demystifying the notion that theory is "too hard" and "too abstract." My purpose here is not to provide the ultimate feminist theory text; others have already done this extremely well. Nor is my goal to reproduce the work of numerous excellent feminist anthologies. The goal here is threefold: to spark your curiosity about theory, to lead you to recognize that theory is something you already do, and to build your confidence around theorizing and critical thinking. Each of these goals, of course, requires thinking through feminisms, debates, theories, and activism. As readers, you will spend a considerable amount of time engaged in theorizing rather than just learning theories. This process makes it possible for you to understand theories, not as grand narratives that need to be apprehended and compartmentalized into units of thought, but as tools with everyday value and application. As you read, you will activate feminist theories and see how they make sense in understanding your lived experiences. Engaging with theory and debates as well as activism in this way is key to developing critical feminist thinking.

Feminisms Matter encourages explorations of power, privilege, self-location, and the locations of others, as well as intersectionalities of sex, gender, race, class, sexuality, age, and ability. To understand the value of feminisms and feminist theories, it is necessary to look at where feminisms come from and where they still need to go. This means that feminisms are still incomplete and that more work needs to be done. The book may be thought of as a road map, giving readers the necessary theoretical tools to navigate this journey. These tools will be developed throughout the text to help strengthen critical analytic skills.

Rather than proposing an all-encompassing definition of feminism from the start, I encourage readers to engage in an experiential understanding, supported by case studies and illustrations, of the key concepts of feminist theories and the herstories of feminist and women's movement. I use the term "women's movement" throughout the book to indicate the plurality and diversity of movements across time and space. Yet, it also recognizes a connection, even solidarity, across borders and issues of concerns in our increasingly globalized world. Others might use "women's movements" in the plural for similar reasons. I am making this point here because of the historical debates around "the women's movement." Of concern for feminists is the implication of "*the*" in "*the* women's movement." Here it implies that there was/is but one women's movement and that this movement is dominated by mainstream, white, middle-class, heterosexual, able-bodied women. This is certainly not the case. Women's movement is everywhere; the goals are diverse; the strategies to achieve these goals vary; anyone can participate; and the ways that we participate are as varied as the goals and strategies we can imagine for change.

The reader will begin to recognize feminism as both a theoretical lens through which to understand the world in which we live, and an interconnected movement to end sexism, racism, classism, and all the other "isms" that plague our communities and our world. Consequently, the book allows the reader to consider the possibility that feminisms are valid theories (or lenses) through which to understand, and to act in, their lives.

Feminisms Matter offers a non-traditional pedagogical approach to women's and gender studies in that it veers from the usual linear trajectory of teaching about women's movement first and learning about theory second. This linearity implies that women's movement existed before theorizing. To present women's movement in ways that are theory-free is misleading. Rather, theory and practice have always been interwoven and inseparable. Accordingly, theories are presented entwined with practices and movements are paired with theories in an attempt to challenge this artificial separation.

The illustrations in *Feminisms Matter* are meant to be provocative, challenging, and in some cases unsettling. It is important to consider these emotions when reading the illustrations. Readers should note that the depictions closely reflect what we encounter in our lived experiences; that is, feminized and masculinized bodies are not marked and represented in the same ways. Feminized bodies may be hypersexualized and masculinized bodies hyper-masculinized. This leaves space for the reader to question how, why, and if such depictions mirror or misrepresent our realities.

Feminisms Matter encourages curiosity and questions among readers. Each chapter is supplemented by study questions, discussion questions, and activities to create further dialogue. These "20-minute workouts for feminist muscles" draw upon many years of classroom experience. They ask readers to examine their experiences of power, empowerment, and disempowerment, and then to question how these experiences may be gendered, raced, classed, or embedded in systemic relations of power. Both exercises and case studies will provide critical insights into popular culture, which occupies a major space in our lives. They are useful ways for readers to frame feminist questions and use feminist theories.

Engaging in critical self-reflection builds readers' self-location in the research process as well as critical engagement in the world around them. Readers will become familiar with how feminisms and feminist theories can frame and inform everyday decisions, such as drinking fair trade coffee, or purchasing clothing that is not produced in sweatshops. *Feminisms Matter* asks: "What is the link? What should we do about it?" This book presents alternative actions to avoid the conclusion that the issue is just too overwhelming to do much about it. Such critical self-reflection serves to challenge preconceived ideas and expose biases.

My purpose in writing this book is to demystify terms, to challenge backlash, to show the practicality and usefulness of feminist theory, to demonstrate that theorizing is an activity we already do, and to make theory visible in everyday practices. The book provides readers with a guide to feminist theoretical thinking and practices to get people, especially young women and men, thinking about social change and getting involved in feminist and social justice movements.

While there are many excellent feminist anthologies and feminist theory texts, this book provides tools on how to "do" feminisms, understand feminisms, and use feminist theory to understand the world and our place in it. I suggest that the process of learning about feminisms and feminist theories will incite readers to "do" feminisms. Feminisms help us understand our education as more than an exercise in memory work. Feminisms engage us in ongoing praxis, the linking of theory and practice at the everyday level. Finally, readers will develop problem-solving skills that they can use in the real world.

The book is reader-friendly, with accessible language and humour wherever possible. Feminists are often depicted as dour and overly serious, not taking time to laugh and enjoy life. *Feminisms Matter* challenges the negative stereotypes about angry, vengeful feminists. It takes back feminism, representing it as a valuable perspective and a substantial tool for enacting social change.

As you read, you will explore why and how theories emerge and why this process matters. It's important to get women and men talking about power: who has it and who doesn't. The discovery that theory is always about some ideas (and not others) and for some people (and not others) will demonstrate the power of theory itself. Different theories have different areas of focus and different levels of analysis. Different feminist theories, therefore, can work together to reveal new understandings. Readers will be encouraged to recognize that what they already do is theory, just without the fancy names and terms. We already theorize to make sense of the world around us, to make decisions, and to solve problems. We develop working assumptions to guide us based on what we know and what we have experienced.

Ultimately, this text encourages the reader to think about the world critically, empathetically, imaginatively, and with hope. My own hope is to encourage thinking, about the world and our places in it, as feminists. *Feminisms Matter* shows us how the world we already "know" can look very different when seen through feminisms. Active learning is the key to understanding feminisms. Education is not for the faint of heart; it is not accessible to all, and therefore, we must be active participants in the learning process. As Adrienne Rich (1977) suggests, we must claim our education.

I myself have never been able to find out precisely what a feminist is; I only know that people call me a feminist whenever I express sentiments that differentiate me from a doormat.

—REBECCA WEST, 1913

CHAPTER ONE

DON'T CALL ME THAT!

FEMINISM AND OTHER "F-WORDS"

The F-word

When you hear the word "feminism" or "feminist," you might find yourself in a quandary. You might be curious, furious, or you might just want to run for cover. Feminism is a word that is frequently used and often abused. Where you hear it, who says it, and the context in which it is used often influences your reaction. How can the "F-word" stir up such emotion?

At the root of such reactions is the bad reputation that feminism continues to experience as a result of the powerful negative stereotypes in everyday culture. The proverbial four-letter F-word has nothing on the other F-words: feminine, female, femme fatale, and of course, feminism and feminist. Even flatulence has a better "rep" than feminism.

We've all heard the stereotypes. Feminists are angry, hairy, combat-boot-wearing, bra-burning, ball-breaking, man-hating, ugly, lesbian, and/or queer. Yet, when I look in the mirror, this is not what I see. I simply see myself, with all my strengths and weaknesses. However, this wasn't always the case. In my pre-feminist days—yes, there was a light bulb moment when I realized that the F-word made sense to me—when I looked in the mirror, I saw mostly my weaknesses, and many of these were related to my being female. I did not seem to embody the so-called essences, the very core characteristics I had been told were critical to being a woman.

1

Illustration 1.1: Is this what a feminist looks like? Stereotyping feminists as ugly, hairy, man-hating, ball-breaking lesbians.

Essentialism, the idea that a woman or a man can be defined by a single characteristic or grouping of characteristics, is just plain screwed up. This narrow thinking leads us to assume that a vagina or a penis can define us. It also implies that having common genitalia makes us the same. How can we get past this essentialism? Well, one way is to think critically about making a distinction between *sex* and *gender*.

Feminists have long used the concepts of sex and gender. Sex, in studies of everything from biology to politics, commonly refers to "what's between the legs." This categorization is largely based on the assumption that the assignment of genitalia is fixed at birth—an assumption that is now questioned, as we will discuss in some detail later, but one that still holds much social power. The real issue is that, by assuming sex is fixed, gender characteristics can be assigned accordingly. The term *gender* is used to express socially and historically constructed assumptions about women and men. These are the social expectations that women and men perform in certain ways in work, marriage, parenting, politics, education, religion, and other areas of life. Gender is what it means to be feminine or masculine in any given time or place. In contrast to sex, gender refers to "what's between your ears."

For analytical purposes, *sex* is used to refer to the biological characteristics that differentiate women and men based on visible differences in genitalia and reproductive capacities. Although they were once thought to be fixed and immutable, medical science has shown that sexual categories can be transgressed. Gender, in contrast, is cultural. It reflects the ways in which the social categories of masculine and feminine are performed. Nonetheless, these categories are often challenged.

We have been socialized to perform particular gender roles aligned with traditional notions of masculinity and femininity. The rigidity of these roles is an important part of maintaining the status quo. Being a woman is equated with being feminine, those characteristics girls and women are supposed to embody: nurturing, irrational, subordinate, passive, domestic, virginal, and dependent. What the f***? As you can see, the other F-word comes in handy, too. Didn't women win the vote almost a century ago?

Yet, when I ask students what characteristics define femininity, the same list quickly arises. This tells me that little has changed in how we are socialized to think about femininity, and these characteristics have implications for how we think about women, men, and ourselves.

But things have changed, and they've changed a lot. If you were to define women, what would you say? Some of you, I'm sure, are thinking that none of these characteristics describe you or the women you know. Some of you might even be thinking that you know some men who would identify with some of these characteristics. And what does that mean about their masculinity? We'll get to that a bit later. I see many young women in my classes, and I have yet to meet one who represents such a model of femininity. I see young women as strong, sensitive, dynamic, outspoken, smart, independent, subjective, rational, and nurturing. My question, then, is why do these sexist stereotypes retain such a strong influence on us, even as we reject them?

How Can Such Definitions Hold Power Over Us?

Words, identities, and concepts are socially and historically constructed. This means that value and meaning are tied to concepts like femininity, masculinity, race, class, and gender, and the value and meaning of such concepts change across time and place. We are taught about the rules and expectations of society and the meaning of these concepts through social and political institutions such as family, religion, culture, education, government, literature, media, film, music, and economic systems. Rules and expectations are rooted in historical practices and patterns. While they are not fixed, they are difficult and slow to change and are therefore formidable barriers.

Social construction can be likened to the construction of a house. The foundation upon which a house is built is important for stability. Similarly, social constructions are produced from history and this history is bound, like the walls and roof of a house, by social, political, and economic structures. These structures direct and define our lives. Like a house, social constructions

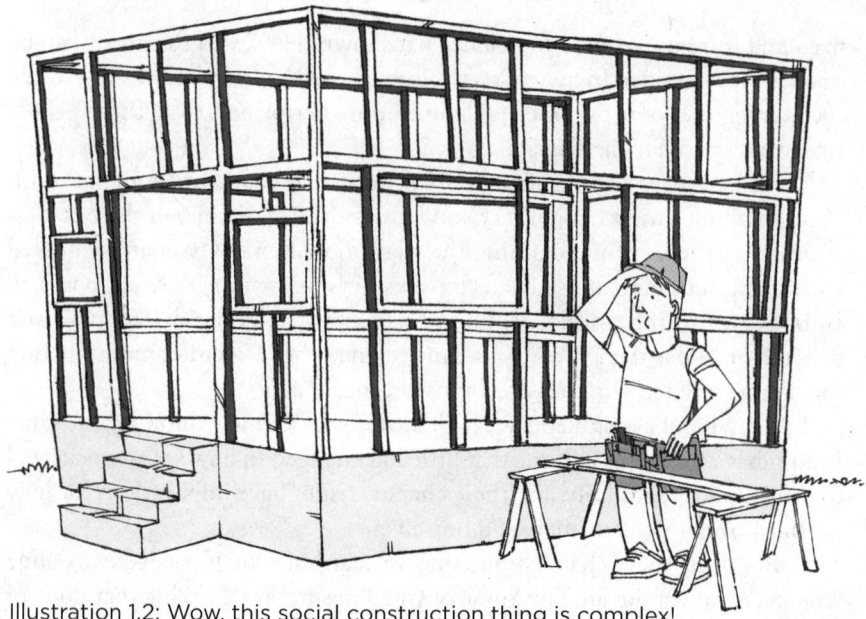

Illustration 1.2: Wow, this social construction thing is complex!

are not permanent; however, they are powerful and difficult to change. It is through social construction that conventional understandings about femininity and masculinity emerge.

Let's explore some of the predictable characteristics attached to masculinity today. The word predictable is important, because it forces us to recognize that there are extraordinary pressures on boys and young men to embody particular masculine characteristics. When asked, students are easily able to list these masculine characteristics. Boys and young men are pushed, prodded, moulded, and contorted to embody masculine characteristics of objectivity, detachment, authority, rationality, dominance, aggression, physical strength, sexual prowess, authority, and independence.

It is interesting to note that masculine characteristics seem to be the opposite of feminine ones. Indeed, if they are paired together, masculine/feminine, we see that masculine characteristics are more socially valued than their feminine counterparts: objective/subjective, detached/nurturing, rational/irrational, dominant/subordinate, aggressive/passive, muscular/delicate, sexual prowess/virginal, and independent/dependent. However, there are problems with this system that affect both women and men. It is not as clear-cut as saying that men embody masculine characteristics and women embody feminine ones. This binary thinking is part of the problem. It imagines that girls and women can only be feminine and boys and men must be masculine. Rigidly linking feminine and masculine characteristics to presumed biological sex helps to reinforce the power of the categories themselves to define us. Indeed, most of us embody characteristics that challenge the stringency of such binary divisions. So why does this type of thinking remain so strong?

Why Are Masculine Characteristics Socially Valued More Than Feminine Ones?

The simple answer is patriarchy. However, patriarchy too is socially constructed. Patriarchy refers to hierarchal historical systems of rule and domination by men. If we look to the root of this word, we find patriarch, which means rule by the father. Patriarchy ensures the power of men—fathers, husbands, brothers, and uncles—and the valuing of masculine characteristics. Patriarchal structures act like the walls and roof of a house to define the spaces of what is possible and to set limits on women's equality. Not surprisingly, if you hold the power, you can set the rules. The power and privilege associated with setting the rules, however, is seldom recognized.

Consequently, women and other marginalized groups are often blamed for their "failure" to grasp equality. For example, women who choose to balance family with a career are frequently blamed for not doing either adequately. On the job, they are passed over for promotion, yet, at the same time, they are judged for missing their child's science fair. If a child has a problem at school, the mother is likely the first to be blamed. And, if a woman's project report at work fails to meet its deadline, her divided loyalties and family responsibilities are likely points of blame. Everywhere women are told that they made their choices and they have to live with them. How women manage to do this is up for debate. Everybody seems to have an opinion, but real solutions are few and far between. An important feminist initiative is to ensure that men are ready, willing, and able to share in family responsibilities. Perhaps getting in touch with their feminine side isn't such a bad idea.

Do we really want men to only embody masculine characteristics? What does this mean for boys and young men? When aggression, physical strength, dominance, authority, and sexual prowess are cultivated in boys and young men, there can be serious consequences. Feminists, both female and male, suggest that these very characteristics fuel male violence against women and other men. The image of a real man as tough is everywhere. Tough is not simply physical, however; it is essential to the social constructions of other masculine characteristics. To be perpetually tough can't be easy. Can you imagine your mother dying and not being able to cry without considering what people will think about your manhood? Can you imagine holding your child in your arms and not being emotionally moved? Boys and men are continually confronted with the dilemma of maintaining the "real man" facade, while at the same time experiencing full and meaningful lives.

Common sayings such as "big boys don't cry" are reminders to men that emotions must be kept in check. Yet boys and men do cry, and they can embody many "feminine" characteristics. For example, they are nurturing, subjective, and emotionally connected. The problem is that displaying these characteristics makes them vulnerable to ridicule, bullying, and pressure to adopt a rigid masculine identity. Everyone knows what we call men who don't conform—wuss, fag, and pussy. This language is both powerful and hurtful. It is powerful because it prevents boys and men from experiencing themselves fully. It is hurtful because having to suppress part of yourself is painful, and because if you don't, the pain could be even greater. But why do the characteristics attached to femininity seem so negative, especially when men embody them?

We must look to the power of patriarchy to understand why feminine characteristics are less valued than masculine ones. At the root of this explanation is the notion of power. If men have historically held power in society, then they have been able to set the rules and construct systems of value that will maintain their power. Patriarchal power exists alongside other forms of power that may undermine or uphold the power of some men. Race, class, religion, sexuality, and other social divisions empower some men and disempower others. Power, in this sense, is exercised as domination over those who are perceived as less powerful: girls, women, and some boys and men. This is not to say that boys and men spend their days conspiring how to wield this type of power. It is much more subtle. Power is already embedded in the ideologies that order society and guide work, play, family life, politics, and economics. It is systemic and therefore invisible, unquestioned in our everyday activities.

Illustration 1.3: I'm the man.

But when women embody valued masculine characteristics, they disrupt the established social order of society. These women are seen as the problem by being too strong, too confident, and too bossy. Such women are often misunderstood as threatening to men, and to the established patriarchal hierarchy, rather than being seen for themselves. We will return to this perception in our discussion of backlash.

One problem in understanding masculine and feminine characteristics is that we often become confused, thinking that feminine equals woman and masculine equals men. These formulaic equations are misleading since each of us embodies both feminine and masculine characteristics. These characteristics make us who we are as individuals. In complex ways, they fit together and make us unique.

You might think of yourself or the women around you, for example, as independent (although "no [wo]man is an island"), aggressive (but in a good way, hard-working, career focused), rational (planning things and writing lists), and nurturing. I have both masculine and feminine characteristics. However, a woman who displays so-called masculine characteristics is quickly labelled a *bitch* or a *dyke*. These are often attempts to silence, dismiss, and discredit her and her ideas. She might even be labelled with the dreaded F-word: feminist.

Feminism: The Root of All Evil

Let's explore this label and the popular notion that feminism is the root of all evil. Infamously, television evangelist Pat Robertson claimed, "The feminist agenda is not about equal rights for women. It is a socialist, anti-family, political movement that encourages women to leave their husbands, kill their children, practice witchcraft, destroy capitalism and become lesbians" (Schwartz and Cooper 1992, A15). Feminists certainly do not advocate that women kill children or abandon their families. Why would he claim such things? Well, feminism is not as simple as it is often portrayed. Its meaning is diverse and informed by individual and collective experiences of the past and present. Most feminists agree that feminism should be used in the plural, as *feminisms*, to reflect its diverse meanings. Since feminisms are multiple, so too are feminists, feminist politics, and the ways in which we come to understand ourselves in relation to other people and the world. Feminism is complex, and because it means different things to different people, it can also be contradictory.

Some feminists, for example, might say that feminism is about equality between women and men. Other feminists would question the very meaning of equality. They would ask: equality with whom? What might this equality look like? For example, if women seek equal wages with men, but black men earn lower wages than white men, what kind of equality would women seek? The debate is likely to get quite heated. For others, feminism can mean the struggle to end sexism. Contributing to feminist debate, we might question whether sexism simply affects women—or are men shaped by sexism, too? What about other social divisions, such as race, class, sexual orientation, disability, and location? Still other ongoing concerns include homophobia, transphobia, colonialism, militarization, war, terrorism, Islamophobia, globalization, and the environment. Do feminisms have anything to say about these issues? The short answer is yes. We will begin to explore many of these feminist issues in later chapters.

Feminism is a complex and fluid concept with multiple meanings, functions and layers, which vary depending on the speaker and their experiences.

Feminist issues change across time and space. The particular historical and cultural context will shape the issues that dominate. For example, in the late nineteenth and early twentieth centuries, many North American feminists supported ending the distribution and sale of alcohol, a position that would be unusual for Canadian feminists today (Cook 1995; Parker 1997). The debates that surround women's movement and feminisms are very important, particularly since constructive debates can enhance feminist theories and practices and make us better feminists. By pointing out weaknesses, gaps, and of course their strengths, feminisms benefit everyone.

While there is no fixed, unchanging, or universal definition, feminism is both a theory and a movement to bring about social change based on that theory. Feminist politics demand a transformation of the existing systems of power, which are complicated by debates about what it means to end oppression and exploitation. This seems like a daunting task. And, with such lofty goals, it is not surprising that feminisms and feminists have run into more than a few roadblocks.

A definition that combines feminist politics with some transformative tools is needed to help us move forward and overcome some of the obstacles to change. I suggest that we begin with a preliminary definition of feminism that combines the two: a means for asking questions, finding answers, and fostering social change that is framed by a movement to empower women and men to make positive changes that improve the lives of everyone. Such a framework begins with a critical lens, a way of understanding and experiencing the world in which we live. This critical lens is an analytic tool that allows us to recognize the complexities and contradictions in life. Like walking out the front door of our socially constructed house for a breath of fresh air, feminism changes our view of the world. Things that we never thought about now become central to our everyday lives, things like power and inequality and how these intersect with gender, race, class, sexuality, age, and ability. Analyzing the world in which we live, and understanding the challenges that we face, are central acts to living feminist lives.

(En)countering the Backlash—I'm Not One of Those F-eminists!

Change is scary, especially for those who like things the way they are. These are the people who benefit from the status quo and are unlikely to give up their positions of power and privilege without a fight. Also, those who don't hold power might be okay with things the way they are because it's familiar and understood. Change that creates a more equitable and socially just world is what feminists of all stripes want. And we take the business of change very seriously. Women's movement, over time, in multiple locations, and across diverse issues, has been very successful in making change, and because of our historic strength, we are encountering increased backlash. Backlash is a strong, antagonistic, or violent reaction against social or political change and is a powerful tool used to discredit feminisms.

Backlash myths about feminism abound, and they are commonly combined with myths about other kinds of social categories including race, class, sexuality, age, and ability. One of the most common myths that feminism challenges is the notion that women are already equal. Clearly we crazy feminists don't get it. Women, racialized groups, the poor, and other marginalized people no longer need equality policies because we are *already* equal. And some critics would argue that women have it better than men, especially white men. Women who have benefited from equality policies in their education, careers, and family lives commonly make these assertions. They are also spread by men who hold these successful female anomalies up as proof of the existing equality among the sexes. A consequence of the "already equal" thinking is that women are blamed if they don't succeed. This is confirmed by Walmart vice-president Susan Chambers, who stated in an interview with *Time* magazine on America's most powerful women, "The main barriers that I see women facing are the ones they create for themselves" (Fastenberg 2010). Many of you might be thinking: well, she's right. But what she is saying is that although she is one of a tiny number of women in high-ranking corporate positions, any woman can be just like her if they try hard enough. This narrow thinking suggests that there are no real barriers to women's advancement. But there are. Let's consider some other myths.

The race myth goes something like this: since the United States elected an African American president, Barack Obama, racism no longer exists in the United States. Likewise, the appointment of Condoleeza Rice to Secretary of State in 2005 served both the gender and race myth. Since *this* black woman "made it," all women, and all black women in particular, are equally able to accomplish such a feat. Underlying such myths are further myths that assume there is a level playing field where everyone is equal from the outset, and the responsibility for success or failure rests with the individual. The idea that "if you can't make it, it's your own fault" is central to backlash. Backlash based on these and other myths is everywhere: in popular culture, government policies, and economic markets. Feminisms work to expose the underlying realities of systemic discrimination and to transform the status quo. This is scary for those with power and privilege.

No wonder there is such popular disdain for feminism. Nonetheless, the packaging of feminism as anti-men, anti-family, and anti-capitalism is overly simplistic. We tend to buy into such anti-feminist rhetoric because we are constantly bombarded with negative messages. This nonsense tries to convince us that feminisms are unnecessary and that women are already equal. On the one hand, these negative messages must be understood as backlash against feminisms. On the other, the potency of anti-feminist backlash tells us that feminisms are powerful and that we can effect social change. Otherwise people would just ignore us. And this is great news for feminists.

I am suggesting that feminisms offer powerful spaces for men to work in concert with women to bring about social change that will benefit everybody. Feminisms allow us to ask different questions, to see the familiar differently, and to find answers in different places. In this sense, feminism is visionary and it is global. It allows us to imagine a world where sexism, oppression, exploitation, and inequality based on differences are eradicated.

You might be saying to yourself right now, "Yeah, right, like that's going to happen." I'm not naïve enough to think that feminists are going to over-throw all the powers that be. I do think, however, that we have to try to make real changes in the ways we think and act in the world, and feminisms can help us on our way.

Conclusion

In this chapter, we have begun the process of exploring feminisms, learning about some of the concepts, language, and issues of concern. We are beginning to see that feminisms challenge social conventions and norms, and this makes feminisms powerful. There are many different feminisms, which means that there is no one way of being or doing feminisms. Hopefully, we are beginning to understand that feminisms are not just for women and girls, but that men and boys need feminisms too. In the next chapter, we will explore some of the social and political changes that feminisms have not only inspired, but also made possible. We will see how feminisms have already changed us and the world.

Questions for Study

1. What are the differences between "sex" and "gender"? Why is it important to understand the differences?
2. What are the negative stereotypes of feminism and feminists? Where do they come from? What is their purpose?
3. How and why is the illustration of the stereotypical feminist both provocative and unsettling?
4. What is a social construction? How are ideas socially constructed? Why is it important to recognize ideas and concepts as socially constructed?
5. What are feminine characteristics? What are masculine characteristics? Do these socially constructed concepts affect your life?
6. What is backlash? Describe your observations of backlash.

7. Do you consider yourself a feminist? What does feminism mean to you?

8. What does it mean to you to be a "woman" or "man" in today's society? How have you come to these understandings?

9. How does patriarchy limit the possibilities for living fully for men, women, and children? What about transgendered people? How does patriarchy affect them?

10. Why is the term "feminisms" a more representative term than "feminism?" Give several examples.

Activities and Questions for Discussion

1. How did you learn about what was expected of you as a gendered boy or girl? Would you change these expectations if you were raising your own child? If so, how? If not, why not?

2. What tasks/chores/activities do members of your family do in your home? Do these tasks/chores/activities reflect gendered social expectations? If so, how?

3. Brainstorm with a partner and make a list of as many negative stereotypes about feminists as possible. Group the list of stereotypes according to the reasons that the stereotypes exist. For each reason, explain why some people believe each of these stereotypes.

4. Why do masculine and feminine characteristics continue to hold so much power in our culture? Who benefits from such definitions and how do they benefit?

5. Before reading the next chapter, answer the following question. Do you consider yourself to be a feminist? Why or why not? Be sure to include explicit examples from your day-to-day activities, such as work, school, and your social life. How are feminisms a part of your everyday experiences? What advantages and/or disadvantages do they provide to you and other men and women that you know?

The trouble is that once you see it, you can't unsee it. And once you've seen it, keeping quiet, saying nothing, becomes as political an act as speaking out. There's no innocence. Either way you're accountable.

—ARUNDHATI ROY, *POWER POLITICS*

CHAPTER TWO

WHAT'S FEMINISM DONE (FOR ME) LATELY?

FEMINIST CONTRIBUTIONS

We made it! We are equal. Feminism is no longer necessary. And, of course, feminism is dead. The struggle is over and we can put our concerns to rest. These are some of the tenets that we often hear. It makes us feel good to think that things are not as bad for women and other marginalized groups as they were in the past. Social commentary of this brand is often paired with the familiar preface for gender equality assertions: "I'm not a feminist but…" What follows is a laundry list of values or aspirations that most people can agree on, such as equal pay, women's equal access to education, ending violence against women and children, women's right to enter the professions of medicine or engineering, and women's right to vote.

I'm Not a Feminist but …

Feminism offers a way to see ourselves and the world anew. Fortified with feminist analyses, we can challenge the negative images that bombard us every day and the bad things happening around us. It enables us to reject the bad stuff and move on to the good. The good is the stuff anyone can get behind, like equal rights, equal pay, environmental justice, and just plain old "I'm OK the way I am" and "I don't have to change who I am for anybody." These ideas are empowering.

I always ask my students during the first class, "How many of you are feminists?" About 10 per cent of students in my large first-year class usually claim this political identity. Yet I am always surprised by how many students look confused at my question. I commonly follow up with more acceptable questions such as how many of you believe in equal rights? Equal pay? Equal access to education? Reproductive freedom? Accessible and affordable child-care? Ending violence against women? Invariably most students raise their hands and I welcome them to the idea that these beliefs might mean they are feminists.

Our reluctance to link feminism to social justice issues is based on the negative stereotypes of feminists that dominate popular culture. Who wants to be seen as one of those card-carrying, angry, loud, man-hating "Feminazis"? Our reluctance to raise our hands and identify as feminists could also mean that we are not sure how others will interpret our version of feminism. Yes, there are many kinds of feminism, and we may not agree with everything other feminists say or do, so we keep quiet. But if feminism at its core includes both theory and practice to end sexism and other systems of oppression, is rooted in social justice, and demands social change, how can we not speak out?

Oh, but we *have* been speaking out! Feminists have been raising their voices for years. Social change doesn't happen easily. It is created through struggle, protest, and a commitment to a better world. It is rooted in concepts of social justice. Feminists have been very successful in making social change and achieving many of their goals. Unfortunately, many of the hard-fought struggles and important gains have become conventional common sense. I say *unfortunately* because such incredible successes make the significant changes in North American societies less visible. Many of the hard-won achievements by women's and other social movements now inform popular understandings of *normal* in North American culture. Most of us accept that with citizenship comes the right to vote regardless of one's gender, race, class, or sexuality, and that equal pay is a good idea, at least in principle. We also think that equality and freedom from discrimination are important goals for any society. However, these seemingly common-sense notions were not always part of our collective consciousness. Consequently, we may take them for granted.

It is important to recognize that in the mid-twentieth century, the women's movement emerged alongside many other social justice movements. All of these movements inspired each other, learned from each other, and created a wider context for social change and the questioning of many well-established customs, laws, and social practices that fostered inequalities and oppressions. As a way to understand the past and to support future feminist activism, we will examine the many links between women's movement and other social justice movements, including the peace movement, civil rights movement, Indian/Native rights movement, and gay/lesbian rights movement.

The purpose here is to provide an understanding of where we were, how far we have come (at least in some ways), and what is at stake.

Social Change and Social Justice

In North America, the 1960s and 1970s were a period of social and political upheaval that made people both hopeful for and fearful of change. In the United States, the government was preoccupied with the Cold War and defeating the Soviet Union. This international focus affected domestic politics. Anti-war and peace movements were visible and vocal, with students and others protesting American involvement in the Vietnam War. The slogan "Make love not war" could be heard on the streets and in the news. Canada did not experience the same level of protest, and its international ambitions were not as intimately tied to victory in Vietnam as it was in the United States, but national debates still ensued, particularly as American draft resisters sought refuge across the border. The oil crisis also emerged in the 1970s. American reliance on oil laid the foundation for a new phase of U.S. imperialism and interventions in attempts to retain control over global oil reserves.

At the same time, the movement for civil rights in the United States was making race relations front-page news. African American students, with the support of local communities and the NAACP, sparked a movement to end racial segregation in the American South when they peacefully sat down at lunch counters reserved for whites and requested service. The first lunch counter sit-in was launched in Wichita, Kansas, in July 1958, and by August of that year, integration was achieved. Buoyed by that success, activists sat down at lunch counters in Oklahoma City a few weeks later (Walters 1996). Other non-violent sit-ins were organized across the American South, including the well-known sit-ins that targeted the Woolworth's lunch counter in Greensboro, North Carolina, and various luncheonettes throughout Nashville, Tennessee, including Walgreens (Turner 2010). These were not the only protests to challenge segregation. Thousands of ordinary people protested everything from segregation on interstate buses to segregation in education and employment throughout the 1960s. Martin Luther King Jr. and Malcolm X, who articulated different ideas about how to bring white supremacy to an end, became the best known spokesmen for that movement. *White supremacy* refers to the belief that white people are superior to all others, which has resulted in the systemic privileging of white people. Federal legislation, culminating in the Civil Rights Act of 1964, made racial segregation in schools, workplaces, and public facilities illegal and prohibited discrimination on the basis of race. It also made discrimination on the basis of sex, religion, or national origin illegal. The passing of the 1965 National Voting Rights Act, which banned voter prerequisites and qualifications such as literacy tests, ended the legal disenfranchisement experienced by African Americans, women, and

Illustration 2.1: Tax evasion? I just wanted to watch a movie!

Viola Desmond—A Canadian Civil Rights Activist

It is perhaps fitting that the little-known hero of Canadian civil rights fought her battle in Nova Scotia, where segregation was socially, but not legally, sanctioned. Often compared to Rosa Parks, who refused to give up her seat on a Montgomery, Alabama, bus in 1955, Viola Desmond had refused to give up her seat in a New Glasgow, Nova Scotia, movie theatre in 1946 (McNeil 2005, 65; Smith 2008, 17).

Viola Desmond requested a ticket for a main floor house seat at the Roseland Theatre; however, the white teller sold her a ticket for the designated black seating area in the balcony. The teller apologized and explained that she was unable to sell Desmond a main floor ticket. Nonetheless, Viola Desmond took a main floor seat in protest of the unlawful segregation policy of the Roseland Theatre. The white theatre manager insisted that Desmond move to the balcony, and when she refused, the white police chief was called. Desmond was dragged from the theatre and arrested. Although the theatre imposed designated "white" and "black" seating, the practice of segregation was not based in law. Since Desmond could not be prosecuted for sitting in a white-designated area, the white police magistrate charged her with tax evasion. Since the

Roseland Theatre charged forty cents for main floor seats, and thirty for balcony seats, and Desmond was sold a balcony seat, she was technically guilty of tax evasion on the difference between the two ticket prices, which amounted to one cent in tax. Shocked and troubled by her arrest and conviction, Viola Desmond launched an appeal with the assistance of the newly organized Nova Scotia Association for the Advancement of Coloured People (NSAACP), the black community, and the black press (Backhouse 1999).

Their collective effort to challenge Desmond's conviction and end racial segregation in theatre seating was defeated in 1947 when the Nova Scotia Supreme Court dismissed the application for judicial review. Viola Desmond continued to be an avid anti-racism activist until she died in 1965, without redress for her conviction.

In 2010, the Premier of Nova Scotia, Darrell Dexter, offered a long overdue apology when Viola Desmond was granted a posthumous pardon. At the announcement ceremony, the first black Lieutenant Governor of Nova Scotia, Mayann Francis, stated, "It is only on rare occasions ... that a society comes together to undo the wrongs of the past" (Parliament of Canada 2010). Efforts are underway to designate a provincial holiday to honour Viola Desmond.

the poor. Making discrimination illegal, however, does not mean that racism ceases to operate. But it was the bravery and creativity of ordinary women and men that inspired the nation and encouraged other oppressed people to create their own movements.

Canada's history of racial exclusion differs sharply from that of the United States. Canada's experience of race relations is much less openly confrontational, and the mass demonstrations, sit-ins, protests, and marches that marked the 1960s in the United States were less visible, although protests did occur. In Canada, no charismatic individual such as Martin Luther King or Malcolm X emerged to represent black Canadians. But slavery, segregation, and racism did happen and racism continues in Canada to this day. Exclusionary practices in Canada relied extensively on unwritten conventions and social attitudes rather than the formal legal structures used in the southern United States.

Canadians often take pride in the romanticized history of the Underground Railroad, which brought many black people to Canada from the United States. Following the second Fugitive Slave Act of 1850 in the United States, which allowed free blacks, former, and escaped slaves to be re-enslaved, many African Americans fled to Canada. In the years following the American Civil War (1861–65), the majority of blacks returned to their communities in the United States, disappointed not to have found the freedom from racial oppression promised in Canada. Many Canadians are unaware of the long history of black people's presence in Canada, which dates back to 1608 when the first named negro servant, Mathieu de Coste, was recorded in Nova Scotia. The first recorded black slave was Oliver le Jeune, who was brought from Madagascar to Quebec in 1632 (Winks 1997, 61). Black people came to Canada in various other ways as well. Following the American Revolution, Black Loyalists, many of whom were slaves who fought for the British, and were therefore seen as trai- tors to the newly established United States, were promised land and freedom by the British in Canada in 1783. The British also exiled some former slaves known as the Maroons, to Nova Scotia in 1796 (Winks 1997; Mensah 2010). This group of escapees had wreaked havoc on the British colony of Jamaica by raiding plantations and liberating slaves.

Native Americans were also actively protesting during the 1960s and 1970s in the United States. Since 1924, Native Americans have held a unique type of dual citizenship. The recognition of Native Americans as members of domestic dependent nations by United States law made them citizens of both the United States and of their specific nations. This meant that Native Americans could vote in state and national elections. While the Supreme Court determined that Indian tribes were independent sovereign entities that retained their right to self-government in *Worcester v. Georgia* (1832), confirming the Court's ruling a year earlier in *The Cherokee Nation v. Georgia* (1831), where tribes were recognized as states in the context of an international system of states, they remained reliant on the United States for external protection. Accordingly, true autonomy and self-government remained elusive, and Indian nationhood remained subordi- nate to the United States government. This struggle continued even after the passage of the 1968 Indian Civil Rights Act, which granted many long-fought-for civil rights. These rights included, among others, the right to free speech, press, and assembly; protections from unreasonable search and seizure; the right to hire an attorney in a criminal case; and equal protection under the law.

The American Indian Movement (AIM) sought sovereignty over Native American lands and for Native peoples with a focus on treaty rights and the ob- jective of preserving tradition and culture. AIM organized the Trail of Broken Treaties march on Washington in 1971, which offered a framework for negotiat- ing tribal sovereignty within the federal system, and its members were key actors in the occupations of historic sites (Deloria and Lytle [1984] 1998; Ward and Vander Wall 1988). Many Aboriginal people living in Canada travelled to the United States to join AIM and support Native self-determination.

Like many Native American groups in the United States, Canadian First Nations, Métis, and Inuit are bound by land treaties and subject to the dictates of the Canadian government, rather than constituting self-determining na- tions. The descendants of those who lived in the area now known as Canada, prior to European contact, are referred to as First Nations peoples. The name signifies their status as one of Canada's founding nations, together with English and French. Métis are Native peoples of mixed North American Aboriginal and European heritage, who self-identify as Métis. Inuit are Native peoples of northern Labrador, northern Quebec, Nunavut, and the Northwest Territories. Together, these three groups are understood as Aboriginal peoples of Canada. But not all Aboriginal groups ceded their lands to the Canadian government, and there are many ongoing disputes with federal and provincial governments over title and land rights. The revision of the 1876 Indian Act in 1951 allowed some traditional ceremonies, such as potlatch and pow-wows, to be practised once again. The 1951 Act instituted changes to Indian Status, which determined who was and who was not eligible to claim Indian Status. The 1951 revision ultimately excluded many women who were born with Indian Status and later lost their Status, as did their children and grandchildren, because they married a non-Indian. Conversely, non-Status Indian women who married Status Indian men became Status Indians. Native people actively challenged this sexist legislation since it prohibited non-Status Indians from having property on Indian Reserves. A Status Indian woman who married a non-Indian man and then later got divorced could not return to her reserve to live, as housing would no longer be available to her (Lawrence 2003; Moss 1990; Green 2001).

Protests and legal challenges led to the passage of Bill C-31 in 1985, which reinstated some women and children's Indian Status. However, even with this bill's revised calculations, Aboriginal people continue to be denied Status as they "marry out." The federal government is therefore increasingly able to shrug off its responsibilities to Aboriginal people. The number of Status Indians will continue to decline as children of Status and non-Status relationships are eventually cut off.

All this history may seem unconnected to feminisms, and to some, perhaps a bit boring, but understanding the diversity of historical movements helps us to imagine this dynamic and socially and politically charged era. It was this environment that supported the development of new feminist thinking and the invigoration of women's movement.

Imagine change brewing all around you, because the 1960s also witnessed the emergence of the gay rights movement. Like the peace movement, this movement emerged in the era of Cold War politics. This context was particularly important as governments of the day increased the state regulation and repression of homosexuality, guided by assumptions about "subversives" and deviant identities as vulnerable to blackmail and communist influences. These views dictated practices that resulted in the expulsion of gays and lesbians from the military and government institutions, as well as heightened policing of gay bars and social spaces in both Canada and the United States (Andersen 2006; Smith 2008; Kinsman 1995, 2010).

After much debate over the legal prohibition of private sexual practices among consenting adults throughout the 1950s, the American Law Institute recognized the necessity of separating religious and moral views from civil responsibilities. A group of legal scholars and practitioners, it published the Model Penal Code in 1962 (Smith 2008; Andersen 2006). The Model Penal Code was intended as a guide for states, which encouraged consistency in criminal law across the nation. Of importance here is that it stipulated the decriminalization of "deviant sexual intercourse," which included sodomy, among consenting adults (Andersen 2006). However, because of the institutional and legal divisions between states and federal jurisdictional power, if gays and lesbians were to claim their civil rights and achieve broad-based social change, it would demand state-by-state legal challenges. Until then, gay bars and bathhouses would continue to be the targets of police raids and harassment.

It was just such an incident that sparked a series of riots that inspired a new militancy among gay and lesbian activists in 1969. The Stonewall riots of June 27–28 marked the first direct resistance to police harassment when a gay club in New York City was raided. No longer willing to accept unequal treatment by law enforcement passively, queer folks fought back.

While gays and lesbians had been organizing in an ad hoc fashion around education, acceptance, and the de-pathologization of homosexuality since the 1950s, the time was now ripe for concerted social change. Moved by the fervour of social movements in 1960s and 1970s, particularly the women's and civil rights movements, in which gays and lesbians were already participating, gays and lesbians shifted their agenda to a more liberatory focus. The political environment too was ripe for change, or so it seemed. In 1965, the Supreme Court struck down *Griswold v. Connecticut*, which had upheld the Connecticut statute prohibiting the use of contraceptives among married couples. In so doing, the Supreme Court recognized the fundamental right to privacy and created a possible legal entry point for gay and lesbian legal activists. In 1967, the ACLU reversed its position and was now ready to challenge the state's regulation of homosexuality through police harassment and discrimination in employment and immigration (Smith 2008; Andersen 2006).

Gay liberation has been celebrated since 1970 across the United States and elsewhere, commonly in June to commemorate the Stonewall riots. Gay Pride parades and events attempt to make homosexuality more visible, celebrate diverse gay identities, and ultimately make homosexuality socially acceptable. In 2003, the Supreme Court's landmark ruling in *Lawrence v. Texas* held that states cannot criminalize consenting adults who engage in sodomy in the privacy of their homes. In effect, *Lawrence* struck down all remaining state sodomy laws (Smith 2008; Andersen 2006). However, gays, lesbians, bisexuals, and trans and queer people remain subject to legal and social regulation in many areas, including same-sex marriage, adoption, child custody, health care, and employment, among others.

In Canada, an amendment to the Criminal Code in 1969 repealed the sodomy laws to decriminalize consensual sex for those twenty-one years of age and over. Interestingly, this amendment was part of a package of legal reforms proposed in 1967 by then Minister of Justice Pierre Trudeau, which also included greater access to abortion and the relaxation of divorce laws. Pierre Trudeau introduced the bill into Parliament and made headlines with his legendary statement, "The state has no place in the bedrooms of the nation" (Smith 2008).

Nonetheless, the unjust Toronto bathhouse raids of 1981 resulted in the arrest of close to 300 men on February 5. Targeting four of six popular gay bathhouses, Toronto police, together with the Ontario Attorney General's Office, engaged in massive raids, employing tactics to terrify and humiliate bathhouse patrons. Following the arrests, police contacted employers notifying them of their employees' arrests. As a result, many of the men arrested lost their jobs (Bérubé 2003). On February 6, the day after the first bathhouse raids, several thousand people marched on the Division 52 police station to protest the targeting of gays and lesbians by police. Weeks later, over 4,000 people gathered at Queen's Park demanding an investigation into the raids. On March 6, gay and lesbian activists, including MP Svend Robinson, author Margaret Atwood, and Reverend Brent Hawkes (who went on a hunger strike until an independent investigation of the raids was initiated), gathered for a Gay Freedom Rally (Thomas 2011; CBC 2012). In the official investigation that followed, police were condemned for their actions and the right to engage in consensual sex in private spaces was confirmed. It is reported that Operation Soap, as the raids were called, and the "policing" of the three subsequent protests, cost taxpayers an estimated $10 million. Pride Day was first celebrated in Toronto on June 28, 1981, with 1,500 participants, and is touted as North America's largest Gay Pride parade, with more than one million people now attending the celebrations.

This brief summary paints a complex picture of social justice movements in the 1960s and 1970s. Women were active in all of these social justice movements and in the struggle for what was then being called women's liberation. While each movement was distinct, it offered the possibility of crossover participation and synergy on multiple issues. Synergy, where one issue is connected to other issues to bolster change at many levels, is evident in the struggle for Native women's rights (see text box Synergy Among and Across Movements: The Case of Native Women's Rights in Canada).

Women's movement has never been homogeneous or linear. A homogeneous movement would assume that all the women who participated were the same—they would look the same, think the same, act the same, and want the same results. However, the women who participated in "Women's Liberation" have always been of all races, ethnicities, sexual orientations, abilities, and classes. Not surprisingly, this diversity has brought a plethora of issues to the table and has resulted in multiple paths and many twists and turns complicating women's movement. It has also resulted in conflicts, debates, and exclusions.

The process of trying to set priorities and frame a cohesive and unified agenda is where women's movement gets its bad reputation as a white, middle-class movement. And, to some extent, this seemed like the case as the mainstream media created celebrities out of prominent white women such as Betty Friedan, who published *The Feminine Mystique* (1963) documenting women's unhappiness as "the problem that has no name." Gloria Steinem (see text box Profile of a Feminist: Gloria Steinem) also became famous during this era, which put her in the position of speaking for all women, as well as Jane Fonda, who became the face of women's involvement in the anti-war movement. As an anti-war activist, Fonda was a hero who steadfastly held to her convictions that the United States government's lies and propaganda needed to be exposed to bring an end to the Vietnam War. Fonda was also seen as a traitor by United States soldiers when she was photographed sitting in an anti-aircraft vehicle during her visit to enemy territory in North Vietnam in 1972. During her visit, Fonda also made several radio broadcasts, which earned her the nickname Hanoi Jane. She has repeatedly apologized for the photograph and remains engaged in feminist struggles. Yet, from boot camp to retirement, military personnel are encouraged to connect real soldiering with Fonda-hating. It may be that Fonda symbolizes the dangerous female who threatens military culture (Burke 2004). While these women may have been the chosen darlings of the media, many more women of various backgrounds were working tirelessly, marching, advocating, and struggling for social change beyond the focus of the cameras.

Women's Movement Is Complex, Multiple, and Diverse

Betty Friedan was the co-founder of the National Organization for Women (NOW) along with the Reverend Pauli Murray, who was the first African American woman to become an Episcopal priest. This pair showed the diversity of women's representation in the movement. As the co-founder of NOW, Friedan also participated in some of the ongoing conflicts, debates, and exclusions that plagued women's movement, particularly in her notorious 1969 reference to lesbians as the "lavender menace." Not until 1977 did NOW embrace lesbian rights as a fundamental feminist goal.

While lesbians were active in the gay rights movement, many also claimed a feminist consciousness. Evidence of this synergy across movements is presented in the radical feminist *Redstockings Manifesto* (1969), which defined lesbianism as a political identity and a choice, which women should embrace. The *Manifesto* called on all women to unite in the struggle for liberation and all men to give up their male privilege and support women's liberation as a goal of humanity. It promoted consciousness-raising to expose and eradicate patriarchy, which it argued was the root of women's oppression.

Synergy Among and Across Movements: The Case of Native Women's Rights in Canada

Aboriginal peoples have historically had a variety of ways of organizing gendered relationships and expectations that varied over time and in different communities. With the creation of the Canadian nation, Aboriginal women's roles and status were defined by laws and customs that were particular to them but not created by them. In Canada, the Indian Act governed Aboriginal Status, and when Mary Two-Axe Early, Jeannette Lavell, Irene Bedard, and Sandra Lovelace lost their Status and were permanently banned from their ancestral lands, like so many Status Indian women who married non-Indians, they fought back. Loss of Status meant that these women were no longer able to live, own property, or be buried on their reserves. They were prohibited from participating in reserve politics through council meetings or elections, or having any say in band decision-making.

Unwilling to accept the exile of any Aboriginal women from their Native lands, in the 1950s Mary Two-Axe Early began her life of activism and protest, founding the organization Equal Rights for Indian Women in 1969 (the forerunner to the national Indian Rights for Indian Women, founded in 1973). Recognizing the dynamic synergy of the time and understanding the importance of the Royal Commission on the Status of Women as a means for change, Two-Axe Early presented a petition before the Commission, challenging the government to rectify the loss of Native women's Status under the Indian Act. Spurred by the contradictions of living on the reserve but not being able to inherit property due to loss of Status, Two-Axe Early testified to the Commission (Early 1994; Green 2001). Hers was but one voice among the many Native women who had lost their Indian Status through marriage. Jeannette Lavell and Irene Bedard took their case all the way to the Supreme Court of Canada. They claimed that the Indian Act was discriminatory under the Canadian Bill of Rights (1960). Disappointingly, the Court ruled in 1973 that the Indian Act was exempt from the Canadian Bill of Rights (Lawrence and Anderson 2003; Bear 1991; Moss 1990).

On the heels of this decision, Mary Two-Axe Early, together with sixty other women from Kahnewake, took their struggle for Native women's rights global. Two-Axe Early and the others attended the United Nations' First International Conference on Women in Mexico City, which marked the International Year of the Woman in 1975. However, when they returned they found that the band council had evicted them from their homes, following government legislation and using the Indian Act. With heightened national and international publicity around the plight of Native women, the band was forced to withdraw their eviction notices, but the issue of Indian Status remained unresolved (Lawrence and Anderson 2003; Gehl 2000).

Again taking sexist discrimination against Native women global, Sandra Lovelace, a Maliseet from the Tobique Reserve in New Brunswick who lost her Status after marrying out, took her struggle to the United Nations. Lovelace and her children had been denied housing, health care, and access to education on the Tobique Reserve. Unwilling to be denied her birthright, Lovelace took her challenge to the United Nations Human Rights Committee in 1977. She argued that the Indian Act violated Article 27 of the International Covenant on Civil and Political Rights, which Canada had ratified the year before. It took four years for the United Nations to rule against the Canadian government. The 1981 ruling was a significant victory for Aboriginal women in Canada, even if it was only symbolic. While the United Nations ruled that the Indian Act breeched Aboriginal women's rights by denying them Status, international agreements and decisions by United Nations committees and courts do not supersede the laws of sovereign countries like Canada (Lawrence and Anderson 2003; Gehl 2000; Early 1994; Bear 1991; Moss 1990).

In the heated debates prior to the adoption of the Canadian Charter of Rights and Freedoms in 1982, feminists and women's groups were instrumental in pushing to have discrimination against women included under Section 15. Discrimination against First Nations women who had lost their Status, however, was not specifically addressed until the passing of Bill C-31 in 1985, which reinstated some but not all Aboriginal women's Status under the Indian Act (Lawrence and Anderson 2003; Gehl 2000; Early 1994; Bear 1991; Moss 1990).

The struggle for Aboriginal women's rights continued in the 2007 case *McIvor v. Indian and Northern Affairs Canada*. Sharon McIvor claimed that her children were denied Indian Status even though their father is a Status Indian. It was alleged that women were discriminated against under the Indian Act. McIvor argued that if it had been their grandfather who was Indian and married a non-Indian, her children would have Status. However, because their father's mother lost her Status when she married a non-Indian and did not regain Status, and their mother is non-Indian, they were denied on the basis of the "two generation" rule of mixed Status parentage—their grandmother and their mother are not Status Indians. The Supreme Court of British Columbia decided in favour of McIvor's claim that Bill C-31 was discriminatory of the basis of sex and marital status. The Court found that McIvor's children were being denied Status because of their grandmother's lost Status through marriage, and recognized that sex discrimination had occurred because McIvor's children would have been awarded Status if their grandfather had been the one who married a non-Indian. The Court ruled that discrimination on the basis of sex, the sex of their grandmother, was perpetrated by the Indian Act. The 2007 McIvor decision found Bill C-31 in violation of Section 15 of the Charter, which prohibits discrimination on the basis of "race, national or ethnic origin, colour, religion, sex, age or mental or physical disability." In 2009, the federal government sought to appeal this decision; however, the appeal was dismissed by the British Columbia Court of Appeal (Hurley 2009).

The Court demanded that the Canadian government amend the Indian Act to bring it in line with the Charter within the year. As a result, the government introduced Bill C-3, the Gender Equality in Indian Registration Act, amending C-31; they claimed this would confer Status on thousands of previously ineligible descendants of Aboriginal women. The Native Women's Association of Canada (NWAC) argues that the bill fails to address the issue of the privileging of men in the second-generation cut-off for Indian Status. Consequently, those who trace their heredity through maternal ties will be denied Status if they were born prior to 1951, whereas those who trace it through paternal ties will be able to gain Status (NWAC 2012).

Ultimately, debates about Status will continue, as Bill C-3 only postpones the inevitable end of Indian Status as mixed-Status marriages continue. It continues a legacy of gender discrimination and legislative violations of the Charter. The McIvor decision recognizes sex discrimination under section 15, but fails to address broader Native identity issues. After the Supreme Court of Canada declined to hear her case, like Sandra Lovelace, McIvor took the struggle for gender equality and equal rights to the United Nations Human Rights Committee in November 2010. She is arguing for a complete amendment of the Indian Act (McIvor and Grismer 2010).

Aboriginal groups in Canada, including the Native Women's Association of Canada, the Métis National Council, and the Chiefs of Ontario, are raising new questions about Native identity that move beyond the Status debates, arguing that as self-determining nations, Aboriginal peoples have the right to define who is and who is not an Indian, not the government of Canada. They contend that Indian identity cannot be measured by "blood quantity" as Indian Status currently attempts to do. Accordingly, Aboriginal people are still in jeopardy of extinction under the Indian Act. Instead, Native identity must be understood as the outcome of a complex configuration of social, cultural, and political forces (NWAC 2012; Chiefs of Ontario 2010; Lavell 2010; Hodgson-Smith 2010).

There are multiple problems that arise from viewing patriarchy as the common oppressor of women. First, this view supposes that men are the targets of feminism, giving credit to the backlash. Second, it fails to recognize the intersections of race and class as culpable in the oppression of all people. Black feminists have argued that, unlike the suburban middle-class white women trapped in their homes of whom Friedan writes about, black women often found their homes a place of refuge from racism and solidarity with men. Working-class women activists have also raised issues of workplace oppression and the role of capitalism as implicated with patriarchy.

In Canada, women were participating in many of the same debates. In 1970, the Royal Commission on the Status of Women Report documented women's inequality in Canada and offered recommendations for its eradication. Recommendations to all levels of government were made, such as the choice for women to work outside the home, the establishment of a universal childcare program, joint parental responsibility for children, implementation of affirmative action policies to overcome the discrimination against women, a commitment to publicly funded reproductive health care, and the establishment of a Committee on the Status of Women.

In response to the Report, the National Ad Hoc Committee on the Status of Women (NAC) formed in 1971 as a national advocacy group. Like the public face of women's movement suggests, NAC's early leadership was white and middle class. This failure to be representative of the diversity of Canadian women fostered friction and dissention among NAC members. It was not until the 1990s that racialized women claimed their place as leaders of NAC. Under the leadership of Sunera Thobani (1993–96) and Joan Grant-Cummings (1996–2000), NAC expanded its focus to address both national and international concerns including racism, refugee issues, global trade, and United Nations programs for women. Unfortunately, NAC has suffered from economic woes. Federal government funding cuts, an end to funding for advocacy organizations, and widespread backlash against feminisms and women's movement have stifled much of NAC's advocacy work, and questions as to whether it still even exists abound. Other feminist organizations have jumped into the fray to support women's movement; however, these too have suffered from slashed budgets and backlash.

Abortion Rights and Women's Movement

Prior to 1969, abortion was illegal in Canada. Many women who sought to terminate a pregnancy had back-street abortions, which were performed in non-medical settings and rarely by accredited doctors. In desperation, women put themselves through dangerous and painful processes to induce miscarriages. Some women threw themselves down flights of stairs, ingested toxic substances, or inserted objects into their cervixes. Such options for terminating an unwanted pregnancy could have devastating outcomes. With no legal access to birth control, single mothers were particularly stigmatized as "bad girls," "loose women," and certainly not the kind of gals that you would take home to meet your mother. While not all feminists were (or are) pro-choice, the issue of abortion has been an important issue for women's movement.

Under such circumstances, we might assume that feminists and women activists would be thrilled when the Canadian government passed an abortion law in 1969. However, this legislation only partially legalized abortion. While the law served as the federal government's response to emergency rooms

Profile of a Feminist: Gloria Steinem

Gloria Steinem is a writer and an iconic feminist, social, and political activist. Born in 1934 of Jewish and Christian heritage, in Toledo, Ohio, Steinem grew up under precarious circumstances. Like many people during the Great Depression, Steinem's father was largely unemployed; however, he was also financially irresponsible, mortgaging assets and placing the family in debt. Unusual for the time, Steinem's parents separated when she was ten years old and one year later divorced, leaving eleven-year-old Gloria to care for her mentally ill mother. Gloria's mother Ruth suffered from depression and hallucinations. Refusing to allow her mother to be institutionalized in a publicly funded facility and unable to afford a private one, Gloria chose to take on the task of mothering her mother at home. Home was a dilapidated triplex that Steinem's mother had inherited in a rough working-class neighbourhood among the shipbuilding, meatpacking, and automotive factories. The two, mother and daughter, survived on meager income from two apartments in the triplex and the money Gloria earned from dancing at the local Eagles and Elks clubs. Steinem attributes her ability to live on the paltry earnings of a writer and the insecurity of becoming a feminist organizer on her parents. She notes, "He taught me to live with insecurity...[she] taught me to remember that disaster could strike" (Marcello 2004, 12).

At the age of seventeen, Gloria moved to Georgetown in Washington, D.C., to live with her sister Susanne. Liberated from the task of caring for her mother, Steinem attended an upscale all-white high school, in contrast to the working-class multicultural one she had attended in Toledo. In 1952, Steinem attended the prestigious Smith College. This period was marked by national and international strife. The United States was already in the early stages of the Cold War, embroiled in domestic anti-communist fanaticism, and threatened with nuclear attack by the Soviet Union. This environment encouraged Steinem to study Marxism during her year abroad at the University of Geneva in Switzerland. However, she came to realize that Marxism in theory and Marxism in practice functioned very differently in her study of the Indian Communist Party (Marcello 2004; Heilbrun 1995).

Having graduated from Smith College in 1956 and abandoned her engagement with a handsome and socially well-positioned man, Steinem's passion for women's rights was sealed. Heeding her mother's words that "once you get a taste of being independent, you'll never want to get married" (Marcello 2004, 48), Gloria accepted a scholarship to do graduate work in India, where she would add to her knowledge about women's rights, Marxism, and Gandhi's legacy of social change through non-violent civil disobedience as political activism. In the interim she left for England but found herself pregnant. At a time when pregnancy for single women was scandalous, and unwed mothers and their children were considered morally reprehensible, Steinem decided to abort the fetus. While abortion was illegal in the United States, it could be obtained legally in London under certain conditions: two medical experts needed to attest to the mother's mental and physical incapacity to carry the pregnancy to term. Selecting this route, Steinem's belief that women must have control over their bodies was confirmed and her pro-choice feminist activism foreshadowed. After completing her scholarship, Steinem attended a radical humanist study camp where she learned about radical change, liberation from social structures, and how actions dictate the end results.

Returning to the United States in 1958, Steinem was still unwilling to accept the traditional conventions of womanhood—marriage, children and jobs as teachers, secretaries and librarians. However, as an inexperienced writer she was unable to land a prestigious journalist position as she had hoped and as a university graduate she was overqualified for more junior positions. Steinem worked in various capacities and freelanced for *Esquire*, all the while making contacts and meeting famous people.

Steinem's first big byline came in 1962, when she undertook an assignment for *Esquire* to write about the effects of the Pill on the behaviour of college graduates and the pressure on young women to be sexual before they were ready (Heilbrun 1995, 95). Steinem's 1963 article "A Bunny's Tale" famously exposed sexual harassment and the objectification of women at the newly opened New York Playboy Bunny Club, where she worked undercover for three weeks. Yet to name herself a feminist, Steinem's article clearly offered feminist insights. In the years that followed, Steinem protested with the Women's Strike for Peace coalition against the Vietnam War and Soviet and American testing of nuclear weapons, and supported both the civil rights movement and the struggle to unionize migrant farm workers, led by Cesar Chavez. In 1968, while attending a radical feminist event on access to abortion, Steinem realized that women deserved political change and that this could be achieved through feminist solidarity (Marcello 2004, 94–110). By 1970, Steinem was speaking about feminism across the country and became a central figure in women's movement in North America. Her good looks and witticisms arguably made her a media darling, but her intelligence and commitment to women's rights made her a feminist leader.

Steinem's feminist accomplishments are many. Her contributions and initiatives include co-founding the National Women's Political Caucus (1971), which advances the numbers of pro-equality women in elected and appointed office at a national and state level, as well as the Women's Action Alliance (1971–97), a national organization to assist women at local levels to organize action projects to eliminate economic and social discrimination. In 1972, she co-founded *Ms.* magazine, which became a leading voice for feminists, and she remains involved with the magazine today. Steinem also co-founded the Ms. Foundation for Women (1973), a national multi-racial, multi-issue organization that supports grassroots projects to empower women and girls, and Choice USA (1992), a national organization to support pro-choice education and leadership. In 2005, Steinem co-founded the Women's Media Center to ensure that women's stories are told and their voices are heard.

flooded by women seeking treatment from botched abortions, feminists and women's groups argued that the partial legalization of abortion was not enough. The law not only limited abortion procedures to accredited hospitals, prohibiting the establishment of women's clinics, but worse, a woman would only be granted an abortion if it were approved by a Therapeutic Abortion Committee. Such committees consisted of four doctors who would determine whether carrying the pregnancy to term would be detrimental to the woman's health. Needless to say, this process took time. And time was something that pregnant women seldom had.

To protest the inadequacies of the law, seventeen activists took to the road in March 1970, with the goal of arriving in Ottawa on Mother's Day, in what became known as the Abortion Caravan (Rebick 2005). What better day to reflect on the effects of pregnancy, both wanted and unwanted, than Mother's Day? The caravan began its journey in Vancouver and travelled east across Canada. It stopped in cities and towns along the way to rally support for the full legalization of abortion. Women waved clothes hangers and bottles of drain cleaner to represent the dangers of illegal abortion and the narrow-sightedness of the new law. The caravan got a lot of press, especially for leaving a coffin on Prime Minister Trudeau's doorstep to represent all the women who had died from illegal abortions. But this was nothing compared to the coverage that the thirty-five feminist abortion activists who chained themselves to chairs and demanded the legalization of abortion on demand received. These women activists so disrupted Parliament that it was forced to close (Sethna and Hewitt 2009).

These were just the first steps in the long and difficult struggle to the 1988 Morgentaler decision by the Supreme Court of Canada, which struck down the 1969 law as unconstitutional. The issue of abortion galvanized women in Canada and made "a woman's right to choose" a reality, with abortion clinics in almost every province.

Canada's struggle for reproductive choice was fortified by the 1973 United States Supreme Court decision in *Roe v. Wade*, which made first-trimester abortions legal. It did so by recognizing that the right of women to make choices about bearing children is central to their ability to participate fully and equally in society. This landmark decision derived its authority from the United States Supreme Court decisions, beginning in the 1920s, that interpreted constitutional guarantees of liberty as the individual's right to privacy in decisions about childrearing, procreation, the use of contraception, and marriage.

Prior to *Roe v. Wade*, it is estimated that anywhere from 200,000 to 1.2 million illegal abortions were performed each year in the United States (Cates 2003). Although determining the effects of illegal abortions and their subsequent complications is difficult to calculate, it has been estimated that as may as 5,000 to 10,000 women died each year (NARAL). The historic verdict settling *Roe v. Wade* was the outcome of laborious work by women's movement, supported by medical, public health, legal, and religious organizations. As we can see, women's movement was as varied as the women and men who participated in it.

Life without Women's Movement

Can you imagine what your life would look like if women's movement had not been so successful? Without women's movement, marriage would still be the crowning achievement of any young woman's career. Convention would still demand that a woman take her husband's name. No-fault divorce would be unheard of. A "broken home" due to divorce would be blamed on the woman's inability to keep her marriage together, and it would still be a social stigma to be divorced or to come from a family where divorce occurred. Women, of course, would be wholly responsible for everything related to the home, except for any major decisions because those decisions would be the domain of men.

Sex, if you were having it, would only be permitted within marriage and then not necessarily a choice. Rape within marriage would not be a crime, but considered a man's right of access to his wife. Unmarried women would be divided into those who do and those who don't. And, if a baby resulted from doing it, the child would be stigmatized for life by its "illegitimacy." Sexual pleasure would be a uniquely male experience and women would still (secretly) be looking for the vaginal orgasm.

Fewer than half of women would work outside the home and they would earn, on average, just $0.52 for every dollar earned by a man. Women's paid employment would be seen as temporary until their real careers of marriage and motherhood began. Women's earnings would not be considered critical to family survival; rather, they would be thought of as "mad money" to be used by women haphazardly and according to their whims. As a result, women would be paid less, as their wages were not considered essential. "Help Wanted: Male" or "Help Wanted: Female" would divide classified ads in newspapers. Women would work predominantly as secretaries, nurses, teachers, domestics, and in other low-wage service jobs. Bosses could ask women if their husbands had given them permission to work, if they planned to have children, or if they intended to have more children. Women workers could be demoted or fired for getting pregnant; and sexual harassment on the job would be a regular occurrence with little recourse. The glass ceiling would be even more visible (Baumgardener and Richards 2010).

Since girls would be educated in "Home Economics" in high school, they'd be able to cook and sew, but changing the oil in their cars or fixing a faulty light switch would have to be left to the boys who took shop class. Of course, to ensure that boys could boil water and sew on a button when they left their mothers, they could take a class in "Bachelor Studies." But once they were married, they could expect to rely on their wives for such menial tasks. Girls would be rewarded academically for their talents of sitting quietly and listening passively. Math and science would be the privileged domain of boys, even if a girl showed some promise or skill. Curriculum and academic testing would reflect boys' experiences rather than girls', and, if girls happened to show up in a textbook, they were likely to be insignificant characters. The phrase "boys will be boys" would be bantered around as if it could explain anything and everything that wasn't quite right. There would be no Little League sports for girls and no mandate to ensure their physical education. If a girl "got herself pregnant," she was the one who would get expelled from school. There would be no women's studies programs, and the fields of critical race studies, sexuality studies, and queer studies would be even more unimaginable.

Gender inequality in medical treatment and research remains a problem. One example of how gender is ignored in the field of medicine is in the area of oral contraceptives. Why isn't there an oral contraceptive for men? Well, apparently scientists are working on it. However, the male pill is still years away from approval (Goodman 2008). So, not only do men not have to take a pill but also women have to put up with the consequences of taking it. We can control our fertility with a little pill, but we have to deal with the side effects of weight gain, headaches, and the possible risks of cancer. Is this gender equality? I'm not advocating for male contraceptives that risk men's health and well-being, that certainly wouldn't be the equality that feminists are looking for. What feminists want are safe contraceptives, whether for men or women. They want more research and better testing before contraceptives are marketed to ensure that they are safe.

Another place where gender plays an important role is in the diagnosis and treatment of cardiovascular disease. Did you know that heart disease is still thought of as a health risk predominantly for men? When women go to the emergency room fearing a heart attack, they could be sent home without treatment, since they don't present with the same symptoms as men. Even when women have all the classic signs—chest pains, nausea, radiating pain in the left arm—cardiac tests can come back as "normal." Indigestion, gall bladder problems, anxiety, or stress are the most common misdiagnoses. Women are made to feel embarrassed about making a big deal of their health concerns and pain. If you're a woman under the age of fifty-five, you are seven times more likely to be misdiagnosed when the problem is really heart disease (Pope 2000). In 2005, only 8 per cent of family and 17 per cent of cardiologists knew that more women die from heart disease than men each year (Mosca 2005). More shockingly, women are five times more likely to die of heart disease than breast cancer and all other cancers combined (Lloyd-Jones 2010).

Speaking of breast cancer, without pink ribbon campaigns spurred by women's movement, awareness about breast cancer and funding for research might not exist. Some caution needs to be raised here, however. As corporations jump on the philanthropy bandwagon, accusations of pinkwashing grow. For feminist critics, pinkwashing refers to the ways in which businesses brand their products as supporting the fight against breast cancer, as a means for boosting sales and ultimately revenues (King 2006; Pool 2011; Landman 2008; Lubitow and Davis 2011). In this competitive environment for donations, there is concern that a greater proportion of the money raised is allocated to fundraising than to research. And researchers are spending more time applying for funds, taking precious time away from their research, than ever before (Johnson 2011). While the management of breast cancer has improved considerably and success rates for remission are high, these results are not universal and women still die from this disease. Is this what success looks like?

Without women's movement, campaigns to end violence against women would be virtually unknown. Take Back the Night marches, the White Ribbon Campaign, and the 16 Days of Activism to End Violence Against Women would not be on the radar. Women would still be encouraged to stay in abusive marriages. There would be no women's shelters for abused women and their children, and rape crisis lines and sexual assault centres would not exist. Even with women's movement, these critical resources are underfunded and often on the verge of closing because of budget shortfalls.

As for finances, without women's movement, married women would be unable to get a loan without their husbands cosigning, and their credit ratings would be tied to their husbands' rather than to them. Single women would have difficulty renting an apartment, since landlords would want steady long-term renters and, after all, a single woman is bound to be married soon. If not married, what would women be doing living on their own? Landlords would need to worry about propriety, for the sake of the good tenants. The fear that single women are loose, that they could be having men over at all hours or even running a brothel would continue to be a widely held and dominant view.

The achievements of women's movement are seldom discussed outside of the classroom, but they are considerable: pay equity; the recognition of unpaid work as real work; affirmative action policies; freedom from sexual harassment on the job; legislation to criminalize rape in marriage; women's right to education in the professions (medicine, engineering, law, and business); and shared responsibility for parenting. Our failure to recognize and acknowledge the difficult struggles of the past, which made these accomplishments part of what we think of as *normal*, is the very reason that they may be in jeopardy in the future.

Backlash against Feminism and Women's Movement

Backlash is a concept that has been discussed in feminist circles since the 1990s, when Susan Faludi wrote *Backlash: The Undeclared War on Women*. Feminism, she argued, was being blamed for anything and everything, from high divorce rates, children's failure in school, job loss, to economic recession. Backlash is an aggressive and violent reaction to social changes that challenge the status quo. By status quo, I mean the power and privilege that dominate societies. Those who have it attempt to keep it at all costs, because they believe that they will be the losers if women's equality becomes a reality. Just imagine, women's movement is moving along, maybe under duress, but still moving forward and, suddenly, those with the most power who are benefiting from the way things are start to get scared. They feel their lives are changing and they are not happy. Have women gone too far? Have women progressed too quickly? Has feminism placed men and women on the defensive? When push comes to shove, complaints are bound to surface, and feminism and women's movement get blamed and face backlash. Feminist concerns about the need for more change and attacks on women's rights are commonly met with dismissal or backlash claims of "been there, done that and we don't need to go there again," "women are (already) equal," and, "affirmative action is reverse discrimination."

Affirmative action policies, such as equity hiring policies, ensure that historically marginalized groups like women, racialized people, and those with disabilities, have an opportunity to participate. This means that some white guy doesn't get the job that he previously could have counted on simply because he is some white guy. Cries of "This is reverse discrimination!" can be heard everywhere. But were we concerned when a woman or person of colour was the one who did not get the job, even when their qualifications were equal or better than the white guy's?

The highly publicized idea that women are already equal, and therefore that no one needs to be a feminist and there is no need for women's movement, can easily be challenged. Just think about women's earnings compared to men's, or the epidemic of violence against women, or inadequacies in health research when men's experience is the measure of treatment. Women are definitely not equal. And, if we have "been there and done that," why do funding cuts continue to plague women's advocacy organizations, shelters, and sexual assault centres? And why is the accessible and affordable childcare that was advocated for and recommended more than forty years ago by the Royal Commission on the Status of Women in Canada and by NOW in the United States still not a reality?

After more than 100 years of women's movement, much work remains to be done. In answer to our demands for equality and social changes, feminists have been basically told "If it ain't broke, don't fix it." These clichés are borrowed when a task is too hard or will take too long to complete. However, if everyone used this excuse, then things would never change, and we already know that things are not fine the way they are.

Yet "I'm not a feminist" still resonates with many.

Conclusion

We have seen in this chapter that the struggle for equality and social justice is a long and as yet unfinished battle. We explored the complex landscape of mid-twentieth century social justice movements—the peace movement, the civil rights movement, the Indian/Native rights movement, and the gay/lesbian rights movement—to show how these were interconnected with feminists and women's movement. It is clear from these struggles that social change does not simply happen. The tremendous accomplishments and social change achieved by feminists and social justice activists required hard work, tough decisions, massive organizing, and innovative theorizing. In the next chapter, we will begin the process of thinking through theory: what it is, and how do we know.

Questions for Study

1. Why are some people reluctant to link social justice to feminism?
2. Make a list of all the American and Canadian social movements. What are commonalities among all of these movements?
3. Why is an understanding of social change and social justice historically essential for understanding the women's movements?
4. How did the Indian Act in Canada deprive Aboriginal women of their rights? How did three women challenge this?
5. Why can women's movements NOT be described as "homogenous and linear"?
6. Why can patriarchy not be solely blamed for women's oppression?
7. What are the significant outcomes of the United States Supreme Court decision *Roe v. Wade*? And why did this momentous decision happen?
8. What benefits have been achieved for North American women by the women's movement? (Hint—reread the section in this chapter, "Life without Women's Movement.")
9. Why is it essential to acknowledge the feminist and social justice struggles of the past?
10. How can the idea that "no one needs to be a feminist anymore" be easily challenged?

Activities and Questions for Discussion

1. Do an informal poll of three to four acquaintances, both male and female, who are *not* in a "feminist" course, and record your answers. Ask each if he/she considers himself/herself a feminist and why or why not. What do you conclude about your informal findings with reference to the ideas in this chapter?

2. Using the Internet, research one of the social movements in this chapter. How are the issues of this social movement linked to feminist issues? Clearly identify the issues and connect these to the whole movement.

3. Visit your local museum. Reflect on the representations of women and men from the past—activities, travel, work, education, family composition, style of dress, sporting events, technologies, and various social divisions. Ask yourself, how would your life be different without feminism?

The first problem for all of us, men and women,
is not to learn, but to unlearn.
—GLORIA STEINEM, "'WOMEN'S LIBERATION'
AIMS TO FREE MEN, TOO"

CHAPTER THREE

HOW DO I KNOW WHAT I KNOW?

EPISTEMOLOGY AND THEORY

In the last chapter, we discussed the complex and interconnected histories of feminist and social justice movements. Feminism, however, is not simply a movement. It is also a theory. So, to understand feminisms more fully, we must also understand what theory is and why we need it. Yes, theory. OMG! Don't run for cover just yet.

We might agree that there are women and men, and that we have theories about how they are different, if they are different, and, if they are different, how and why it matters. These theories lead us to think about inequality. And, if there is inequality, we might begin to wonder if inequality is a problem or just the natural order of things. We need to ask ourselves: How do we know? To move forward to understand and/or change the world, we need theory.

To ensure that the struggles of the past are not forgotten and the achievements undone, we must place ourselves in the picture. In order to do so, we must develop more than a passive understanding of history. We have to develop analytical and theoretical ways of thinking about the present as well as envisioning our future. You might think that theory has no place in your everyday life, or that it is simply a perplexing jumble of ideas and names of people who are long dead. You may believe that theory is too difficult and abstract and that you are being forced to take theory courses merely to meet departmental or disciplinary requirements. However, you may be surprised to find out that you are already doing theory but not calling it that. In this chapter, we will explore some everyday examples of doing theory and discuss what theory allows us to accomplish.

Facts, Assumptions, Opinions, and Theories

Theory allows us to explain events and phenomena that we observe in relation to broader frameworks of understanding. Theory helps us to make sense of the universe and our place in it. It can also help us to develop new ways of understanding the world. Theory is more than descriptions of events, observations, or experiences, although these are important components. Theory shapes our analysis of how and why things happen the way they do. Theories also define key concepts from which to develop an analysis.

Theory is something that we do every day. Indeed, everyday theorizing is the foundation for all critical thinking, as opposed to just giving your opinion. While we all have opinions about how things work and why things happen the way they do, opinions do not necessarily make good theory. An opinion is a statement based on a person's perspective, understanding, feelings, beliefs, and desires about an event, issue, or situation. It is *subjective*, which means that it is informed by the person or subject who is speaking. Opinions, therefore, are deeply personal and emotional interpretations rather than objective, unbiased, and substantiated information or facts. Opinions are knowledge claims that assume an air of truth. But they often fail to make convincing arguments. For example, you could tell me that in your opinion, eating liver is good for me because it is a super-food that can boost my energy, libido, and brainpower. However, there is nothing that you could say to convince me to eat it if I think it tastes awful. Our differing opinions both contain some validity, but are they based on facts?

Facts are thought to be irrefutable, indisputable, and provable. They are the basis on which we can make valid arguments. Facts are the evidence, commonly published in academic journals, for making particular claims. They are based on empirical data, which is information discovered through the use of our five senses: sight, hearing, taste, touch, and smell. Since we can determine that something exists and is therefore accessible for others to observe, we think of it as a fact. Empiricism is an epistemology, a way of knowing, that acknowledges direct observations of the world as valid ways to generate truths about the world. However, facts are not as indisputable as we might first think, and "truths" are often proven to be false.

Epistemology and Other Confusing Terms

So we already recognize, understand, and apply theory in our everyday lives. When we watch TV shows such as *Law & Order* or *CSI*, we theorize about who

Law & Order and *CSI*: What TV Crime Shows Teach Us about Theory, Facts, and Opinions

In criminal investigations, pieces of what might be called "hard evidence" at a crime scene (a dead body, fingerprints, blood, or a smoking gun) are often considered to be the facts of the case. They are collected based on the five senses, and they are discernible to others as well as us. We could assume, then, that we already know the facts of a case by looking at the hard evidence. But do we?

If we find blood at the scene of a crime, we might assume that it is the victim's, but is that a fact? Many other questions about the blood remain. Was this the primary crime scene? Was the body moved? Is anyone else's blood also present? Is the blood fresh? What do the shapes of the blood spots or splatter patterns mean? Our TV crime detectives must apply further tests to determine these answers. The crime scene provides the place to start, but investigators must be careful not to make hurried assumptions, since doing so might lead to the wrong conclusions.

Eyewitness testimony is not necessarily reliable evidence about what actually occurred. Witnesses will report what they have seen and heard with a sense of certainty. However, when there is more than one witness, stories of what has been seen and heard may differ. Eyewitness testimony has proven over time to be riddled with problems. For the most part, witnesses provide honest accounts and know that perjury is against the law. Nonetheless, research shows that human memory is fallible. Witnesses may remember events erroneously and even embellish their testimonies with fabricated details. Testimony is therefore a mixture of facts, opinions, and assumptions.

In these TV programs, as in life, detectives analyze the crime scene by drawing on past experience, research, and statistical evidence, as well as theory, to solve crimes. TV audiences also learn about theories. In theories of violence, for example, we discover that the perpetrator in a murder case is commonly someone known to the victim. This is theory based on experience. In the case of violence against women and children, a family member is statistically more likely to have committed the crime than a stranger. Careful analysis, which is critical in doing theory, must still be done. This analysis is complex, relying on facts, opinions, and theory for its conclusions. Such processes of analysis are grounded in larger frameworks, which draw on scientific and criminological theories of criminal behaviour, among others.

might have committed the crime, how they did it, and why. It seems that theorizing, then, is based on asking questions and finding answers. The answers become what we know. The question, is then, How do we know what we know?

As members of a society, we are constantly exposed to various social institutions that teach us about our world. This is how we learn. Not surprisingly, when we think about learning, we immediately recall our elementary and high school education, and now our university and college lives. But we don't just remember the in-class lessons; we also think of our life lessons from peers and family members. Perhaps we recall our participation in clubs, in organized sports, and street games like hide-and-seek. We might also participate in religious communities. As we grow up, we begin to recognize our civic rights and responsibilities as citizens of societies and nations. These are our experiences of learning and coming to know. Social and political institutions like family, education, religion, culture, customs, and traditions, as well as government institutions (such as departments of citizenship, health, revenue and taxation, Indian affairs, and heritage) shape what we know and believe. Through our experiences of social institutions, we learn about the rules, regulations, and social and cultural expectations that guide our lives.

When talking about knowledge in the classroom and other academic spaces, we use the term *epistemology* to refer to the theory of knowledge, or how we know what we know. The suffix "ology" is added to the end of a term to refer to a field of study such as soci*ology* or psych*ology*, or it can refer to a collection of knowledge or way of thinking about a specific term, in this case epistem*ology*. *Epistemology* encourages us not only to ask how we know what we know but also to raise other questions about the nature of knowing (Harding 1987; Alcoff 1998; Naples 2003). Epistemology asks:

- What is knowledge?
- What knowledge is valuable?
- How is knowledge acquired?
- What are the possibilities and limitations of knowing?

Let's do a little test of how we know and what we know with this example about capitalism. We have all heard of the term *capitalism* and we know that we live in a largely capitalist world, but do we consider this term a theory? Indeed, capitalism is a theory that has been discussed by many, including Adam Smith and Karl Marx. While we may not know the specific tenets of capitalism, we are already engaged in its practices. We are raised from a very young age with a basic understanding of money, a key component of capitalism. Either we have it or, in the majority of cases, we don't have enough of it. Our parents teach us about money through everyday activities like going to the grocery store or the food bank, the bookstore or the library. We may shop at retail clothing stores or second-hand ones. We, or our parents, may own our homes or rent them, or in some cases neither, forcing us to live in shelters, cars, and on the streets. Buying and selling goods and services are foundational to capitalism, and we participate in these activities every day. But still we don't really think of this as doing theory, or even as practising capitalism. Yet learning about capitalism is embedded in the games we play, including board games and virtual games. Monopoly teaches us about investing, acquiring properties, and building hotel and motel businesses, while the Game of LIFE takes us through the stages of our lives from youth through to college, marriage, and retirement. In both games, players are taught about the perils of bad choices (and bad luck), with the consequence of going to jail in Monopoly or ending up on the Poor Farm in LIFE. Alternatively, the winner of both games is rewarded with money, living on Park Avenue in NYC in Monopoly or moving to Millionaire Acres in the Game of LIFE. In virtual play and gaming, the world of capitalism is also firmly present. For example, in the online games Second Life (SL) or World of Warcraft (WoW), virtual goods and skills are exchanged for money; capitalism is the foundation (Dyer-Witheford and de Peuter 2009).

We are also well aware of key concepts of capitalism, money, markets, competition, supply, demand, and, of course, profits, through other everyday avenues. While we may not be business tycoons or entrepreneurial superstars, we have been primed to value and strive for these jobs through our social and cultural experiences. We "know" that competition, at all levels, is the key to success. We already understand that we must work to make money to buy the things that we need and want. As workers, we learn that the more money we make, the more we can spend and the better our lives will be. As consumers, we are the engines that drive capitalist markets. It is our demand for products that ensures their supply. It is also our labour that makes products for the market. Our various positions within capitalism give us an understanding of the laws of supply and demand for goods.

We also have an understanding of markets and competition through our experiences as consumers and workers earning money to buy things. We know, for example, that when new products are launched, they will be expensive and that people seem to always want what is new, even if it is only slightly better than what they already have. We also know that over time, the price of these must-haves will drop. We may not consciously think about why this happens. However, we do understand that as more of these products enter the market, the greater the competition. With competition, we know that sellers will have to lower their prices to sell more and meet their profit goals. We may not really care why prices decline, but we want them to since this affects how much money we have to spend. The increased production of goods can result in lower production costs. The nightly news reminds us of the importance of markets with flashes of numbers from the New York, London, Tokyo, and Toronto stock exchanges. Most of us can't make sense of these numbers, but we are reassured nonetheless when we are told they are going up. The concept of the market, the interaction between supply and demand, is central to the theory of capitalism, and we are already engaged in it. Capitalism is the dominant social, political, and economic system. We may not know all the ins and outs, but we do know about it.

From our experiences and our multiple and diverse locations within the big picture of capitalism, we can begin to understand the concept of theory as something that we already do every day.

There's No Way I'm Already *Doing* Theory: Theorizing the Every Day

If theory is a way of thinking about and understanding our experiences in relation to the past and in preparation for the future, so that we can figure out what is likely in store for us, everyday theorizing might look something like this. You are a university student who has a class to attend at 11:30 in the morning. After a late night of studying (or perhaps partying), you accidentally turn off your alarm and go back to sleep. Suddenly you awaken with only a few minutes to get to class. What do you do? You might contemplate taking a taxi, which would mean that you could get there on time. However, your decision might be influenced by your budget. For example, if you take a taxi, you won't be able to pay your rent. Consequently, you eliminate this option. You might think that if you hurry to get ready, and run (assuming you're able-bodied) to catch the bus, you will arrive with seconds to spare. However, your experience tells you that when you get off the bus, if the traffic light changes to yellow, you still could be late. You decide to take the risk, hurry, and take the bus. The light changes to yellow. Now what do you do? You again theorize your situation. Should you cross the street anyway? You must assess the oncoming traffic. You will need to quickly hypothesize how fast the cars are travelling and calculate if you can move fast enough to make it across without injury. While you are theorizing the situation, you will also evaluate the consequences *if* you arrive late to class. Last time someone was late, the professor was annoyed and made her sit in the front row. It was embarrassing. The time before, someone slipped into the back of the class, but there were no seats on the aisles, so several of your classmates were disturbed and there was quite a bit of noise with papers shuffling and people huffing in annoyance. The professor noticed the late arrival, frowned, and continued on with her lecture. Still, it was a bit embarrassing. To avoid all this theorizing next time, you might resolve to get to bed earlier, get up when the alarm rings, and arrive to class on time. This is theorizing. We may not recognize everyday decision-making as theory because we are unaware of the assumptions behind our actions, and we make these choices unconsciously. Consequently, we don't recognize that our choices are grounded in theory.

Subjectivity and Objectivity: This Is Not the Way I Thought It Worked

In the story about being late for class, knowledge about what would happen if you were late is based on personal experience. This type of knowledge is referred to as subjective knowledge. This means that the knowledge you have about lateness is influenced by you as a subject.

We might think that theory is provable, something like the experiments that we proved in our high school science classes. You might recall an experiment to determine the pH of a liquid. The theory is that if you dip litmus paper into a liquid, you can determine whether it is alkaline or acidic depending on whether the paper turns blue or red. The results are observable, and they can be replicated successfully without changing. We consider our observations to be objective. This means that we, as a subject, did not influence the outcome of the experiment. So whether I am Christian, Muslim, Buddhist, or agnostic, male or female, the results of the litmus test will remain the same. But life is not like that.

It is important to recognize that theory is always about something and for someone. This means that theories have power. They are not neutral or objective; rather, they are contextual and subjective. The questions that we ask and the theories we choose to use to answer them are also subjective. Not all theories can answer the same questions, and different theories may answer the same questions differently. Theories therefore have an epistemological basis. Capitalist theory, for example, is written for the powerful, and the rules of capitalism, reinforced by our cultural practices such as games, uphold these positions of power. In contrast, critiques of capitalism are written about and for those who have less power, those who have been excluded from power, and those who are exploited under capitalism. But what does all this have to do with feminism?

What Is Feminist Theory and Why Do We Need It?

Feminist theory provides frameworks for understanding our lives, the means to envision the way things could be different, and strategies for taking action and making change. As early as the eighteenth century, feminist theories, although not named as such, sought to explain women's experiences and everyday lives. By the 1970s, feminist theorists began to expand their frameworks to address issues of gender, race, class, sexuality, ability, age, colonialism, imperialism, and power, as we will see in chapters 5 and 6. We can imagine using feminist theory like a camera lens, one that we can use to focus our analysis and see issues, situations, or events differently. A feminist lens is an important concept because it allows us to zoom in for a close-up view of particular situations and experiences, but it is also a way of zooming out and seeing the world more

Illustration 3.1: What do you mean hit the F-stop button? This F-start sure gives me a better view.

broadly. It is because of this adjustable lens that feminists are able to ask different questions and hopefully produce new answers.

As with all other theories, feminist theories reflect the interests, values, and assumptions of those who create them. A feminist epistemology, therefore, is a reinforcing process of knowing and acting as a feminist. Many feminist theorists recognize the dangers of subjectivity and counter it by insisting on *self-reflexivity* (Harding 1987, 2006; Hartsock 1987; Alcoff 1998; Naples 2003). Self-reflexivity is a process whereby you critically examine the causes and effects of your ideas, words, and actions. Self-reflexivity for feminists necessitates an evaluation of the ways we think and act, as well as our positions of power and privilege. It demands that we hold a mirror up to ourselves and question whether we are measuring up to our feminist principles and goals, however we define them. Feminist theorizing, therefore, allows for multiple and varied approaches for understanding the world in which we live. These theories are flexible and adaptable rather than fixed and unchanging explanations of how the world works. Feminist theories incorporate diverse perspectives and strive to correct past mistakes or omissions.

There are many different feminist theories: liberal, socialist, radical, anti-racist, postmodern, postcolonial, queer, and transnational. Different theories can offer us different perspectives and insights into our research and our lives. Topics addressed, ways of seeing things, explanations, and strategies for change may differ according to the particular feminist theory, and choosing one does not necessarily mean excluding the others. Each of us must begin the process of choosing a theory, or theories, that make sense to us and best help us understand the world and our place in it. This means finding yourself and your experiences in the theories that we will be examining and using them to express your ideas and your perspective on the issues. Before you know it, you will be making links between these theories and the way you see the world. Imagine what it could look like.

When we are attuned to thinking critically, we begin to realize that our ideas are rooted in convictions that are both subjective and theoretical. You have a politics, too, and it just might be feminist.

Feminist theorists use key terms and concepts to analyze, understand, and explain our experiences and ask different questions. Unlike many other theories, these questions place women and marginalized people at the centre of analysis. Some of the key terms and concepts used by feminist theories are gender, patriarchy, masculinity, femininity, equality, equity, sexuality, power, and empowerment. We have already defined some of these terms in past chapters, such as gender, patriarchy, masculinity, and femininity, and we will expand on these and explore others in coming chapters.

Conclusion

In this chapter, we have begun the process of theorizing. We have seen through various examples that theories shape our everyday lives. It isn't really as hard as we might once have thought because, while we may not have been calling it theory, we were already doing it. We have also discovered that politics and subjectivities are attached to every theory. Feminism is not simply a theory, it is a politics, and it shapes how we understand the world in which we live. An emphasis was placed on the importance of theorizing about issues, subjectivity, and locating ourselves (self-reflexivity) in the debates. In beginning this process and using theory to explore the everyday, we can build critical analytical thinking skills to interpret what we know, what we think we know, and how we know it. In the next chapter we will further develop our understandings of power, politics, and intersectionality.

Questions for Study

1. What is the value of theory in understanding feminisms? List at least three ways.
2. What is theory? Give an example of everyday theorizing in your life.
3. What is epistemology? List four central questions that epistemology asks and/or answers.

4. How is subjective knowledge different from objective knowledge? Provide an example of each.
5. How does a theory have "power"?
6. Why theorize about feminisms? What do feminists theorize about?
7. How is self-reflexivity central to feminist theorizing?
8. What are institutions? How do institutions maintain gender inequality?
9. What is power? What is privilege? Where do power and privilege operate? How do power and privilege affect your life?

Activities and Questions for Discussion

1. Gender transgression: Create and perform an activity that challenges gendered expectations and behaviours. To do this you must first critically reflect on the ways that you engage in gendered behaviour. Make a list of your gender conforming behaviours and spend a day transgressing them. Write a short critical reflection on this experience. You might want to consider the following questions:
   • Where do you place yourself on the gender continuum?
   • How do you "perform" your gender in the social world?
   • What gendered expectations did you seek to disrupt with your gender transgression?
   • How is your gender raced, classed, and otherwise mediated by social categories?
   • How does your experience relate to feminist ideas about gender and society?
2. Have you ever been in a situation where friends or family members are talking about an issue about which you have a different opinion? You might have kept quiet about your views, or you might have confronted them with your opposition. Afterwards, you likely just continued about your day. Rethink this situation: engage in an exercise of critical self-reflection to explore how you might have handled this situation differently to create a different outcome.
3. Do an Internet search to find activists working in an area that you are interested in. Find out what they are doing, how they got involved in their work, and what the impact/status of their activism is today.

Until all of us have made it, none of us have made it.
—ROSEMARY BROWN, IN LUXTON, "FEMINISM AS A CLASS ACT"

CHAPTER FOUR

MAKING MY HEAD SPIN
CRITICAL INTERSECTIONALITY

Intersectionality is a conceptual tool for analyzing differences. It allows us to think about multiple identities and how they may be interconnected in complex ways. It is also a tool for understanding how multiple systems of oppression may be interrelated. Feminists use the concept of intersectionality, a term coined by legal scholar Kimberlé Crenshaw, to consider how interlocking systems of oppressions, complex identities, and social inequalities affect people's lives (Crenshaw 1989). The concept of intersectionality has long been used by black feminists to explore the lives of racialized women (Moraga 1983; Lorde 1984; hooks 1984; Collins 1990, 1993).

In saying that identities are multiple, feminists recognize that each of us can appreciate multiple aspects of our identity. Identities include the many social categories we use to define ourselves and others such as lesbian, Aboriginal, able-bodied, wealthy, educated, immigrant, or criminal. We are likely to identify with a particular gender, race, ethnicity, sexual orientation, age group, and ability. Our identities are also shaped by our experiences and social locations. Often the term *positionality* is used to refer to our locations in our communities and the world, based on our class, geopolitical place, nationality, citizenship, religion, and level of education, to name but a few (Alcoff 1988; Anzaldúa 1987). For example, you might be living in Canada, in your first year of university, born in South Africa, a Buddhist, and struggling to pay for your living expenses, yet able-bodied and employed. All of these locations and experiences add to your understanding of yourself and the world around you. Feminists use the term *situated knowledge* to express knowledge gained by our positionality (Harding 1989; Smith 1987). Donna Haraway's (1988) influential work led feminists to explore how such knowledge is *located* in lived experiences and contexts. Is your head spinning yet?

We are all complex individuals with multiple identities. This does not mean, however, that we are fractured or that we can divide ourselves into various component parts as needed, acting differently according to which identity we are wearing at the time. Rather, our complexity lies in the ways in which our multiple identities simultaneously create our whole selves. This complexity makes us unique, but it also allows us to relate to others who share both similar and dissimilar identities and experiences.

Categories, Binaries, and Other Ways of Knowing That Don't Quite Work

Let's examine some more of the concepts and categories used in intersectional analyses. One way of processing and sorting information and experiences is by placing them into categories. This processing informs our way of knowing by relating information and experiences to other similar and dissimilar information and experiences. Feminists have always struggled with the imperfections of ways of knowing and categories of analysis because they are multiple and socially constructed (Grosz 1987). In chapter 1, we discussed the idea that gender, patriarchy, masculinities, and femininities are socially constructed. Recall that the concept of social construction can be understood through the metaphor of building a house. While most houses have foundations, walls, and roofs, these elements are also what makes houses enormously different. Differences in climate, location, the availability of building materials, architectural styles, environmental policies, and building codes all affect the house. They classify and sort the variety of housing options, yet they remain within the overall category of housing.

Categories such as sex, gender, race, and class have long been used to classify and explain everyday experiences. Such analyses depend on distinct categories and on reinforced *binary* divisions, meaning that they fall into one of two possible categories (Fausto-Sterling 1981; Harding 1986). Accordingly, the category of sex was subdivided into male and female, race was often thought of as a division between white and black, and class could be divided into elites and working people. Through binary codification, feminists and other social scientists imagined that they could understand and explain what they observed. However, the limitations of such distinct categories and sorting into *either/or* are obvious. By the 1970s, feminists had begun to question the sex/gender binary that divided sex, the biologically presumed categories of man or woman based on reproductive capacity, from the socially constructed gendered understandings of masculine or feminine (Firestone 1970; Millett 1970; O'Brien 1981; Irigaray 1985; Fausto-Sterling 1993). What happens when something is better classified somewhere in between the binaries or when neither binary nor the space in between is sufficient?

Since the 1980s, intersectionality has revealed the limitations of binary thinking (Moraga 1983; Lorde 1984; Crenshaw 1989; hooks 1984; Collins 1990, 1993; Mohanty 1986, 2002; Haraway 1988; Harding 1989). Intersectionality recognizes that the multiplicity and diversity of experiences and social locations, or positionalities, is central to analysis. It is important to acknowledge that experiences and positionalities exist within frameworks of *power*, which are systems of inclusion and exclusion, structures of domination and subordination, and hierarchies of privilege.

What's the Connection? It's All about POWER

Power is a central concept for everyday theorizing. People are likely to think that some people have power while others don't, but they may not consider why this might or might not be the case. We simply think this is the way power operates and we don't question it. So, when asked to define power, many of us conjure up images of domination over others. We think of power as the way a pie is carved up and divided: the bigger the slice, the more power one has. The winners are those with more power and the losers are those with less power. According to this scenario, power is *zero-sum* or equal to one pie, which means that power is finite, with only so much to be had (Tickner 1988; Keohane 1989). When the pie is divided and one person's piece is bigger than the others' pieces, the person with the biggest piece holds power over the others. We simply think this is how the world works, and it is this thinking that underpins the rules of capitalism. For example, we are socialized to imagine that money is power and that more money or a bigger piece of the pie equals more power.

Images of shared power or *empowerment* are less likely to come to mind when we are considering power. Power, however, is not simply possessed and wielded; it is also something that can be struggled against and it can also be shared. The kind of power that feminists are concerned with is shared power. This is called empowerment, a type of power that enables people to live more fulfilling lives. According to visions of empowerment, power can be attained through knowledge. For example, we might be counselled to get a good education because "knowledge is power." And, if we choose, this power can be used for good rather than evil. This sounds a bit melodramatic, so let's consider knowledge like feminists might (Keller 1987; Haraway 1988; Collins 1990; Rowlands 1995). Knowledge is not zero-sum. The acquisition of knowledge does not reduce the knowledge that others can also possess. Knowledge can be shared with others and, as others gain knowledge, they can also be empowered. Most feminists envision empowerment not as something simply conferred on an individual but as something that can be shared with everyone.

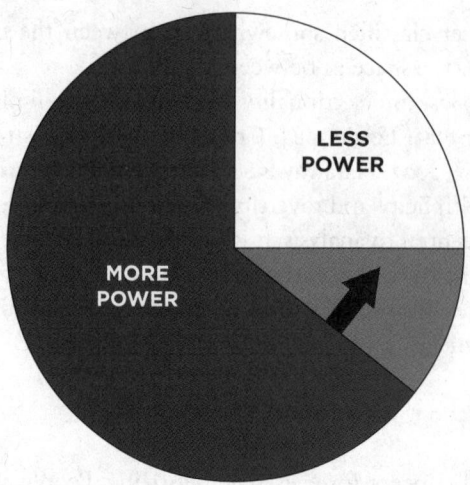

Figure 4.1: Power over others: how we get a smaller piece of the pie in the zero-sum game.

Consequently, empowerment is collective, expansive, and beneficial rather than merely satisfying for the individual. Empowerment increases the social, economic, political, and spiritual strength of individuals and their communities. It is not finite like a pie. A piece for one person doesn't leave less for everyone else.

Understanding power in all its complexity is important for feminists because it offers an inroad to the analyses of systems of inclusion and exclusion, the structures of domination and subordination, and the hierarchies of privilege. Systems of *inclusion and exclusion* are divisions or barriers that prevent people from joining and belonging (Keller 1987; Spelman 1988; Linklater 1992; Walker 1992; Tickner 1993). They are a way of ordering society and there is power embedded in such systems. If you wanted to join a club, for example, you would likely have to meet particular requirements and follow the rules of membership. If you are a member of a soccer team, you might be required to wear a uniform. Membership is not always simple, however. What happens when students resist or confront social expectations? What happens when boys bring their male partners to proms or girls wear tuxedos instead of conventional party dresses? Too often they are met with sanctions, exclusion, and punishment.

The categories of analysis themselves—gender, race, class, sexuality, age, and ability—have boundaries and rules that define appropriate membership. Simply put, these are the markers or identifiers that are often used and abused to maintain the status quo. In such systems, power and surveillance operate to control actions and behaviours and to maintain social order. *Surveillance*, the

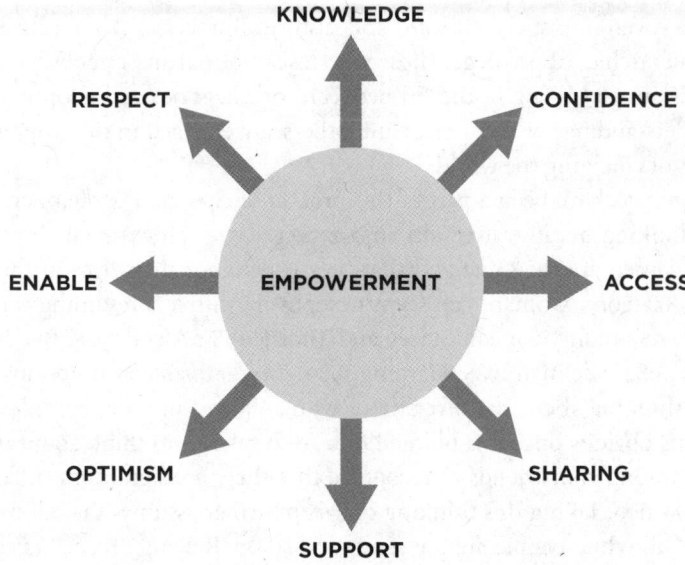

Figure 4.2: Empowerment: More than zero-sum.

everyday monitoring that we experience by family, friends, teachers, bosses, and community members, as well as *self-monitoring*, works to ensure that we follow the rules that maintain hierarchies of privilege.

Hierarchies of privilege order society based on ensuring that advantages flow to the dominant group in society: those who make the rules and hold power over others (see, for example, hooks 1984; Lorde 1984; McIntosh 1989; Collins 1990, 1993; Tickner 1993). In North America, that group is overwhelmingly white, male, heterosexual, able-bodied, and economically affluent. Hierarchies of privilege exist in oppositional categories of difference that rely on notions of "us" versus "them," as well as zero-sum power. In this sense, one is male or female, white or not, masculine or feminine, heterosexual or homosexual, young or old, able-bodied or *dis*abled. Imagine these rigid binaries as policed boundaries that reinforce separation and difference, preventing our understandings of common-alities. Like all hierarchies, power is embedded in the dividing line between the two binaries. In each pairing, privilege rests with the first in the twosome. At first we might see these divisions as quite natural rather than socially constructed. What about those who don't fit comfortably within these rigid categories? On closer examination, we recognize that there is fluidity, flux, and interpenetration, as well as a resistance to such categories. This is also about power, the power to determine "normal" and the power to change what is accepted as "normal." But there isn't a powerful group of rich, white able-bodied heterosexual men sitting around in a room somewhere dictating the rules of normal. Rather the rules are woven into social customs and historical processes that create and reinforce hierarchies of privilege. Those who resist normal and established binary categories, instead living in the "in between" of categories and adopting more fluid understandings of themselves and others, are engaged in the empowering processes of changing the world.

Feminists have been a part of this process of change. They have critiqued binary thinking because it results in a *homogenizing* process, which assumes that all women are the same and that they experience their lives in the same way. The category "woman" can seem deceptively simple, presuming there are no *differences* among women (Stacey and Thorne 1985; Alcoff 1988; Butler 1988; Mohanty 1984; Spelman 1988; Harding 1989). *Universalizing* assumptions block us from thinking about the diversity of women's lives in more complex ways. This seems obvious once it is pointed out. All it takes is to think about the differences among your friends to recognize that there are significant differences among women. Taking this thinking one step further assumes that all men are the same, all white people are the same, and so on. Relying on such *essentialist* thinking erases the diversity of experiences within and outside categories, preventing more complex theorizing. Unquestioningly accepting binary categories as natural and normal reinforces unearned privilege.

Unearned privilege or advantage should be contrasted to merit. In North America, we tend to think that our society operates as a meritocracy. Members of society earn their status, and create their advantages, and successes are always earned rather than simply conferred. This means, for example, that on the job, we assume that our hard work, education, and job performance should always be measured and rewarded with success, promotions, and salary increases. However, this is not necessarily the case. Assumptions about gender, race, sexuality, age, and ability influence all aspects of our employment, from hiring and performance evaluations, to promotions and even salaries. For example, the unearned privilege of whiteness could mean that an applicant gets the job based on their perceived skin colour. This is not necessarily a conscious decision on the part of the hiring committee; nonetheless, the effect of screening out non-white candidates occurs every day in various sectors of the economy. Interviewers have set criteria for particular jobs; however, the interviewer's *assumptions* about the qualifications of potential employees are complex. Recent studies in Canada and the U.S. found that there is considerable employer discrimination against applicants with ethnic-sounding names or with experience from foreign countries (Bertrand and Mullainathan 2004; Oreopoulos 2009).

Exclusions can occur even before an interview is offered, particularly if an applicant's name fails to convey whiteness or if their nationality or citizenship status is other than Canadian or American. Ability also raises unfounded assumptions by interviewers, because of the commonly held view that a disability makes one a poor employee or that hiring someone with a disability will result in high accommodation costs to the employer. Such assumptions discount the qualifications and abilities of individuals who already contribute significantly to both the economy and their communities. Excluding candidates based on their age is frequently done through a careful reading of the résumé, which indicates when candidates completed their education and therefore indicates their age.

Consider how this newspaper story demonstrates the power of whiteness and class to reinforce unearned privilege. At President Barack Obama's first state dinner in 2009, Michaele Salahi and her husband arrived at the White House gala without an invitation. Nonetheless, the couple was admitted without a fuss because, at a glance, the Salahis conform to the assumptions about wealthy and important people: a beautiful willowy blond and a handsome tuxedo-clad gentleman. The couple was able to have their pictures taken with the President and other key political figures, confirming the belief that they belonged at the dinner. Regardless of our particular location and experiences, it is a struggle to challenge the assumptions and stereotypes that we have internalized. While the admission of the Salahis was a blunder on the part of the Secret Service, the possibility of such a breach in security demonstrates the power of unquestioned assumptions that reinforce unearned privilege (Givhan 2009).

"Privilege" in these examples refers to an unspoken and invisible advantage that is not earned but conferred based on markers of identity—gender, race, class, sexuality, ability, and age. Assigning these markers seems *natural* and *normal* to us; however, in so doing, we mistakenly see the characteristics or properties that we assign to people as intrinsic to them rather than recognizing ourselves in the process of constructing peoples' identities. Because we assume a *naturalness* or a *normalcy* to the categories that we assign, the categories remain unquestioned and our assumptions about the categories remain invisible. Consequently, considerable authority continues to reside with white, heterosexual, able-bodied, economically affluent men; unearned privilege rules and the perception of a meritocracy in North America remains unquestioned. However, feminist critiques work to dismantle unearned privilege by exposing how hierarchies of privilege operate as systems of exclusion and inclusion and are rooted in notions of difference. Differences are generally associated with race, ethnicity, class, sexual orientation, sexualities, religion, nationality, age, and ability.

Difference has been a stumbling point for feminists, both in terms of theorizing and within women's movement. The problem has been to recognize and value difference and diversity while at the same time rallying solidarity around commonalities to construct both theoretical insights and forward political agendas (Collins 1986, 1990; Mohanty 1995, 2002; Barrett and Phillips 1992; Braidotti 1994, 2011; Lorde 1984; Zinn and Dill 1996). Differences are

What's in a Name? Exclusions, Discrimination, and Racism in Employment

Two recent studies, one in the U.S. and one in Canada, are important in understanding exclusionary hiring practices based on perceived race and ethnicity. In the U.S. study, Bertrand and Mullainathan (2004) sent 5,000 fictitious résumés in response to 1,300 job advertisements in Chicago and Boston newspapers in the areas of sales, administrative support, clerical, and customer services. The purpose of the experiment was to measure and compare callback rates for white and African American applicants. Fictitious résumés were created and half were randomly assigned very white-sounding names, such as Emily Walsh or Greg Baker, while the other half were given very African American-sounding names such as Lakisha Washington or Jamal Jones. Gender and skill sets were equally distributed in both groups to ensure that these characteristics did not negatively influence the results.

The results were disturbing. Researchers found large racial differences in callback rates. For every 10 résumés sent out, applicants with white-sounding names received one callback but those applicants with African American-sounding names received one callback for 15 résumés sent out. This 50 per cent gap in callbacks is statistically significant. Bertrand and Mullainathan also found that blacks need 8 additional years of labour market experience to equalize the callback rates of whites. Suggestions of widespread discrimination in the U.S. labour market are supported by the findings that racial gaps in callback rates hold across all the occupation and economic sectors. Bertrand and Mullainathan concluded that differential treatment by race still appears to be significant in hiring practices in the U.S.

In a similar Canadian study, Philip Oreopoulos (2009) wanted to find out why skilled immigrants, who were accepted as immigrants on the basis of their skills, continue to struggle in the labour market. Oreopoulos sent out 6,000 fictitious résumés to online advertised jobs in the Toronto area over a period of seven months. Fictitious résumés were created to represent recent immigrants from Britain and Canada's three largest sending countries (China, India, and Pakistan), as well as non-immigrants with non-ethnic-sounding names. Résumés were also randomized by country where the applicant received his/her degree, foreign versus Canadian work experience, and language fluency (including French). Fictitious résumés were constructed by using actual résumés of recent immigrants and online submissions to ensure that they reflected the skill sets of recent immigrants. English-sounding names for fictitious résumés were selected from among the most popular in Canada (Smith, Martin, Brown, Wilson, and Johnson). These were randomly matched and equally distributed with male names (Greg, John, Matthew, or Michael) and female names (Alison, Carrie, Emily, and Jill). An equal number of fictitious résumés were created with foreign-sounding names randomly .

chosen from the most popular male and female names in China, India, and Pakistan.

Oreopoulos' study found that applicants with English-sounding names, with Canadian education and experience, received callbacks 40 per cent more often than did applicants with Chinese, Indian, or Pakistani names. The results of this study suggest that potential Canadian employers discriminate against applicants with ethnic-sounding names and foreign experience.

produced and reproduced through oppressive structures such as patriarchy, racism, colonialism, Eurocentrism, heterosexism, transphobia, and ableism. Indeed, it is impossible to understand gender, race, sexuality, age or ability as analytic categories that are separated from the oppressive structures that form interlocking systems of oppression (Moraga 1983; Moraga and Anzaldúa 1983; Mohanty 1984, 2002; hooks 1984; Lorde 1984; Collins 1986, 1990, 1993; Anzaldúa 1987; Crenshaw 1989). Without such contexts, analyses will be incomplete and ineffectual for theorizing or movement building.

To more fully understand interlocking systems of oppressions, we must understand the implications of colonialism, Eurocentrism, patriarchy, and heterosexism as structural barriers or inhibitors of social justice and change (Mohanty 1984, 2002; Moraga 1983; Grewal and Kaplan 1994; McClintock 1995; Shohat 2001). *Colonialism* refers to the processes by which a people, empire, nation, or state conquer, acquire, and control another people, their lands, culture, and wealth. Beginning in the fifteenth century and extending into the twentieth, empire- and state-building on the part of European and other nations proceeded under an imperialist direction by establishing colonies around the world. This domination meant not only the acquisition of gold, silver, and raw materials but also the possession of lands and control over people through domination, oppression, war, rape, pillaging, trickery, and unequal trading practices. Colonialism is not so easily defined merely by this set timeframe. Its legacy of domination, oppression, exploitation and inequality continue today as neocolonialism: the ongoing unequal relationships between former colonies and colonizers. In North America, *neocolonialism* is used to express the unequal relationships and continued oppression of indigenous peoples. More broadly, neocolonialism refers to the ongoing legacies of colonization and dependency that reinforce the structural disadvantages of the Global South vis-à-vis the Global North in a globalized world (McClintock 1995; Misra 2000; Bacchetta 2001; Krishna 2009).

Eurocentrism is also an important concept to explain ongoing processes of inclusion and exclusion. It is premised on the view that Europe is the centre of the world and "civilization," and everything can and must be measured against this standard. Accordingly, anything non-European is relegated to subordinate status and assumed to be inferior. Eurocentrism, therefore, is a way of looking at the world that reaffirms privilege to Europeans and their descendants. The term Eurocentrism is often used interchangeably with Western-centrism to reflect the extension of power beyond Europe. Such a perspective assumes whiteness, maleness, and heterosexuality as the primary and only valuable identity markers.

If we take all these concepts together, we can begin to understand how intersectionality helps us to conceive such complexities while recognizing that their effects vary according to different historical time periods and in different geographic and political spaces. As this complicated messiness of identity plays out in people's lives, differences and commonalities become even more important to work through if social justice and change are the goals of feminisms.

Feminists engaging with intersectional analyses assert that race, class, sexuality, age, ability, and gender are interlocking and interdependent sites of (possible) oppression that are simultaneously experienced rather than independently or sequentially experienced. Adding "possible oppression" recognizes that we can hold positions of advantage and disadvantage as well as power and powerlessness, simultaneously. We can also be both oppressor and oppressed (Miller 1996). Our particular experiences are diverse, complex, and even contradictory. So while affluent, heterosexual men hold some advantage in certain circumstances, working-class men, racialized men, gay men, or transgender men may be disadvantaged in similar situations. Likewise, while women in general hold less power in North America, white, affluent, heterosexual, and well-educated women are likely to hold much more power than others. Consequently, each of us can be both oppressor and oppressed, depending on the situation and our actions.

Take for example, a well-educated North American Latina woman who hires another Latina woman as the caregiver for her children. This may be an equitable relationship if the caregiver is well paid, receives benefits, and is fairly valued for the work that she performs. However, the employer could become the oppressor should these conditions not exist. Further, if the caregiver does not have citizenship status in the country, often referred to as working "under the table," the caregiver is more vulnerable to oppression and exploitation, even if both women are Latinas. This simplified analysis demonstrates the need to be self-reflexive and to recognize our positions of unearned privilege and dominance as well as our experiences of subordination and marginalization.

I Think I'm a Good Person, but ...

Understanding intersectionality as a conceptual and analytical tool is useful, but understanding its implications for self-reflexivity is another thing. For us to grapple with the messiness of intersectionality in our everyday lives, we need

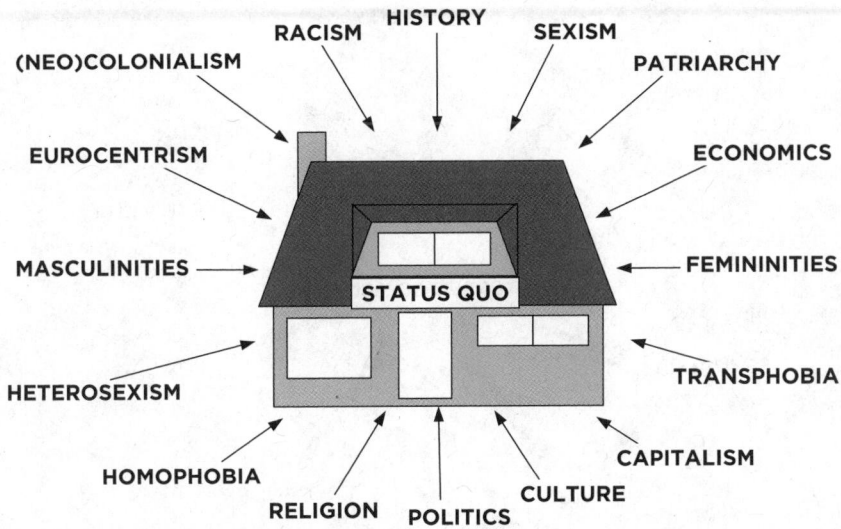

Figure 4.3: Structural barriers to social change.

to recognize the multiplicity of experiences and diversity of social locations as well as our own *positionality* in any analyses. Struggling with intersectionality when social and popular conventions assume gender, racial, and social equality already exists is all the more difficult for us. Because we have been raised in a racist, patriarchal, and heterosexist society, racism, sexism, and homophobia permeate every aspect of our conscious and unconscious thinking.

When concerns about racism, sexism, or homophobia are raised, we hear the outpouring of denial around us, even coming, perhaps, from ourselves. We might even be offered tokens of proof that equality exists. For example, those who disclaim the existence of sexism and racism might suggest that Oprah Winfrey's success is evidence that black women can gain heretofore-unprecedented social, economic, and political power. The problem with such evidence is that it assumes that Oprah is representative of all black women and it mistakenly presumes that if Oprah can do it, so can all black women. What people who offer such evidence fail to recognize is that one or even many examples don't prove the case. While Oprah is the highest paid woman in the U.S., according to *Forbes* magazine's 2010s list, it is still true that African American women are paid significantly less than white women in general, and white men in particular. Sexism is systemic and institutionalized, and it invisibly reinforces social assumptions and reaffirms that men are fundamentally superior to women. Racism operates in similarly insidious and undetectable ways to reify social assumptions that one race is intrinsically superior to another. So, while Oprah's success is indisputable, the ways in which sexism and racism have nonetheless played a part in her life are less clear without more information and in-depth analysis.

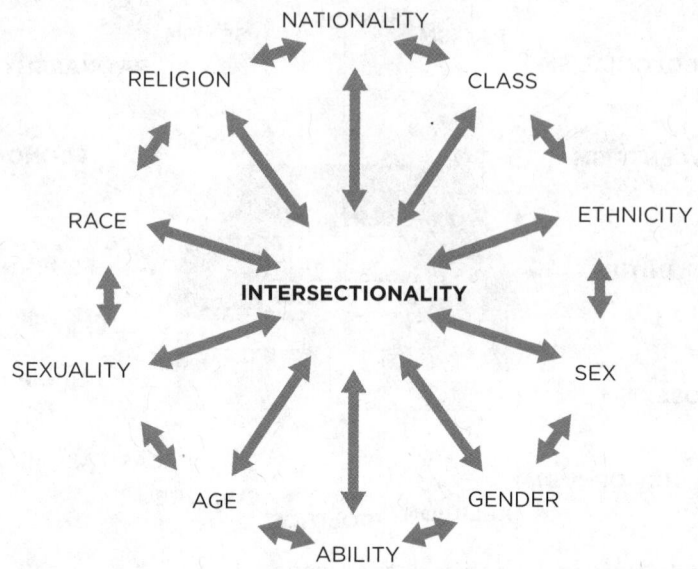

Figure 4.4: Thinking through intersectionality.

No individual is raised in North America without internalizing the assumptions that operate through the oppressive structures of sexism, racism, classism, heterosexism, and ablism. In this sense, we are all, at least to some extent and in different ways, sexist, racist, classist, heterosexist, ableist, and ageist because of the social, economic, and political environments in which we have been socialized. Consequently, we can readily understand stories and jokes that are infused with racist, sexist, homophobic, and other stereotypes. Indeed, the very telling of such stories and jokes serve to remind us of the power hierarchies that continue to exist. Take, for example, "dumb blond" jokes.

You might giggle at the comic featured in illustration 4.1, which at first glance seems harmless enough. On closer examination, however, the blond is not without a gender identity. She is clearly assumed to be a woman, otherwise it would not seem funny and it would be challenging masculine privilege. The joke, however, is not just about a blond woman or even blond women in general. It is a statement about all women that reinforces their presumed subordinate position. Think about replacing the blond character in the joke with another identity, perhaps a black woman or for that matter a black man. The humour immediately disappears because the racism embedded in such a joke is quickly exposed. The sexism in the blond joke is much more subtle.

What happens if you call someone out for their sexism, racism, or homophobia? Depending on where you are located, you might witness some fancy backpedalling. A quick dismissal of your concern is not uncommon, including: "Can't you take a joke?" "I didn't mean anything by it," and of course,

Illustration 4.1. Is this joke really funny?

"I don't really think that way ... but it *is* funny, isn't it!" No one wants to be called a "Debbie Downer" for ruining the fun, but each of us has a responsibility to ensure that oppression is not reproduced and that we are not participants in its reproduction.

Sexism, racism, classism, ableism, and homophobia are part of our everyday language. Comments like "that's so lame," "that's so gay," and "trailer trash," and even the commonly referred to men's sleeveless T-shirt as a "wife beater," expose sites of oppression and power structures that regulate our everyday lives and consciousness. When we begin to recognize that each of us has internalized assumptions and stereotypes that maintain systems of oppression, we can begin to act differently. Understanding how oppression works and how we unwittingly and perhaps unwillingly participate in its continuation is not about guilt, blame, or shame. These emotions fail to produce social change and can even prevent us from taking action in our own lives. When we become conscious of our participation in oppressive activities, through our thoughts, language and actions, it becomes our responsibility to make a deliberate effort to reflect on our own positionality, question our privilege, and then act differently. To become more attuned to our unconscious selves, we need to engage in processes of consciousness-raising.

Raising Consciousness: Critical Self-reflection, Empathy, and Imaginative Thinking

Consciousness-raising is central to various feminisms. By the mid-1960s, women were engaged in a feminist politics, sometimes referred to as "rap sessions," "bitch sessions," and, of course, "consciousness-raising" (Morgan 1970; Driefus 1973; Koedt 1973; Sarachild

1978; hooks 2000). Initially, these sessions were organized around kitchen tables so that women could subversively gather, as they regularly had in the past to exchange recipes or household and childrearing tips, without raising concerns from men and even other women about what exactly they were conspiring to do (Chicago Women's Liberation Union 1971; Jones 1980). Consciousness-raising groups met to discuss and analyze women's experiences of patriarchy and sexism, their experiences of violence, exploitation, and exclusion, and to develop a feminist politics for change (Redstockings 1969; The Combahee River Collective 1977). Consciousness-raising was a grass-roots initiative that expressed the ideas of feminisms in a language and way that women could understand and use in their own lives.

This concept of raising consciousness more generally expresses the process of individuals becoming more aware as thinking, feeling, and caring people (Freire 1970). It is a process in heightening one's awareness, whereby the links between the personal and the political are exposed. Many third wave feminist groups have adopted consciousness-raising techniques and practices to raise the consciousness of young women, and are applying these to current social and cultural contexts (Sowards and Renegar 2004). Raising one's consciousness, however, is not only or simply a group act, as in feminist consciousness-raising groups, where we can learn about and from others. It is also an individual self-reflective process that helps us begin to recognize our positionality and our relationships to other people.

One of the ways that we can move forward and make social change is to engage in *critical self-reflection* (Lorde 1984). By engaging in this process, we acknowledge that all knowledge is partial and that it is produced under and within particular social conditions. This is to say that we are products of our social circumstances. The act of critical self-reflection, and it is a conscious act, demands an interrogation of ourselves as complex identities produced through and in particular social, historical, political, and cultural locations. It demands the recognition of our multiple positionalities and experiences as advantaged/disadvantaged and oppressor/oppressed (Narayan 1988). In so doing, we are able to see how our ideas, assumptions, theories and actions, as well as inactions, affect others. Finally, critical self-reflection pushes us to think and act differently. By beginning with ourselves, we are better able to empathize with others.

Empathy requires careful and respectful listening to the experiences, ideas, and concerns of others, in a way that recognizes and validates that what the speaker is saying really matters. Invoking empathy allows us "To walk a mile in someone else's shoes." It permits us to imagine ourselves under different circumstances in a deeply subjective way. It suggests that we question how our life might be different if we were born a different sex, race, class, gender, sexual orientation, or ability. By practising empathy, we can become more fully attuned to both the differences and commonalities among us. This is a thoughtful process that allows us to imagine ourselves quite differently.

At the same time, we need to adopt caution so that we do not fall into the trap of *appropriation*, where we might assume that listening to the stories of others means that we truly know what their lives entail (Lorde 1984; Narayan 1988, 2002; Spivak 1988; Alcoff 1995; Ahmed 1998; Loomba 2005). We need to keep our positionality in mind and critically reflect on how our experience influences the stories we hear and (re)tell. We need to listen carefully, yet think critically about what we learn so that we can have a fuller understanding of the lives and experiences of those we seek to know. We must also be careful not to assume that knowledge shared is now ours to be used without concern for, or credit given to, the people doing the telling. Such actions serve to reproduce unequal power relations. Finally, empathy must not be confused with sympathy, which invokes feelings of pity and assigns helplessness to others (Lorde 1984; Narayan 1988, 2002; Spivak 1988; Sylvester 1994; Alcoff 1995; Ahmed 1998; Loomba 2005). Rather, by listening empathetically, we are able to acknowledge alternative positionalities that help us better understand the complexities of people's lives and generate new ways of acting in the world for social change.

Conclusion

In this chapter, we have begun to see how intersectional analysis can help us to understand differences, identities, knowledge, and power, in more complex ways. We can start to see that we have a role to play in social change and that using critical self-reflection gives us the opportunity to examine our positions and the positions of others in various contexts. This allows us to consider that we might be both advantaged and disadvantaged in various situations. We might even be both oppressors and oppressed. Beginning to recognize these complicated positions empowers us to think about the world and our place in it in more complex ways. Intersectional analysis has been necessary to advancing feminist theorizing, a process that we will start to explore in the next chapter.

Questions for Study

1. Define the following terms and provide an example for each:
   - positionality
   - multiple identities
   - situated knowledge
2. What is intersectionality? Why is intersectionality a useful tool for feminists?

3. What are the limits of binary categories for understanding everyday experiences? What are the deficits in this type of either/or analysis?
4. How is power most commonly understood? How does this differ from feminist understandings of empowerment?
5. What does it mean when power is "zero sum"? Use an example from your own experiences.
6. How do you think women's rights and opportunities have been limited by the following. Give a definition and a few examples for each:
   • hierarchies of power
   • homogenization
   • universalizing
   • unearned privilege
7. How does intersectional analysis provide a tool for questioning the status quo?
8. How is the "dumb blond" cartoon problematic? What does it say about women? How does this illustration reinforce stereotypes of the various characters represented?
9. Why is critical self-reflection important for feminists? How could critical self-reflection be useful in your role as student, son/daughter, parent, partner, employee/employer?
10. Why is appropriation of someone else's experiences a pitfall, especially for feminists? How can others' lives and experiences help us critically reflect on our own experiences and our understandings of feminisms?

Activities and Questions for Discussion

1. Write three to four paragraphs about your identity. Be sure to take into account the significant aspects of your positionality, situated knowledge, and where you are located.
2. Pie charts are a common way to diagram zero-sum power. However, empowerment cannot adequately be charted the same way, because knowledge can be shared with others as you and they are empowered. Consider a situation in your life where you were empowered by sharing and receiving knowledge from those around you. Diagram your empowerment. (Be creative.)
3. Take five minutes and write about inclusivity and exclusivity in a situation you have witnessed at school, at home, or in your work life. What were the power dynamics in this situation?
4. Imagine that you are a manager in a high-tech company and that you need to organize a team of three others to review 250 job applications for 15 new jobs at the company. How will you ensure that your team does not make inappropriate assumptions about qualified job applicants on the basis of gender, race, sexuality, age, and ability? Make a list of some of the strategies you would use to make sure your team hires the best qualified candidates.

5. Unpacking *Your* Privilege: Fold a piece of lined paper in half parallel to the lines on the paper. The fold will represent equality. For each marker of difference where you fit into the privileged category you will move three lines up and place an X. For each marker of difference where you are not in the privileged category, you will move three lines down and draw an X. Always begin from the last X and move from there up or down. Where do you fit on the equality line? As a group or class, positions of privilege can then be plotted onto a larger graph to expose the diversity of locations within your group/class. This exercise can also be done with everyone standing in a line and taking one step forward or back, depending on everyone's experience of privilege. In the end look around, reflect on your location and that of others. What does this mean? How can you work towards redressing inequalities? The social markers of privilege might include white, male, heterosexual, able-bodied, middle/upper class, citizenship, Christian, young, full-time student, the number of hours one works per week while attending school, among others.

CHAPTER FIVE

SO MANY DETAILS AND SO MUCH READING
FEMINIST THEORIES

Thinking through the intersectionalities of identities, the complexities of people's lives, and the very real struggles that people face every day is not simple. Nor is it easy to understand how people confront and resist oppressions, exploitations, and marginalization. Yet resistance on multiple fronts continues and theories help us to understand not only the struggles towards social justice but also the triumphs of achieving justice. Feminist theorizing, then, is an ongoing process. It does not assume that *one* theory can address all the complexities of women's and men's lives in vastly diverse social, political, economic, and geographic spaces or across all historical time frames. Feminist theories provide us with the tools to think through complex issues, ask particular questions (of issues not even on the radar), develop strategies for social change, and critically analyze where we've been and where we might be going.

Feminist theorizing happens when dialogue, argument, and critical thinking take place between feminists and different feminist theories. Such interactions are not only necessary but also central to the processes of enhancing analyses and strategies for change as well as envisioning how such change might look. These highly charged exchanges of arguments and ideas can extend beyond feminist theorists to include activists and other social theorists. At first glance, the list of theories and names of theorists in every discipline can seem overwhelming. The amount of time and energy that people have put into thinking and writing about theory is enormous.

Feminist theories offer us not only frameworks for analyses or lenses through which to see the world, they also offer us guiding principles, a politics for acting in the world. In the sections that follow, we will explore multiple feminist theories—liberal, Marxist, socialist, radical, and anti-racist—and discover some of their guiding principles. It may appear from the following that the history of feminist theorizing goes from liberal to Marxist, to socialists, to radical, to anti-racist theory. However, this is not the case. Feminist theorizing is much more complex and multilayered than it appears. Multiple theories exist at the same time, alongside each other, sometimes colliding, and sometimes not. To develop a fuller picture of this complexity, we will explore both the theories themselves and their critiques. An analysis of the ways in which feminist theories have been, and can be, challenged will help us to begin questioning how different theories might influence the ways in which we think.

That's So Liberating ... Or Is It?

From the late eighteenth to the early twentieth centuries, feminist theories simply sought to explain women's experiences and everyday lives. Although many feminist theorists assumed that they were speaking for all women, their focus was commonly on particular women—white, affluent and middle class, Western, heterosexual, able-bodied women. There were many feminists, however, who did not fall into this category. They were concerned with the lives of black women, working-class women, and prostituted women. Take for example, Ida B. Wells (1862–1931) who exposed the "protection of white womanhood" as an excuse for the lynching of African Americans (Royster 1997), or Dr. Augusta Stowe-Gullen (1857–1943), daughter of Dr. Emily Stowe, who was one of the best known members of Canada's suffrage movement. Augusta was the first woman to graduate from a Canadian faculty of medicine and was an equal education (for women), child labour, and suffrage activist (Bacchi 1983). Emma Goldman (1869–1940), was an anarchist, a women's rights and labour activist, who confronted the moral panic about "white slavery," in reference to prostitution, by exposing the economic realities of capitalist exploitation. She argued that women of all colours could experience such exploitation and that this might lead to prostitution (Goldman 1969). Another important feminist was Mother (Mary Harris) Jones (1837–1930), a radical labour organizer and founder of the Industrial Workers of the World (IWW), who fought for workers' rights, especially the rights of poor women and children working in vile and unsafe factories (Jones 1983). And, there was Crystal Eastman (1881–1928), who argued that a woman's freedom depended on her ability to choose whether to marry and have children, as well as on her economic independence from men (Eastman 1978). As we can see, not all feminists had the same starting point.

Liberal feminist theory, for example, was guided by the principles of the Enlightenment and classical liberalism of the late seventeenth and eighteenth centuries, represented by Western philosophers Thomas Hobbes, John Locke, and Jean-Jacques Rousseau, who extolled the virtues of liberty and freedom. The guiding principles of liberty and freedom assumed that all men should be equally free to pursue them. These ideas led some thinkers to say, in effect, "Wait a minute; men should be free? Where does this leave women?" Where, indeed, were the women? Without citizenship rights or legal personhood, women were simply counted among men's many possessions. Presumed unable to think for themselves as "the weaker sex," women were subject to the whims of the men they were bound to—fathers, uncles, husbands, and sons. Early feminist thinkers, although they were not yet named as such, began to contemplate their sites of oppression. The principal site of oppression for liberal feminists was patriarchy, rule by men. If, as the boys above argued, men should be free and equal, why shouldn't women be free and equal, too? The problem with the liberal theories of freedom and equality, liberal feminists contended, is that they excluded women. Men were regarded as rational actors, maximizing their individual interests in a competitive environment where other men were acting just like them. Such theories either assumed that "man" referred to all humanity or they excluded women altogether. These were not bad ideas at the time, if you happened to be a man. However, by excluding women, not only were the liberal philosophers exposing a huge weakness in their theories but also they were entrenching the subordination of women, through binary thinking.

Liberal feminists challenged these ideas by arguing that women were equally capable of rational thought and deserved to be included in all aspects of society. The assumption we examined earlier—that Western society is a meritocracy—clearly shows in liberal feminist thinking. Moreover, a focus on the experiences of women in North America or Europe is also evident. The positionality of these feminists as white and privileged does not get them much beyond their immediate goals of civic equality. For liberal feminists, equality meant equality with men, but not with all men. This limited view of equality focused on white, elite, Western women, who demanded equal access with white men of their class to all aspects of social, economic, legal, and political life.

Embodying many of these demands was Mary Wollstonecraft's *A Vindication of the Rights of Woman*, which was published in 1792 in Great Britain. It echoed many of the ideas of the French Revolution but extended those principles to women. Wollstonecraft's arguments about women's rights, equality, and education, as well as the debunking of the myths of women's dependence, female helplessness, and feminine frailties, provided a conceptual road map for future feminist theorizing and activism. Consider Wollstonecraft's views on marriage, which she argued was principally a property-based relationship. Because women didn't receive the education and social opportunities that

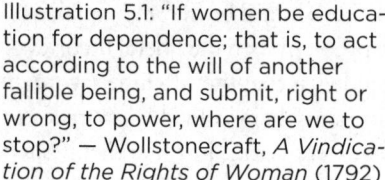

Illustration 5.1: "If women be education for dependence; that is, to act
according to the will of another
fallible being, and submit, right or
wrong, to power, where are we to
stop?" — Wollstonecraft, *A Vindication of the Rights of Woman* (1792)

Illustration 5.2: The independence
to think outside the boundaries of
femininity and to image the horrific
was revolutionary in 1815 when
Mary Shelley published *Frankenstein*.

could make them independent, they needed to marry to ensure their economic security. It was this inequality that led Wollstonecraft to condemn the
romantic relationship of marriage. Instead, Wollstonecraft suggested that a
lasting marriage should be built on friendship rather than physical attraction
(Tomaselli 2012). Yet Wollstonecraft was also a problematic figure because she
had her first child with a man to whom she was not married. Many thought
her to be a libertine and a loose woman with no moral restraint.

Wollstonecraft's legacy continued even though she died from complications in giving birth to her second daughter, Mary, who became Mary Shelley,
the author of the gothic novel *Frankenstein*. Perhaps not surprisingly, Shelley
was haunted by her mother's death and this plays out in the themes of creation
and motherhood, which permeate *Frankenstein*. For example, Shelley's monster
sputters over the grave of his creator: "I, the miserable and the abandoned, am
an abortion, to be spurned at, and kicked, and trampled on." Shelley also took
care to include some of her mother's concerns about the unequal education of
women in her novel. Another character in *Frankenstein*, Safie, was instructed
by her mother to aspire to higher powers of intellect and independence of
spirit.

Building on Wollstonecraft's work, liberal feminists began to locate the
source of women's oppression in patriarchy. It was patriarchy after all that
named men as the subjects of writing and as the writers of subjects. This is a
rather roundabout way of saying that men were the ones doing the writing. The

implicit assumption was that men were thinkers and "doers," while women were passive onlookers. By simultaneously celebrating men and their accomplishments, women were relegated to wifely and motherly duties.

By the beginning of the twentieth century, liberal feminists had theorized this division between the public sphere where men resided, and the private, domestic sphere of the home, where women were confined, as further evidence of women's oppression. In addition to describing and analyzing women's lives, liberal feminists' vision of equality came with strategies for change. Initially, liberal feminists imagined a woman's plight could be transformed if she were given access to education, the vote, and ownership of property. And since politics seemed to be the place where men were excited to be, women wanted to be there, too. Women would show men that they were independent thinkers and doers, once given the opportunity. Surely with these goals accomplished, women would demonstrate that their rationality was equal to men's and then they could be taken seriously. Many women therefore fought for—and achieved—these goals. Today, in the twenty-first century, it seems ludicrous to us that women were ever forbidden to go to school, vote, own property, and run for political office here in North America.

Gaining access to education, winning the vote, holding political office and owning property did change some things for many women; and, in many ways, society was transformed. With the enactment of married women's property rights laws across North America, between 1839 and the early 1900s, married women gained control over the management and disposal of their property and the ability to direct and control any income that they earned. These achievements marked a change in married women's legal identities, which previously fell to the authority and power of her husband (Backhouse 1988; Flexner and Fitzpatrick 1996; Amott and Matthaei 1996; Chambers 1997). When women won the vote, they were recognized not only as citizens but also the winning of the vote changed the very definition of citizenship itself. When women were educated and entered the professions, their entry introduced fundamental social changes. Even with such enormous transformations and fundamental changes, the concerns of many women were not yet addressed.

For the most part, liberal feminist thinking focused on the lives of white, privileged, Western women who were presumed to be heterosexual. Liberal feminist theorists didn't necessarily seek to transform society; they simply wanted to be included and to have more access to the public sphere so that they, too, could pursue the "good life" that men were enjoying. However, by demanding women's inclusion and equal access to the good life, liberal feminists began to transform society. By the mid-twentieth century, liberal feminists expanded their theorizing to include the economy—at least a small part of it. Liberal feminist theory attributed women's oppression to their economic dependence on men. They further contended that women's sole responsibility for the home, as wives and mothers, prevented women from accessing paid employment on an equal footing with men. Women's equality, they argued, was dependent not only on paid employment but also on accessing jobs and sectors of the economy that so far had been restricted solely to men. As liberal feminists fine-tuned their theories, they began to work for and within political institutions to create initiatives that would support working women: affirmative action policies, pay equity, childcare, and sexual harassment policies.

The logic of liberal feminist theory—to overcome women's oppression through gaining equality with men and championing women's rights—is legitimate. However, without questioning the very foundations of classical liberalism—individualism, patriarchy, capitalism, Eurocentrism, and the supremacy of science—little was likely to change for most women. Like its classical forefather, liberal feminist theory had its flaws and exclusions as well. More feminist theories were definitely needed.

You Mean the Old Guy Was a Feminist? Marxist Feminism

Recognizing that liberty and freedom were not simply goals for some men, feminists began to rethink the sites of women's oppression. Building on Karl Marx's theory of class struggle and capitalist exploitation, Marxist feminists argued that women were an oppressed class due to their economic dependence on men within the capitalist system. They linked the situation of women to the situation of the working class (proletariat), which, Marx theorized, was exploited by both its relationship to capitalist production and its state of being controlled by an elite (bourgeois) class.

In the nineteenth and early twentieth centuries, feminisms were influenced by anarchism and Marxism. The two had similar understandings about class struggle and ending domination; however, their end results differed. Whereas anarchists advocated for the militant elimination of all forms of hierarchy and domination, including all forms of government, Marxists supported the end of bourgeois domination through class struggle and anticipated its end through the revolutionary rise of the working class and a socialist state (Mann 2012). For early Marxist feminists, building on their understandings of class struggle, men were understood as the elite class who controlled women as a subordinate class. They recognized that capitalism relied on both women's productive and reproductive labour.

Accordingly, Marxist feminists located women's oppression in their relationships of production, not only in the exchange of their labour in the capitalist economy (paid employment) but also in their reproductive work (bearing children, raising children, cooking, cleaning, sewing, knitting, caring for the sick and the elderly in their homes), work for which they were not paid. Following the theory set out in *The Origin of the Family, Private Property and the State* (1884), Friedrich Engels, extending from Marx, argued that women were *un*equal to men under capitalism because men were able to control capital (material goods—land, livestock, tools, and everyday goods such as food, clothing and household products) and the production of goods (what, where, how, and how much was produced) both within and outside the household. Motivated by the desire to accumulate wealth and the need to ensure that their wealth, once accumulated, remained in the hands of their legitimate (biological) heirs, men attempted to control women's reproductive capacity through patriarchy. In this sense, Engels suggested that the origin of women's oppression was in men's patriarchal control over private property, wherein men were the propertied class and women were the propertyless one (Tong 2008).

At the same time, because of their reproductive capacity and childrearing responsibilities, women were tethered to their homes, unable to travel any distance, or for any length of time. During the Industrial Revolution (1750–1850), as capitalism expanded away from home-based production and as ownership of private property centralized in the hands of men, women not only lost power in comparison to their male family members but also their reproductive work was devalued because it was economically unproductive, which simply meant unpaid. Following this logic, Engels determined that women's oppression would be eliminated through economic independence from men. This independence could be achieved in two ways: first, by women's entrance into the paid economy and, second, by the socialization of housework and childrearing. A key feminist thinker of the time, Charlotte Perkins Gilman, wrote *Women and Economics* (1898). She contended that it was not motherhood that kept women tied to the home but housework, and that this was the primary obstacle to women's independence. Gilman argued that "sexuo-economic relations," a term she used to explain the division between public and private spheres, demanded transformation. She advocated for a more collective homespace, wherein well-paid professional workers would perform childcare and household duties, resulting in the empowerment of all family members (Mann 2012).

Marxist feminists, using Engels' analyses, argued that women make an important contribution to society through their reproduction *of* the labour force itself. Women bearing children, Marxist feminist theory contended, meant that capitalists were assured of future workers. In socializing children under capitalism, mothers were also raising compliant future workers. Moreover, in expending their unpaid energy to care for husbands and fathers, women were providing capitalists with refreshed and happy workers. Surely, as critical to capitalism as women's work was, it should be both valued and paid. And, if not paid, which seemed probable and perhaps as some feminist contended would further isolate women in their homes, then women should at least be liberated from the double duty of paid and unpaid work.

By the 1970s, Marxist feminists had developed important concepts for theorizing women's inequality and oppression. The *sexual division of labour,* which explained how and why the economy was segregated into "good jobs" and "bad jobs," was key to understanding women's oppression (Armstrong and Armstrong 1983; Acker 1990). Good jobs are those that were both highly valued and well paid. Not surprisingly, these jobs were overwhelmingly reserved for men and defined as skilled work. In contrast, bad jobs, those which women were expected to fill, were poorly paid, less valuable, and assumed to be unskilled. That seems about right, don't you think? Women's paid employment in bad jobs, Marxist feminists theorized, emerged as extensions of their reproductive labour in the home (see, for example, Reed 1970, 1984; Blumberg 1978, 1984; Philips and Taylor 1980; Fox 1980; Fox and Fox 1986).

Women's skills, learned and perfected in the home, were devalued as "natural talents," offshoots of their sex. Anyone who has knit a sweater, prepared dinner according to a budget, cleaned the house and done the laundry while simultaneously teaching the little ones to pee on the potty knows that some real skills are needed. These skills are not simply the individual ones required for each task but also entail an extensive knowledge of time management, child development, educational practices, environmentalism, and economic budgeting.

Gendering Marxist Feminist Theory: Building Socialist Feminisms

Marxism is frequently associated with countries such as China and the USSR, which were thought to be existing socialist states. For such countries, socialism entailed a wide array of political and economic philosophies about the paths to post-capitalist (non-capitalist) society. Consequently, socialist theorists worked from various theoretical frameworks, not always starting with Marx. In short, socialism emphasizes the common economic good of society, public ownership of the means of production, which in practice led to state-directed political and economic development. In contrast, capitalism emphasizes privatization of the means of production, economic accumulation of individual/corporate wealth, and the absence of state intervention. However, it was not until the 1960s, 1970s, and 1980s that feminists began to differentiate between Marxist and socialist feminisms. They were no longer convinced that a socialist state alone would end women's oppression (Mann 2012).

Socialist feminist theory added to the array of socialist philosophies by integrating patriarchy, in addition to a critique of capitalist exploitation, into the analysis of women's oppression. Linking patriarchy and capitalism, together and separately, socialist feminist analysis extended Marxist feminist analyses. Recognizing two systems—patriarchy and capitalism—at play in women's oppression some socialist feminists saw these as *separate systems* of oppression, where one had dominance over the other. According to feminists like Canadian Margaret Benston (1969) and British scholar Sylvia Walby (1989), *either* capitalism *or* patriarchy could be identified as the *primary* source of women's oppression. This perspective recognized that patriarchy pre-existed capitalism as a source of women's oppression, for example, in feudal time. Accordingly, patriarchy operated independently from capitalism. And capitalism oppresses women differently than patriarchy (Walby 1989). Other socialist feminists, such as Zillah Eisenstein (1978) and Heidi Hartmann (1976, 1981), recognized that patriarchy *and* capitalism were *interdependent*, linking the two systems into one by naming *patriarchal capitalism* or *capitalist patriarchy* as the reasons for women's oppression.

Among socialist feminists who see patriarchy and capitalism as *separate systems* in women's oppression, there is a debate over which one is the primary and which is the secondary. When socialist feminists contend that capitalism is the primary site of women's oppression and patriarchy is secondary, they do not suggest that women's oppression is simply reducible to economics. They recognize that a woman's status is complex. It is rooted in both her productive and reproductive capacities. However, they argue that it is her integration into capitalism that is the primary source of her oppression. Other feminists advocating the separate systems approach argue the opposite.

When patriarchy is seen as the primary site of women's oppression, socialist feminists such as Alison Jagger recognize that "a woman is always woman, even when she is working" (Tong 2009, 114). In contrast, under capitalism, a worker is oppressed regardless of his/her presumed biological sex. Accordingly, patriarchy accounts for the differential oppression of women and men under capitalism and thus patriarchy must be understood as the primary site of women's oppression.

Some socialist feminists, such as Katharine MacKinnon, who recognize patriarchy as primary, assert that women are alienated (a Marxist concept that recognizes the separation or distancing of the worker from the product they produce) through production differently than men (MacKinnon 1989). Extending this analysis, some feminists contend that women's bodies under patriarchy can become the product itself. Women's actions towards their bodies—primping and preening, dieting and exercising—while couched in terms of personal choice, are intrinsically produced through patriarchy—the "male gaze," gendered social expectations, heterosexual relations, and gendered violence. Through such processes, women may become alienated from their bodies and their selves. In this sense, women's bodies can become commodities, and self-worth may become tied to the value that patriarchy attaches to particular women's bodies.

Although seemingly contradictory in terms of which is *the* primary site of women's oppression, capitalism *or* patriarchy, socialist feminists who adhere to the separate systems analysis ultimately recognizes both capitalism *and* patriarchy in understanding women's oppression. Moving past the age-old question of "Which comes first, the chicken or the egg?" some socialist feminists recognize that capitalism and patriarchy cannot be easily separated. They suggest that capitalism and patriarchy must be understood as interdependent systems, which mutually and variously contribute to women's oppression. By recognizing the interplay between capitalism and patriarchy, socialist feminist theory contributes to an understanding of women's oppression as complexly rooted in *patriarchal capitalism* (Tong 2009).

These socialist feminist approaches challenge the class analysis offered by Marxist feminists. They argue that class is not a "gender-neutral" category, in which men and women are undifferentiated, nor is it possible to categorize women as a class, since this would presume that *all* women are the *same*—undifferentiated by race, class, sexuality, age, or ability. It is only through the recognition of a sexual division of labour under *patriarchal capitalism*, which acknowledges the different locations of men and women within it, that the power embedded in the system can be revealed. Recognition that the *gendered division of labour* is mutually reinforced by capitalism and patriarchy allows these socialist feminists to analyze why, even today, exploitation continues in the economic sectors that remain largely occupied by women—retail, service, administration, childcare, teaching, and nursing.

Without transforming capitalism itself and eradicating patriarchy, socialist feminists argue that this no-win situation for women will continue. Socialist feminists insist that women's equality and liberation can't be attained simply through paid employment. They contend that when women are actively engaged in paid employment, their workload doubles. Not only are they now responsible for "bringing home the bacon," they also have to cook it when they get there! Socialist feminists call this overload the *double day* or the *second shift* (Armstrong and Armstrong 1978; Hochschild and Machung 1989). Women's work in both the private and public spheres, therefore, supports the saying "A man works from sun to sun, but a woman's work is never done." In the 1980s, this *woman's* dilemma was popularly repackaged as the superwoman identity.

Superwomen were those who embraced the notion of having it all and doing it all. Superwomen were those who could successfully manage their homes, families, and careers. They were popularly held as the ideal to which all women should strive. While superwomen benefited from feminist efforts that expanded women's employment opportunities, they could just as easily remove themselves from feminist struggles for equality and against the double day because of their successes. While the concept of the "superwoman" has been used as a term of empowerment—women can have successful careers and a fulfilling family life—we could also consider this term a form of backlash. On the one hand, who could argue with the evidence that women can be successful and manage both careers and families? On the other hand, the costs of having it all and doing it all are excessive and in most cases unsustainable. Consequently, superwoman becomes an untenable identity. And, by measuring a woman's value, ability, and contributions against "the superwoman," any individual woman will undoubtedly come up short. This is backlash. Because the superwoman identity is unattainable for the majority of women, setting it as the standard is an aggressive attack that harms all women. We will return to a discussion of gendering work more extensively in chapter II.

Socialist feminists theorized that women's oppression could be ended through a process of socialization, where housework and childcare were supported communally through state-funded programs and subsidies. An example of how this would look was articulated in 1972 when Selma James and Mariarosa Dalla Costa published *The Power of Women and the Subversion of Community*, launching the international "Wages for Housework Campaign." The feminist argument that women's work in the home should be fairly remunerated by the state resulted in mass rallies and symposiums across the United States and Canada throughout the decade. By the late 1970s, however, many champions of women's equality abandoned Wages for Work under criticisms that the costs would be too high and that the campaign unintentionally reified women's positions as housewives.

Contributing considerably to women's choices about having children, staying home to rear children, and when and whether to return to work, has been and continues to be the availability of affordable, accessible, good quality childcare. In the province of Quebec in Canada, childcare has been long subsidized by the state. Quebec's political agenda to increase the population of its distinct society as a French-speaking population within a continent of anglophones is a powerful underlying reason for its pro-family policies. Accordingly, many families in Quebec currently pay only CDN$7 per day per child for daycare in various contexts, including public state-run programs, private childcare centres, and smaller home-based sites. And, for those parents who don't have subsidized childcare, there are tax credits available from the provincial government. Yet this formula for childcare is not without its critics. Many feminists argue that institutionalizing toddlers and imposing strict modes of childcare that are not necessarily child-centred, such as early toilet training, which is commonly a prerequisite for children entering childcare, is not the best or only way to support families with young children.

In the 1970s in the United States, Congress passed a similar policy that would have provided Americans with nationally funded daycare centres. American women had been fighting for government-sponsored childcare since the federally funded nurseries, under the New Deal, were closed at the end of Second World War, in an attempt to send women back to their homes and make room for returning soldiers in the workplace (Mann 2012). Perhaps not surprisingly, the Comprehensive Child Development Act was vetoed in 1972

Illustration 5.3: And, after all this crap is done, I still have to prepare my presentation for tomorrow. Superwoman? Who needs it!

by then president Richard Nixon. He argued that communal responsibility for childcare would push the U.S. towards communism, a shift that was untenable in the ongoing climate of the Cold War. If such state-funded programs were to be implemented across Canada and throughout the U.S., could you imagine what a difference they would make in the lives of women and working families? State-funded childcare would alleviate a considerable amount of stress around the double day and it would contribute to the financial security of all families with young children. The debates around childcare continue and a diversity of options needs to be explored.

Socialist feminists' theories and strategies for redressing women's oppression, however, were still missing important parts. The very structures of patriarchy, including the notion of the nuclear family, separate spheres of influence for women and men, the public versus private divide, and compulsory heterosexuality had yet to be tackled. While making inroads into women's oppression and engaging activists, socialist feminist theory nonetheless remained within the frames of Eurocentrism. It still had its flaws as well as exclusions.

That's So Radical!

When I hear the word "radical," I am always reminded of the 1995 film *Who's Counting? Marilyn Waring on Sex, Lies and Global Economics*. Feminist economist Marilyn Waring said that she hoped that people would think that looking at the world through women's eyes would be viewed as radical. Indeed, the word radical comes from the Latin *radix*, which means "root." What better way to understand women's oppression than to look at its roots? Radical feminism, like other feminisms, identified patriarchy—rule by men—as the problem. Radical feminist analysis of and solutions for the problem, however, differed from other theories' interpretations of patriarchy in the following respects.

The radical feminist theories of the 1970s and 1980s posited that patriarchy was more than just the hierarchy of men over women and masculinity over femininity. They contended that patriarchy was embedded in social, political, and economic institutions that were difficult to change. It was not enough, they argued, to work within the system to change laws and policies as liberal feminists were doing. Nor was it sufficient to simply provide economic and political critiques as Marxist and socialist feminists were doing. Radical feminists identified women's oppression in men's control over women's bodies. For them, patriarchy was a culture of control and domination over women's bodies and their sexuality.

By defining the *nuclear family*, the family consisting of mother, father, and children, as itself a patriarchal institution, radical feminists challenged the "natural" and "normal" concepts of romantic love, nuclear families as the building block of society, and the idealization of motherhood. They identified these ideas as powerful cultural tools of patriarchy, enslaving women to male desires. This control prevented women from achieving their liberty by reinforcing their vulnerability and dependence on men. Under patriarchy, romantic love was always heterosexual, monogamous, and unique (women pledged themselves to their husbands forever and their remarrying was frowned upon even if they were widowed). Patriarchy defined love between women as illicit—unlawful and illegitimate—and this sanction was authorized by the state (and religious institutions) through the issuance of marriage certificates for heterosexual unions. In this sense, the state was also a patriarchal institution that reinforced male power and privilege.

Once married, as constructions of "the good woman" dictated, prevailing models of motherhood would further control women's lives. The emergence of the nuclear family as an independent unit ruled by "the head of the household," a man, further reinforced patriarchal authority. Early radical feminists contended that the all-consuming work of mothering, however "natural," was oppressive for women. They recognized that reproduction tied women to mothering. But it was patriarchy that conflated motherhood with womanhood, making motherhood the ideal for women to achieve. In this sense, woman equals mother. This idealization of motherhood oppressed women because, as the socialist feminists argued, it placed an overwhelming majority of work in the private sphere on women.

Radical feminists theorized that this sexual division of labour objectified women's bodies as mere possessions and "toys" for men. Men's sexual desires therefore defined women's sexuality as heterosexual. Radical feminists theorized that as objects of male desire, women's bodies were rendered always available to men. Consequently, sexual consent on the part of women was unnecessary. The belief that consent is redundant has created what feminists call a *rape culture*, a culture in which rape is commonplace, even as it is unacceptable. A *rape culture* endures today because of *some* men's perceived male entitlement and their dismissal of the necessity of explicit consent for sex. The construction of femininity as subordinate to masculinity, radical feminists theorized, further heightened and eroticized the power differentials between women and men. Patriarchal control, radical feminists argued, also legitimated men's violence against women both in the home and outside it. They stipulated that in the *misogynist* (woman hating) cultures of North America and Europe, rape, and the fear of rape, worked to maintain men's power over women. While radical feminists raised questions about rape, sex and violence, these concerns continue to be key issues for a wide variety of feminists and feminist theories.

In the 1980s, discussions among feminists about violence and misogyny erupted into *the sex wars*, debates over pornography and prostitution in North America. Radical feminists such as Catharine MacKinnon (1989, 1993) and Andrea Dworkin (1981, 1992) argued that both pornography and prostitution were oppressive for women. MacKinnon defines pornography as sexually explicit pictures or texts that subordinate women. According to this definition, pornography celebrates and eroticizes the sexual subordination of women, and thereby, legitimizes it. Feminist opponents of pornography argued that it socializes boys and men to experience sexual arousal often through the violent and/or degrading depictions of women. The creation of these images harms the actresses and models in the images and, by extension, harms all women. This socialization, radical feminists argued, perpetuates misogyny and patriarchal power at the expense of women. In the early 1980s, MacKinnon and Dworkin participated in the creation of anti-pornography laws, which were adopted in several U.S. jurisdictions (MacKinnon and Dworkin 1997). The laws defined pornography as a violation of women's civil rights and allowed women who believed they were harmed by pornography to seek civil action against producers and distributors of pornography. It allowed the police and courts to define what was degrading. The laws, however, were almost immediately rendered unconstitutional by the United States Court of Appeals for the Seventh Circuit. In Canada, feminists were outraged when similar laws were used to justify customs officials' seizure of lesbian and gay publications being imported into Canada (Karaian 2005). Many feminists fiercely opposed these laws and the thinking behind them, arguing that the police and courts should not be charged with deciding what sexual images people were allowed to produce and see. Many feminists created their own sexual images to counter misogynist, mainstream porn. The 1980s saw a whole genre of feminist magazines, videos, and writing about sexuality. These debates remain important in feminist theorizing even today.

The objectification of women's bodies defines cultural expectations of beauty. Over time, Western beauty ideals have been variously defined, including in some eras women having pillowy thighs and double chins, but always under patriarchy, the male gaze defines it. Accordingly, beauty regiments, including dieting, wearing makeup, hair styling, plastic surgeries, and shaving various body parts, are prescribed by patriarchy. Media images of idealized beauties—women who are white, blond, blue-eyed, and stick-thin (surgically enhanced large breasts don't hurt either)—are used to sell everything from household appliances to cars. Through these processes, women have been trained to regard themselves as never beautiful enough but, of course, capitalism has the remedy for this, too—more cosmetics and surgeries. For racialized women, skin lightening and cosmetic surgeries, ranging from narrowing noses for black women, to creating hooded eyelids for Asian women, have become the sought-after procedures, all of which are embedded in the Western ideals of beauty defined both by whiteness and the male gaze. Women have bought and continue to buy into these beauty ideals, turning the beauty business into a multi-billion-dollar industry. Radical feminists have proclaimed an end to such controlling patriarchal practices since the 1980s. They called for women to see beauty more naturally in themselves and in other women rather than succumbing to torturous regimes, yet they failed to recognize or address the racism embedded in Western beauty ideals. They called for a new way of thinking; they called for an understanding of the personal as political.

The personal is political was the rallying cry of radical feminists throughout the 1960, 1970s, and 1980s. It was more than a saying; it was a call for women to analyze their experiences and to recognize how oppression affected them as well as those around them. In consciously acknowledging these interconnections,

Illustration 5.4: Slutwalks take off in 2011.

women of all backgrounds became involved in political action for social change and engaged in women's movement as part of the process of theorizing. *The personal is political* supported the other feminist slogan of the era: *Sisterhood is powerful*. This call to women's activism was coined by Kathie Sarachild in the 1960s (Redstockings 2001). It was also the title of Robin Morgan's anthology of defining second wave feminist writings (Morgan 1970). These powerful phrases link together feminist theory and practice. Not surprisingly, they continue to resonate with many feminists today.

What could be more personal than a woman's sexuality? Under the umbrella of radical feminism, a theory of *lesbian feminism* took on this very question. Locating the root of women's oppression in *compulsory heterosexuality*, Adrienne Rich famously argued that women are not naturally heterosexual but rather socialized not to question their sexuality (1980). By not considering the possibility of an alternative sexual orientation, women simply accept their heterosexuality. As a patriarchal institution, heterosexuality is always already assumed. This privileging of heterosexuality, and in so doing the institution of marriage, means that women's bodies, labour, and children all fall under the authority of men as the head of the household in patriarchal society.

Accordingly, this radical theory of lesbian feminism identifies heterosexuality as central to the maintenance of patriarchal power. By tying women to

Slutwalks—Challenging Rape Culture

Slutwalk activism erupted overnight in Toronto and it is spreading. In Australia, the Netherlands, New Zealand, Argentina, Sweden, Britain, Mexico, South Africa, and India, women are responding to the often-heard advice for preventing sexual assault by challenging victim-blaming messages.

The first Slutwalk took place in Toronto in April 2011 in response to a sexual assault prevention lecture where a Toronto police officer advised women that they should "avoid dressing like sluts in order not to be victimized" (Millar 2011). A shocking comment, but nothing new. Women have long been told they are the cause of rape, rather than the men who commit the crime.

Women are constantly told: to protect yourselves; always walk in pairs; don't go out at night; cover your drinks so that you don't get slipped a roofie; don't drink too much; don't wear short skirts or plunging tops; and keep your legs crossed! Instead, why not tell men: one of you is a rapist, until we know who it is, men, don't go out after dark or you could be suspect; monitor your friends' behaviour because one of them could be a rapist; and always walk in pairs so that you have someone who can vouch for your good behaviour (Doe 2005). Of course these recommendations to men sound ridiculous and even accusatory, but so is the advice to women. There is a need to change the rape culture that exists and the Slutwalk is such an attempt.

Some critics have taken exception to activists' use of the word "slut." Black feminists, in particular, have argued that "slut" has different associations for black women, ones that are embedded in the histories of slavery, immigration, and racist representations. Accordingly, the term "slut" cannot be liberating for racialized women (Black Women's Blueprint 2011). Yet Slutwalk feminist activists argue that they are reclaiming the term "slut" as a way of challenging the negativity of the term and the victim blaming that surrounds it. Reclaiming terms, such as bitch, dyke, and whore, have a powerful history. Kathleen Hanna, lead singer of Bikini Kill and a member of third wave activists Riot Grrrl (see chapter 10), writes such words on her body and clothes as a way to bring attention to feminist concerns about rape, incest, and women's objectification by the media.

Critics have also raised concern about the attire worn by some activists, who don low-cut and short-cropped tops and leather, lace, and fishnets. Dressing like a slut, a term they argue has no redeeming qualities, serves to hypersexualize and objectify women's public persona. Activists counter such criticism by arguing that what a woman wears is never an invitation for rape (Murphy 2011). Women can enjoy their sexuality without expectations on the part of men. Not surprisingly, in Toronto's cold, drizzly April weather, the overwhelming majority at the rally was fully clad to ward off the chill. Nonetheless, the perhaps risqué outfits worn by Slutwalk participants is intended to parody the advice given to

women to prevent sexual assault. The message is a powerful and play-ful attempt to challenge the prevailing *rape culture* and the censure of women's sex positive stance.
See, for example:

http://www.youtube.com/watch?v=0V-8DWkkZAM&feature=related
http://www.youtube.com/watch?v=PmiwMVqUV94&feature=related
http://www.youtube.com/watch?v=W9bHRKd6b-U&feature=related

men through heterosexual institutions, women as a political force are unable to unite against their oppressor. By recognizing what Rich called a *lesbian continuum*, women could be united (Rich 1980). This is not to say that all women should choose to be lesbians. Nor did all lesbians uniformly accept these claims. The lesbian continuum, however, was a term designed to recognize women's relationships with each other, not only as lovers but as family, friends, and caregivers. By redefining lesbian politics more broadly than merely sexual relations between women, lesbian feminism offered a space for feminists to work together.

As radical as it was, this lesbian feminist theory was also divisive among feminists and in mainstream culture. Some lesbians wanted to emphasize not the politics of patriarchy but rather the sexual meaning of lesbian choices, to celebrate that sexuality rather than equating a powerful sexual choice with a political stance, which might have little to do with sexual desire. Nonetheless, lesbian feminism as a stream within radical feminisms played a critical role in theorizing women's oppression, violence against women, gendered assumptions about masculinity and femininity, and sexuality. It is unfortunate that these important contributions are misappropriated by *backlash culture*, which attempts to trivialize, undermine, and devalue feminisms, and to stigmatize and stereotype all feminists as hairy, fat, ugly lesbians. Calling all feminists lesbians is backlash and an effective way of silencing women. Because many heterosexual women fear the label lesbian, they withdraw from feminist struggles rather than supporting all feminists, including lesbians. This is a divide-and-conquer strategy that needs to be challenged as backlash.

Another theory that fell under the umbrella of radical feminism was *cultural feminist theory*, which emerged in the mid-1970s and exposed women's oppression in gendered constructions that devalue feminine attributes. By devaluing women's nurturing and caring capacities, for example, gendered constructions of authority and scholarship as masculine domains, have discounted women's ways of knowing. The weakness of cultural feminism, however, rested on its essentialism. Mary Daly (1978), a key cultural feminist theorist, linked "female energy," or her term Gyn/Ecology, to the *essential* life-affirming, life-creating condition of the female spirit/body (Alcoff 1988). Cultural feminists called for centres run "by women for women" and "women-only spaces" to challenge negative gendered constructions. Examples of women-only spaces include consciousness-raising groups, music festivals such as the Michigan Womyn's Music Festival, rape crisis centres, lesbian communities, university/college women's centres, and some women's organizations. These were, and are, places where caring, nurturing, and empathy were and are valued. Yet they have not been without their problems. Often, such spaces policed women's ideas and activities according to unwritten rulebooks that were far from transparent and this made it difficult for many women to feel comfortable. Power still operated and the women who had it could easily wield it. Nonetheless, they had the potential to be places where women could feel safe from men, the male gaze, and patriarchal obligations.

Many feminists also criticized women-only spaces and events, such as the annual Take Back the Night marches, as separatist because they excluded men. By excluding men, these feminist critics argue, Take Back the Night organizers were defining men as the problem, rather than locating the problem in the structures of patriarchy. By segregating men, women were deprived of possible allies in the struggle against patriarchy. Segregation essentialized sex, reifying biology as the defining essence of gender, thereby excluding many "women." Transgendered people did not find a safe place in women-only spaces, even when they identified as female. These spaces were also a difficult fit for racialized women who commonly aligned with men who shared their racial identity. Accordingly, not all women found these spaces inviting or empowering.

Radical feminisms still seemed to be exclusionary. Criticisms of essentialism, homogenization, and Eurocentrism came from women of colour and Third World women and grew in the 1980s. Indeed, what about racialized women? What about women beyond the continents of North America and Europe? Many radical feminists failed to recognize or respect these women's experiences and ways of knowing. Clearly, radical feminisms had their flaws and exclusions, too.

Still Left Out: Anti-Racist Feminist Theory

So far, the feminist theorizing we have been discussing emerged from the experiences of mostly white and middle-class women. These analyses centre on North American and European geopolitical spaces. Accordingly, feminisms and women's movement were failing women of colour by excluding them from the analysis and marginalizing them in actions. Calls of racism, imperialism, and Eurocentrism were launched at these exclusionary feminists and feminisms. *Imperialism* has classically been defined as the extension and establishment of economic, political, and cultural authority and control over territories that are beyond national borders. Imperialism and Eurocentrism are embedded in the

Prostitution and the Himel Decision

Prostitution, per se, is not illegal in Canada. However, laws around prostitution make some of the activities associated with it illegal. The Criminal Code of Canada makes it illegal to:

- keep a common bawdy-house (s. 210), which is defined in s. (197(1)) as a place that is (a) kept or occupied, or (b) resorted to by one or more persons for the purpose of prostitution or the practice of acts of indecency;
- live on the avails of prostitution (s. 212(1)(j)); and,
- communicate in public place for the purpose of engaging in prostitution (s. 213(1)(c)).

In the landmark case *Bedford v. Canada,* 2010, it was argued that these above sections of the Criminal Code breach the Canadian Charter of Rights and Freedoms, s. 7, which states: "Everyone has the right to life, liberty and security of the person ..."

Alan Young, lawyer for the applicants—Terri Jean Bedford and Valerie Scott, both former sex workers, and Amy Lebovitch, active in sex work—argued that these three sections prevent prostitutes from conducting their lawful trade in a safe environment, making prostitution a dangerous business. The applicants further argued that these laws were unconstitutional in that they violated the "right to liberty" because sex workers risk the possibility of imprisonment if convicted of these offences. They also asserted the constitutional right to "security of the person" is compromised by these laws and contributes to the violence experienced by sex workers.

Evidence was offered by the applicants, much of which was produced by or for the Canadian government bodies, to demonstrate that together and separately these sections of the Criminal Code prevent sex workers from "screening" potential clients, hiring security/bodyguards, or working indoors under relatively safer conditions and locations. The applicants argued that in several Canadian cities—Toronto, Victoria, Windsor, Calgary, and Edmonton—municipalities are collecting licensing fees for massage parlours, where it is understood that the sale of sexual services is likely. This places municipalities in violation of the law in contention.

Lawyers for the Crown (representing the Canadian government) argued that prostitution contradicts the moral values of the majority of Canadians. Adding to this, they contended that whether prostitution is practised indoors or outdoors it is an inherently risky business. While the conviction of Robert Pickton in 2007 of the second-degree murder of six sex workers, who had disappeared from Vancouver's Downtown Eastside, made it clear to the Canadian public that street-based sex work was excessively dangerous, the same claim could not be made about indoor work. A 2009 Angus Reid survey, in which more than half of the respondents supported the decriminalization of prostitution provided it was an act was between consenting adults, countered the state's assertion that the majority of Canadians opposed prostitution on moral grounds.

Justice Susan Himel made it clear that it was not the court's responsibility to determine the morality of prostitution or whether or not there was a constitutional right to sell sex (Bedford 2010, para 25). It was the court's job to decide if the three sections of the Criminal Code violated the Charter. On this basis, Justice Himel found that the law prohibiting communication served to endanger sex workers by forcing them to hastily conduct transactions and to work in more isolated conditions and desolate locations in violation of the Charter rather than protecting the public from social nuisance as it was enacted to do (Himel 2010, para 503). Justice Himel ruled that "the bawdy-house provision, the living on the avails of prostitution provision, and the communicating provision ... violate s. 7 of the *Charter* ... and are, therefore, unconstitutional" (Bedford 2010, para 506).

The Ontario Superior Court decision has implications for other provinces as well. Accordingly, the heated legal debate and court challenges are unlikely to end here. The Crown asked the Court to suspend its decisions for eighteen months, but was only given a reprieve of thirty days to convince Justice Himel to stay her decision. The case, as of August 2011, is in the process of appeal and in all likelihood could be brought before the Supreme Court of Canada.

---

terms used to describe those who are excluded—people of colour and *racialized* people. In this context, *racialized* refers to power dynamics that exist in white supremacist societies, wherein only non-white people are presumed to have a race. These terms cast a shadow of "otherness" across people who challenge the insights and legitimacy of the knowledge offered by racialized people. *Otherness* is a term used to refer to those who are systematically excluded from the dominant group, based on sex, gender, race, ethnicity, religion, nationality, sexuality, or ability. Otherness is rooted in the power relationships embedded in binary terms such as woman/man, gay/straight, and black/white. These terms are continually contested by feminist theories because they reinforce existing relationships of power and privilege.

By the 1980s, anti-racist feminist theorists—black, Latina, Asian, and Indigenous—were arguing that the failing of feminism was in the assumption of the universalizing category of "woman" (Moraga and Anzaldúa 1983; Lorde 1984; Crenshaw 1989; hooks 1984, 1991–1992; Collins 1990, 1993; Mohanty 1983, 2002; Harding 1986). Liberal, Marxist, socialist, and radical feminisms all spoke of "woman" as an undifferentiated category. This homogenized category presumed that all women experienced oppression in the same ways. For black feminists, theorizing needed the analysis of both gender and race. They argued that theorizing from the perspective of white privilege, as all feminisms had so far, was both racist and exclusionary. Both gender and race were sources of oppression for racialized women whose voices were not represented among mainstream feminist theories. Some black theorists rejected the very label "feminist" for this reason, preferring instead the concept of *womanist* (Walker 1983). The denunciation of the feminist label challenges assumptions about who *owns* feminism, who *is* a feminist, and who *defines* feminism. Womanism is not a rejection of feminist libratory goals per se but rather a rejection of the power hierarchies that exclude racialized others and remain unchallenged in feminist theorizings.

Womanism is just one trajectory of black feminist thought. Early on, black women were thinking about and problematizing the intersections of race and gender. The origins of this feminist theorizing go back to Harriet Tubman, a former slave who became one of the most famous "conductors" on the Underground Railroad. She made ten trips to assist more than 300 black people on the journey to "freedom" in Canada between 1850 and 1860 (Hendrick and Hendrick 2010; Clinton 2004). Another important black feminist was Sojourner Truth (1867). Born into slavery, she became a noted abolitionist in the 1840s and a powerful public speaker on women's rights until her death in 1883 (Washington 2009). Black women continued to theorize about race and gender into the 1900s. Take, for example, civil rights activists like Fannie Lou Hamer, who famously stated that she was "sick and tired of being sick and tired," inspiring black activism. Hamer was a member of the Student Nonviolent Coordinating Committee (SNCC) and an organizer around civil disobedience in protest against segregation in the American South during the 1960s. She continued to struggle in the antipoverty movement and for the provision of childcare. And, of course, there was Rosa Parks who was talking about women's issues and organizing against racialized sexual violence in the 1950s (Lee 2002; Gore 2011). So, while the 1980s marked a particular claim to black feminist thought and anti-racist feminist theorizing, there were many parallel stories of black feminist theorizing and their critique of feminist and other theories.

Still, in the 1980s, when anti-racist feminisms began to take a more prominent role in feminist theorizing, many white feminist theorists had little knowledge of the rich history of black women's feminist theory and activism. Few white feminists had linked feminist theorizing to Sojourner Truth's confrontation with white feminists, in the 1860s, because they wanted to exclude black men and women from the vote, or to Ida B. Wells when she called on white women to stop the terror of lynching because supposedly chivalrous white men claimed it was required to protect the sanctity of white womanhood. Much feminist theory failed to reflect the lived experiences and history of black feminists. Black feminists, for example, disputed the notion of the family as a site of patriarchal oppression (hooks 1990; Carby 2000; Collins 2000). Challenging socialist feminist contentions, they asserted that black families had historically served as places for solidarity for black women with black men, offering a safe haven from, and a space for resistance to, the forces of a racist society. During slavery, black women were never aligned with white women who were their owners and oppressors but with their own family members, reaching across gender lines for solidarity with black men who also experienced racial oppression. Black feminists suggested that the histories of colonization, slavery, and Eurocentrism had institutionalized a raced, classed system that resulted in the marginal economic status of many women and men of colour. Moreover, they argue that racialized stereotypes of masculinity and femininity could be traced to experiences of colonization and slavery.

The stereotypical depiction of black men as *hypermasculine*—physically intimidating, emotionally tough, sexually virile—invokes images of the savage to be tamed, or the rogue slave to be subdued, or unbridled sexual prowess to be disciplined because this virility posed a threat to both white women's purity and white men's sexual integrity (Collins 2004; hooks 2004). Today, these characteristics are (re)presented in images of urban black youth as "gangsta" or rapper. The stereotypes for black women are equally complex. The contradictory images of "mammy" and hypersexualized exotic temptress remain. Mammy is the derogatory naming of black women who either worked or were enslaved as servants and caregivers in white homes, particularly in the southern U.S. Mammy remains a part of cultural memory, famously enacted in the 1939 film *Gone With the Wind*. Hattie McDaniel, the first black person to be nominated for an Academy Award, won the Oscar for her portrayal of Mammy in the film. The mammy image continues to evoke particular constructions of black women as unintelligent, infantile, illiterate, submissive, passive, and yet caring and loyal workers who are ideally employed as domestics, caregivers, and service providers (Jewell 1993).

Stereotyping of this nature has real consequences by constraining black women's economic opportunities and career prospects. And, white women who hired black domestics at low wages directly benefitted from black women's subordination. At the same time, the seemingly contradictory stereotype of the hypersexualized black woman endures. Once the exotic object of sexual desire and conquest by colonizers and slave owners, the image of black woman as promiscuous, erotic, and sexually available permeates popular culture and current stereotypes. Black mothers, for example, as both "bad" mother and "not" mother by comparison to her white counterpart, permeate popular thinking. Stereotypically, she is denounced as a "bad" mother; a woman who has several children with multiple men, has no concern for the paternity or the economic needs of her children and, therefore, is a drain on the state (Ladd-Taylor and Umansky 1998; Brand 1999; Tyree 2009; Pietsch 2010). This image has been institutionalized through current daytime talk shows such as *Jerry Springer* and *Maury Povich*. At the same time, black women are seen as "not" mothers, particularly in their work as nannies, caregivers, teachers, and nurses. In this sense, the *authentic* mother identity is reserved for real (white) mothers, a narrowly constructed essentialist identity that precludes Others.

Accordingly, black feminist theorists have demanded an intersectional analysis that can take into account issues of gender, race, class, and sexuality. Anti-racist feminists recognize that these multiple and intersecting sites of oppression operate in different ways in different women's lives. Consequently, they could not simply be "added on" to existing feminist analyses; rather, what was required was a fundamental rethinking of feminist theorizing. As a place to begin this analytical process, anti-racist feminists called for critical self-reflection among feminists to recognize their participation in the exclusionary practices of sexism, racism, classism, and homophobia in their daily lives.

Social change, then, starts with our self and our relationships with the people around us. In such a process of analysis, we recognize that we all have a gender and that we are all subject to race and class. These individual facets of who we are may be more or less important in different settings; however, they nonetheless structure all of our relationships. Cherríe Moraga contends that Chicana feminism is a theory of the flesh that is born out of the physical realities of life, skin colour, ties to the land, and sexual longings that form a necessary politics in an attempt to bridge contradictions of *feminista* and *Chicana* (Moraga 1981). African American feminist Patricia Hill Collins argues that the purpose of acknowledging the multiple aspects of our identities is not to rank or impose more hierarchies on our oppressions, as simply "adding on" race or class or gender or sexuality would do. The purpose is to explore our complexities and our locations within various structures of power (Collins 2001). Then we can begin to challenge our positions as both oppressor *and* oppressed, not simply as oppressor *or* oppressed. This either/or thinking reinforces a hierarchy of oppressions that people experience, which is not useful if the goal is to create real social change. Canadian feminists, such as Himani Banerjee (1993, 1995, 2001), Enakshi Dua (1999), Sherene Razack (2002), Yasmine Jiwani (2001), Sunera Thobani (2007, 2010), Njoki Wane (2002, 2007), and Agnes Calliste and George Dei (2000) are also engaged in anti-racist feminist theorizing. They contribute to uniquely Canadian anti-racist feminist theories on nationalism, multi-culturalism, immigration, violence, labour markets, and education.

Conclusion

In this chapter, we have begun to see how theories can help us to understand issues, struggles, changes, and triumphs. Feminist theory is not singular but plural. Feminist theorizing is in a constant process of change as new issues and concerns emerge and as past deficiencies in theorizing are exposed. Yet, as new feminist theories develop, old theories do not simply become relics of the past. Depending on the issues and perspectives of the feminist doing the theorizing, all theories can still be useful. One theory does not fit all situations, all goals, all concerns, all people, or all places. In the next chapter, we will explore theories that move us from universalizing to queering, and globalizing feminist understandings.

Questions for Study

1. How is feminist theory created? Why should feminist theory be viewed as a process and not an end product?
2. What is liberal feminist theory? What are its goals? What are its flaws?
3. What did Marx and Engels argue were women's contributions to society? What are the important concepts that Marx developed for theorizing about labour? How have Marxist feminists adopted and adapted these ideas in their theorizing?
4. Why do some socialist feminists argue that it is necessary to transform capitalism and eradicate patriarchy? What are the processes of socialization, regarding housework and childcare that socialist feminists support? What is missing from socialist feminist theories?
5. What views do radical feminists hold about patriarchy and its role in women's lives? Why do radical feminists challenge the ideas of "natural," "normal" and "mother"? How does compulsory heterosexuality maintain patriarchal power? What is missing from radical feminist theories?
6. What is the lesbian continuum? Do you have to be a lesbian to be included in the continuum?
7. What is misogyny? In what ways is misogyny evident in North American culture? What is rape culture and how is it supported by social constructions of femininity?
8. Should sex work be legalized? What are the advantages and disadvantages for sex workers and others? How does the Himel Decision, which dictates Canadian legislation on prostitution, affect your argument?
9. What does it mean to say the personal is political? Use examples with reference to cultural ideas of beauty, health, and work.
10. What are the advantages and disadvantages of women-only spaces? Are women-only spaces still needed? Why or why not?
11. Anti-racist feminists would argue that the racializing of women and men limit their opportunities and power as a group and as individuals. Give some examples of the processes of racialization. How can institutionalized racism be combatted?
12. Why do some black theorists reject the label feminist? How does the term womanist address their concerns? How is womanism distinct from feminism?

13. How do negative stereotypes repress black women and black men? How have activists countered these negative stereotypes?

Activities and Questions for Discussion

1. Make a study chart on a letter-size piece of paper. Create a theory chart using boxes to write down details about each of the theories discussed in this chapter. At the top of the chart, boxes should be labelled: theory, description, aims, famous names, cites of oppression, accomplishments, centres of power, critique, and other. Down the left side of the page write the names of each of the theories. Fill in each box to make a study guide for yourself.

2. How do you define pornography? Some feminists argue that "pornography" is a legitimate expression of sexuality. However, many feminists argue that it legitimates misogyny and perpetuates patriarchal power at the expense of women. On what side of the debate do you stand? Explain why, with clear examples from the media and popular culture.

3. Test your political views. Pick an issue currently in the news and decide which feminist theory is best suited to critically analyze this issue? And why?

4. Conduct an Internet search of women-only spaces on campus and in your community. Select one space. What does this space offer women? Is the exclusion of men from this space valuable? If so, why? If not, why not?

Social justice projects are not either/or endeavors where one can say, "We have our movement and you have yours— our movements have nothing to do with one another."
—PATRICIA HILL COLLINS, *BLACK FEMINIST THOUGHT*

CHAPTER SIX

FROM UNIVERSALIZING TO QUEERING AND GLOBALIZING THEORIES

In the previous chapter we noted an ongoing dialogue among feminist theorists and activists. The dialogue continues in this chapter with the exploration of post-modern, "Third World," postcolonial, queer, and transnational feminist theories. The purpose here is to introduce some current feminist debates and discover some of the key questions and arguments being raised in these debates. We will also reflect on some of the limitations and critiques of these theories as a way for us to think about feminisms. We will question how different theories, feminist and otherwise, might influence the way we think, not only about theory but also about everyday life at home and abroad.

Theory is not something that we do in an abstract, disinterested, or ob-jective way. Theory, any theory, is about producing knowledge. Perhaps more importantly, it is about producing particular knowledge, an understanding of things through specific frameworks or lenses. At its heart, then, theory is about *knowing* the world in which we live. And, it is intimately linked to ques-tions of epistemology that were addressed in chapter 3. Men have traditionally done much of this knowing and theorizing. In the last chapter, we saw how the Enlightenment and classical liberal theories from the late seventeenth to nineteenth centuries, which extolled the virtues of liberty and freedom, were raised anew in liberal, Marxist, socialist, radical, lesbian, and anti-racist feminist theories. The theories explored in this chapter will further challenge the construction of modern white men as *knowers*. Different feminist theorists ask the important questions: *Who* can know, *what* is known, and *how* does knowing resist *and* produce social change? These theories are therefore grounded in the real experiences of knowledge that occur at the margins, not simply at the centre.

Enlightenment, Modernism, and the Search for Universal Truths

To raise questions about knowing, it is necessary to return to some of the ideas so convincingly argued by what have been called DWM (Dead White Men). This somewhat demeaning acronym, DWM, refers to Western white male social and political thinkers and is used to challenge the sexism, racism, and classism inherent in their thinking. Reason, rationality, progress, science, and liberty, the principles of the Enlightenment and classical liberalism enshrined in the theories of DWM, are the bases of *modern* Western thought. Each of these principles tells a story about *what* and *how* we know. These narratives shape the questions we can ask and the answers that can be given. Western thought presumes that the world is "out there" as something tangible, observable, explainable, understandable, and able to fit easily into distinct categories of knowing. The narratives of reason, rationality, science, and progress signalled that the world—land, resources, the environment, and people—belonged to (white) *man* to be controlled and harnessed for *his* use and exploitation. This view spurred the production of certain types of knowledge and employed scientific theories to legitimate *man*made imperialist agendas, for example, the "settling" of North America and the colonization of Africa, Asia, Latin America, and the Caribbean.

Western thought and even science itself, however, were neither disinterested nor objective. The production and products of knowledge were routinely justified by pseudo-scientific theories. For example, the gendered norms of masculinity and femininity were "scientifically" linked to the biology of sex. Science also offered rationality to racially imposed hierarchies by deeming non-white "races" less advanced and not fully human. Such thinking made the imperialist practices of colonization and slavery not only possible but also a justification for European forms of slavery. To this day, science continues to drive technological advancement. Science, conceived as Truth, reinforces its own supremacy and its unquestioned authority. If science says it's so, it must be so! We have come to expect science and technology to provide the answers to modern problems such as curing debilitating diseases, creating new gadgets that soon we will be unable to live without, and finding resolutions to the environmental devastation that surrounds us. We ask science: How will we run our cars in the future without oil? How will we heat and cool our houses without cheap renewable resources? What is the cure for HIV/AIDS? These seemingly good questions, however, are not that far away from other questions like: How can we build a better bomb? How can we make our borders more secure from terrorists and illegals? How can we attain eternal youth? How can we ensure that women can have babies well into their sixties? How can men ensure their masculinity remains intact when their penises cease to function on demand? Science is expected to find the answers to these and so many other questions, as if all things are knowable and fixable, as if all questions and answers have no agendas.

The realm of science is populated by scientists who are invested in the questions they ask and the answers they seek. Knowledge, in this sense, is political. It has a specific agenda/goal, and it is embedded in particular power structures—the military-funded research laboratory, the corporate-controlled academy. The overarching stories, that have long persuaded us to believe what is presented to us at face value, to know without questioning, to participate in imperialist practices, to act as oppressors and to claim our innocence in the process, no longer hold as transcendent truths. The *metanarratives* or *master* narratives of modern Western thought—reason, rationality, progress, liberty, and science, the very idea of truth as unchanging and universal—have lost their innocence (Lyotard 1984).

"They're at the Post and They're Off"

"They're at the post and they're off" is a phrase used to launch horse races. It seems appropriate here as a launch into new ways of thinking—about theory and about the world in which we live. The "post" in horse racing is not a division based on a specific historical time. And, in many ways, the "post" in postmodernism doesn't signal the clear demarcation that the start gate provides in a horse race. The post in *postmodernism* marks a shift in thinking from sameness and universals to a recognition of the many differences within sameness; to the idea of *not* sameness by *postcolonial theorizing*, and to the permanent destabilization of knowing by queer theorizing. Don't close the book just yet; things will become clearer as we work through some of the key concepts of these theories.

Postmodern theory emerged out of the horrors of the Second World War, where the narratives of science, rationality, and progress also permitted the rise of Nazism, fascism, and Western imperialism. These narratives sanctioned, for example, the Holocaust, which resulted in the genocide of six million European Jews, in the name of racial purity. These narratives legitimized human experimentation at the expense of people's lives. They also rationalized the making and ultimately the dropping of nuclear bombs on the Japanese cities of Nagasaki and Hiroshima as an acceptable means to an end. These narratives are not innocent. Postmodern theory was also a response to the massive changes in technologies, computerization, mall culture, consumerism, and globalization, which postmodernists saw as a distinct break from modern industrial societies (Mann 2012).

In the 1960s and 1970s, key postmodern theorists, such as Jacques Lacan, Jacques Derrida, Michel Foucault, and Jean-François Lyotard, sought to destabilize the metanarratives that enabled such tragedies and challenge the modern view of a single truth or reality. For postmodernists, all claims masquerading as universal truths need to be questioned and the underlying agendas of such truth claims need to be exposed. Uncertainty about the stories told by Western thinkers need to be voiced. Challenging existing claims about knowledge, postmodern theorists suggest, is an act of subversion and resistance. Postmodernists use *deconstruction* to expose the power and politics embedded in metanarratives, uncovering seemingly transcendent truths as socially constructed. Deconstruction is the process of breaking down or taking apart the terms, concepts, and ideas that uphold truth claims (Derrida 1976). If truths are socially constructed—built in the way a house is constructed—then they can be deconstructed.

This process exposes the assumptions and power hierarchies that are invisible on the surface. Closer examination, through deconstruction, often reveals that current truths rely on unsubstantiated, even false, past truths. If these past truths are left intact and the assumptions upon which they are built remain unquestioned, they become evidence to sustain current truth claims. Without questioning the basis for truths, claims about knowledge are in effect *made* real, and their constructedness is *made* invisible. Deconstruction, therefore, is both a political tool and an analytical method for exploring knowledge. Throughout this chapter examples of active deconstruction are offered to help us develop our skills. Take for example, the changing meanings of words and language.

Language is critical in the process of producing knowledge. It is through language that we convey our ideas. Language is the basis of all discourse and conversation. The words we use in conversations, in discourse, are assumed to be static, stable, and unchanging. If they weren't, how would we understand what was being said or what we were saying? Postmodern theorists argue that the meanings of words are not necessarily fixed and that meaning emerges in context (Derrida 1976). So, while a chair may always be a chair, there is a great diversity among types of chairs, their size, design, purpose, and the materials used to make them. Accordingly, when we go to the store to buy a chair, there needs to be a discussion about what kind of chair we want to buy. The meanings of words can also change over time. Back in the 1970s, "gay" was just another word for happy and carefree, "queer" simply meant odd, "fag" was a cigarette, "drag" was something you did to a sack of potatoes, and the F-word, actually both F-words, was never used in polite company.

Many people never think about the power or politics embedded in language or discourse. Or do we? Most of us know how to recite the nursery rhyme "Sticks and stones may break my bones but names will never hurt me." Perhaps, then, we are not as innocent as we claim. Perhaps words, language, and discourses are less objective and more subjective/purposeful than we would like to admit.

Postmodern theorists took on the supremacy of objectivity, which lay at the core of modern thinking. They challenged the idea that knowing is unconcerned and unaffected by personal interests. Postmodern theorists recognized that preserving the separation between the knower and how we know was critical to maintain the metanarratives of Western thought. To overcome this separation, Michel Foucault suggested a deconstruction of the *self* (or the *subject*) as thinker, knower, and doer (Foucault 1980).

This questioning is both epistemological and ontological. Recall that epistemology questions how we know what we know. Ontology is slightly more complex. It questions the state of being. Being, in this sense, is a questioning of our existence, how we exist and whether there are different kinds of existences. Is being a woman, or a man for that matter, the same as it was in 1900? Are the expectations the same? And, how do we know what is expected? Is being rich or poor the same everywhere? What does it mean to *be* anything? These questions lead us towards thinking differently. And, if we start thinking differently, we might ask different questions, such as How do I know my self? What choices do/did I make? How were these choices made? Is there (hidden) power in my choices? Whose interests do my particular choices serve? When we begin to think in these ways and challenge the idea that we know "in a vacuum," unaffected by our experiences and the experiences of those around us, the belief in objectivity becomes increasingly absurd.

By asking epistemological and ontological questions, we politicize our subjectivity (the way we think as individuals) and expose our own biases. In this way, we can begin to see how culture and discourse shape what we think, who we are, and how we understand ourselves. Michel Foucault's historical writing about medical institutions, prisons, and asylums during the fifteenth to the eighteenth centuries provides insights into the ways in which we create, shape, and monitor ourselves. He argues that we are socially conditioned to conform to expectations and even ways of thinking. We don't want to stand out as different. In Foucault's words, we *discipline difference* and in so doing, we manufacture conformity and sameness. The processes of self and social *surveillance*, he asserts, demonstrate the productive power of discourse. *Productive power* is the power to produce something, an idea, an action, or a way of knowing and being (Foucault 1980).

Let's explore for example, some of the binary categories used in Western thought—objective/subjective, man/woman, straight/gay, young/old, white/

black, rich/poor, colonial/native, and winner/loser, among others—and ask the question, Is there productive power in naming and defining these categories? Postmodern theorists suggest that discourse gives these categories meaning and therefore that they have productive power. If we consider *discourse* to be what we *say* (language) about things in conversations and how we *do* (practise) things in our everyday lives, discourse might be said to be language-in-action (Blommaert 2005). Accordingly, both language and practice have power. This power is embedded in power structures that define the rules about what we can say and do in particular historical moments (Hall 2001). If language and practices are discursive (related to discourse), then we can imagine the possibility of changing meanings and practice through discourse. This means that through what we say and how we say it, as well as what we do and how we do it, knowledge is produced. This is productive power to which postmodernists refer.

Accordingly, discursive power is not the same as repressive power or power over (see chapter 4), which is often observable as physical threats or acts of violence by the police, military, or intimate partners. Productive power is at once less visible and more influential. It permeates our lives without us seeing the source or sites of power. To expose the insidious nature of productive power, postmodernists ask, for example, what does it mean to see our *self* through the imposed categories that uphold particular truth claims and knowledge systems? Postmodern feminists ask, What does it mean to see ourselves as *already* sexed, gendered, raced, and classed beings? How are these imposed and established identities embedded in power relations, and for the most part, remain unquestioned by those who assume them? In this sense, *already* defined categories define who we are, how we behave, and what is expected of us. Postmodern feminists attempt to answer such questions and to expose the power in naming and labelling. For this reason, according to postmodern feminists, the very categories that construct and define us require deconstruction (Irigaray 1985; Haraway 1985; Alcoff 1988; Butler 1990). To do this deconstruction, we must become participants in discourse rather than objects of it.

As a way to participate in discourse, postmodern feminist theorists began to deconstruct the phallocentrism and heteronormativity that sustain Western universalist thinking. This way of thinking, they argued, demanded deconstruction because it was so embedded in the dominant or hegemonic culture. This is to say that phallocentrism and heteronormativity are ideological. They hold a great deal of power because they seem like common-sense ideas and remain unquestioned because of hegemonic culture.

Postmodern feminists, therefore, contended that binary systems of inclusion and exclusion dictated by hegemonic culture were vested with the power to erase differences. *Phallocentrism*, meaning the vested power of the phallus or penis, they argued, constructed the proverbial modern man at the expense of women. Luce

Irigaray (1977) used the term *phallogocentrism* to expose the singularity of the category sex, which presumed one sex, man, against which all is measured. The erasure of woman from discourse was a consequence of the phallo(go)centrism and the hierarchy implicit in language. For example, the "universal male" is implied by the words *man* and *mankind* but has long been taken to include "woman" as well. Yet feminists connect the use of the word man with actual power. They contend that by using man as a universal, women are implicitly excluded from having power. This feminist assertion is supported by the U.S. Declaration of Independence, which states, "All men are created equal." "Men" in this context was not a universal term since it clearly did not apply to women, who at the time could not vote, or to people of African descent who were legally defined by slavery as free or enslaved. Or take, as another example, the term "seminal," a word used to indicate a foundational or influential development or idea. The term is derived from the word semen, perhaps the ultimate phallocentric word.

Phallocentrism also prevails in popular discourses about masculinity, which instill particular ideas about how men and boys should *be*. The discursive practices that mark men as *man*ly—asserting, for example, that "big boys don't cry"—must be exposed for their productive power. This is what is also referred to as *discursive power*, the power we don't see or really think about and, therefore, the power that is most difficult to resist.

Discourse is about the power to name, and, as postmodern feminists argue, it is through naming that phallocentrism prevails. Even while still in the womb, we begin to talk about the child differently when a girl is expected than when a boy is anticipated. The kicking that occurs in the womb enters discourse. Kicking for the unborn boy is talked about as a symbol of athletic prowess. Athleticism is understood as a clear marker of masculinity, so we talk about the probability of a future soccer player. Such conversations expose the false gendered assumption that girls are not athletic and don't play soccer. The idea that it is unfeminine for girls to be athletic is part of this thinking. It conjures images of a masculine muscular female and, worse, the possibility of the butch lesbian. When the girl in utero kicks, she is more frequently defined as a ballet dancer or as some other clearly feminine-gendered identity. The idea that ballet is not athletic and therefore not masculine is complicated, however, when boys and men are dancers of ballet. When dance enters discourse, it is understood as a feminine activity. Consequently, when performed by boys and men, their masculinity, indeed, their sexuality is suspect. Accordingly, discourse is not simply gendered but also heterosexed. It assumes heterosexuality and *disciplines* homosexuality.

Judith Butler's theorizing of gender as a performance is a critical contribution to postmodern feminist thinking. In her, dare I say, seminal book *Gender Trouble* (1990), Butler proposes that it is not biology but performance, like an actor on the stage of life, that determines gender. While feminists had long argued that gender was socially constructed, Butler's insights delinked biological sex from gendered identity. She argued that gender is something that we do, something that we perform. Gender is a parody for which there is no original (or correct) form. It is not fixed but rather fluid. If this is the case, as Butler demonstrates, then it follows that all identity markers—race, sexuality, class, age, and nationality—are performances.

Despite the focus of postmodern theorists on deconstructing and challenging universal truths, critics argue that it remains decidedly Eurocentric in its focus. Cornel West, for example, argues that postmodernism's valuing of individuality and concentration on the (male) self reproduces the Western universalizing thought that it seeks to challenge. Postmodernism continues to theorize from a position of middle-class, heterosexual whiteness. From this primary identity, it deconstructs language and categories to make room for different identities (Flax 1987; Brodribb 1993; West 1993; Collins 1998). However, difference remains within the binary of what is and what is not the same and a call for critical reflection of the exclusionary practices of feminist and postmodern theories remains.

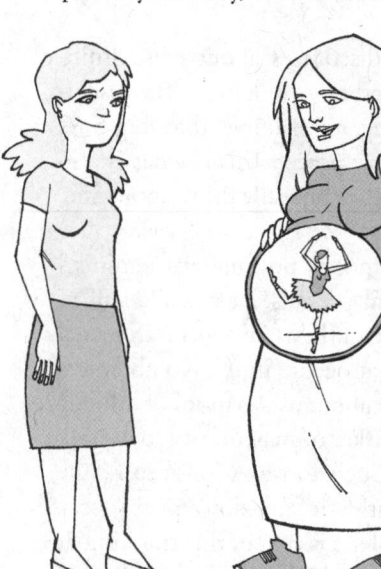

Queer Theory

Queer theorists have reclaimed the term "queer" from its derogatory use in the past to exclude alternative sexualities, and queer activists have worked to remake the term as celebratory of, and unifying for, lesbian-gay-bisexual-transgender-two spirited-intersexed-questioning (LGBTTIQ) people. This acronym has

Illustration 6.1: I'm sure it's a boy.

grown over the past forty-plus years from LGB to LGBQ to LGBT to its current configuration. Queer theorizing emerged in the 1990s to resist "regimes of normal," not in opposition to heterosexuality but to challenge the normalizing tendencies to see Others as the same as "normal," only different (Warner 1992; Duggan 1992). The concept of "queer theory" is attributed to feminist film theorist Teresa de Lauretis, who raised questions about women's ability to speak about themselves, feminist (self) and other representation, gender transgression, and queer sexualities (Mann 2012). Building on various feminist theories—for example, Simone de Beauvoir's understanding of woman as the deviant "Other" by comparison to man (Beauvoir 1952) and Adrienne Rich's concept of heteronormativity (Rich

1980)—together with postmodernism, queer theorists make the argument that binary systems of inclusion and exclusion are vested with the power to erase all that does not fit comfortably into established categories. Also following postmodernism, queer theory focuses on individual truths and a self-understanding that demands the separation of sex from gender and sexuality to allow for greater insight into the complexities of each. It recognizes that compartmentalizing people's experiences gives us only a partial understanding of who we/they are, an understanding that tends to universalize and fix identities. It is a way of skewing things so that we can look at and understand them differently.

Queer theory, while not necessarily explicitly feminist, has much to contribute to feminist theorizing. Of particular importance is the recognition of the separation of biological sex from gender and from sexuality. This has allowed feminists to contemplate multiple and complex identities. Queer theorizing offers the possibility that effeminate men do not have to be defined as homosexual, just as masculine women are not to be presumed lesbians. Transsexual, transgendered, and intersexed identities become not only possible to embody but also visibly embodied. The act of *queering*, to make the previously unacceptable normal, has allowed new understandings of the ways in which the boundaries that define sex, gender, and sexuality shift over time (Halberstam 2005). It is in the shifting of boundaries, and social norms, that the categories themselves transform and new ones emerge. Queer theorists, for example, reject traditional categories such as "biological" male/female or "genetic" male/female. Rather, they insist on the term *cisgender*, borrowing from the Latin *cis* meaning "on the same side," which signifies that our personal gender identity, the way we define our gender, matches our assigned gender at birth *and* our biological bodies (Schilt and Westbrook 2009). As Riki Wilchins (2004) argues, women who are police officers or military personnel, who work in construction, or who are body builders need no longer be gendered masculine or lesbian. Similarly, men who stay at home to raise children or who work in nursing, daycare, and eldercare are no longer assumed to be effeminate or gay. To restablize the binary categories we have become so comfortable with, we modify them to reflect such changes. Queer theorizing is part of this process.

Queer theorists assert that identities of sex, gender, and sexuality are fluid rather than fixed (Rubin 1984; Butler 1990, 1993; Sedgwick 1990; Duggan 1992; Warner 1992; Kinsman 1996; Halberstam 1998, 2005). Accordingly, being a biological woman does not demand a feminine gendered identity or heterosexuality. Yet there is still some expectation of these for a "normal" woman. When someone identifies as a biological man who performs masculinity and heterosexuality, how do others understand them? This one is easy: they are a man. But what if one identifies as a man, performs masculinity and has sex with women, and yet is biologically female? Language only allows for the category "man" or "woman." You might then say that they are a lesbian. But not all lesbians perform masculinity nor do they identify as men. Clearly things are more complex than these categories allow. The limitations of the identity "man" or "woman" and all the assumptions that go with it are complicated. However, when we're not sure exactly which category people fall into, it makes us uncomfortable because of the social and cultural expectations we have that gender identities should be fixed and that we should just as easily fit people into categories.

For most of us, conforming to social and cultural expectations means not standing out as being different. This too is a performance. The gendering of masculine and feminine identities is learned throughout childhood with the bouncing of boys and the rocking of girls; with toy trucks for boys and dolls for girls; and the colour coding of blue for boys and pink for girls for everything from room colours and clothing to toys and tableware. Lois Gould's book *X: A Fabulous Child's Story* (1978), tells of the difficulty of raising a non-gender specific child, a "baby X." Without pronouns to refer to baby X, without knowing with which toys baby X should play, without knowing what clothing in which to dress baby X, without knowing what *is* a "baby X," all the people around baby X—parents, teachers, aunts, uncles, and peers—feel uncomfortable. The story reveals the centrality of imposed gender systems to the ways in which we come to know. In 2011, a real-life example of nurturing gender ambiguity was documented in Canada when the *Toronto Star* reported that a couple in Toronto, Ontario, was trying out this experiment by raising their own "baby X." In the wake of the story's publication, the couple was bombarded both with praise for recognizing the self-defined fluidity of gender and criticism for failing to provide their child with a gender identity. Nonetheless, the parents' hope was to hold off the either/or decisions of pink versus blue, trucks versus dolls, and male versus female until their child could make up its own mind (Poisson 2011).

Arguably, everything we do and every move we make is marked with gendered meaning. Our gestures, voices, fashions and accessories, dispositions, athletic abilities, body shapes, weight, musculature, and aesthetics are all telltale signs of gender. The way we throw a ball, the way we wear (or don't wear) makeup, the way we sit, stand, and walk are all subject to gendering. Gendering is something that we *do* (perform), not simply something that is *done* to us.

I think about when I was young and the neighbourhood girls would get together to play house. I was drawn to playing the father role, which for me in hindsight was my attempt to challenge gender norms, both masculine and feminine. As the man, I recall standing taller, sucking in my stomach so that my chest would swell, anchoring myself firmly with my feet apart, holding my head up high to oversee the situation, while at the same time my friend, the pretend mother, my presumed wife, sat rocking the doll we named Susie. What

Illustration 6.2: Who says what toys are appropriate for girls and boys?

did performing a gender identity in this way say about my femininity? Was I simply performing a well-studied imitation of socially constructed masculinity? Was I queering gender? Today, would I be diagnosed with gender identity disorder (GID) as is so often the case in children as young as three years old (Wilchins 2004)? Was I in the wrong body? Or would my performance be understood as play and part of the process of knowing and becoming myself? And did my performance say anything about my sexuality?

As early as the 1980s, radical feminists were arguing that heterosexuality was constructed as compulsory. Adrienne Rich (1980) suggested that many people will never question their sexual orientation because they presume that they are heterosexual. However, without considering alternative sexual possibilities, the confirmation of one's heterosexuality is not really a choice. But what if we do question our sexuality? Such questioning might (or might not) lead us to the debate as to whether there is a biological or genetic link to sexuality (Hamer and Copeland 1994; Conrad and Markens 2001). This debate has political implications, particularly for the gay rights movement. If a biological link were found, then homosexuality could be reconstructed within scientific discourse as a naturally occurring condition rather than as a deviant behaviour or choice. Queer theory, on the other hand, is uninterested in this debate because it rejects identity politics, which attempts to impose conformity around particular identities. For queer theorists, the "gay gene" would erase the diversity and fluidity of emerging identities.

Judith Halberstam (1998, 2002) contributes to queering gender binaries by offering the concept of *female masculinity* as an alternative masculinity.

She suggests that masculinity, as one of the core structures of gender binaries, needs to be de-naturalized from "male" bodies and uncoupled from maleness. Female masculinity refers to a wide range of identities from tomboyism to queerness. For many girls the tomboy identity is associated with a desire for the independence, self-determination, and mobility assumed by boys. In this sense, it is tolerated and to a certain degree encouraged when it is understood as a liberating identity for girls. However, should the tomboy identity extend from girlhood into adolescence, and thereby threaten "womanhood," regimes of gender conformity are quickly imposed. Social fears around "proper" femininity and homosexuality—indeed, any sexuality as many presume that the tomboy is at least for the moment asexual—ensue. Accordingly, the tomboy is punished when she fails to fit into compliant heteronormative femininity.

The tomboy identity, however, fails to capture the complexities and diversity of female gendered bodies and subjectivities. Halberstam (1998, 2002, 2005) contributes to the understanding of complexities by exploring the notions of passing and performing gender for particular female masculinities—queers, who embody the diversity of butch lesbians and MTF (male-to-female) transgendered people. Halberstam's purpose is to disrupt the comfortable binary of male and female and to expose the fluidity of each as a stumbling block for the acknowledgment of multiple genders. Many queer theorists offer the "third" category of "gender neutral" or "gender ambiguous" as a way forward; however, Halberstam argues that the third category reifies the other two—male /female— and prohibits the emergence of a multiplicity of gender identities because "everyone" can presumably fit within the modified gender triplex—male/female/ gender neutral. Adding a third category simultaneously expands the fluidity of "male" and "female" and homogenizes "gender neutral."

The concepts of passing and performing gender become especially visible in bathrooms. Halberstam (2002, 2005) explains that the gender identity of most people is readily detectable. Those who seem in some way gender ambiguous, however, are subject to surveillance, especially in public bathrooms. In women's public bathrooms, masculine or butch females, and ambiguously "female" gendered people (those who don't easily pass as "female"), are commonly questioned, stopped at the door, so to speak, of gender binaries. Common "friendly" reminders of female gender expectations such as "Ooops, I think you're in the wrong room," to more aggressive remarks like "Is *that* a man? In *here*?" reassert gender boundaries that make female masculinity unimaginable. Those who experience such policing often feel violated and humiliated by such processes of exclusion (Mottet 2002–2003; Coyote 2011a, 2011b).

The men's bathroom is also a place of some difficulty to negotiate if you don't readily pass as male. However, the context for men's bathrooms is different, for they are spaces of male social interaction and homoerotic sexual interactions. Halberstam (2002) argues that the codes that operate in male bathrooms are sexual, whereas the codes in female bathrooms are feminine. She suggests that female/feminine gender coding is clear in the language use to refer to them (e.g., the little girls' room) and the practices expected to take place therein (e.g., powdering one's nose or checking one's lipstick). The coding of men's rooms as sexual spaces may account for lower levels of surveillance and the acceptance of a broader spectrum of "maleness." However, for those individuals who are FTM (female-to-male) transgendered and for those who do not easily pass as male, there is the risk of verbal and physical assault (Namaste 2000, 2005; Turnbull 2007; Girshick 2008).

So, what do those who are gender non-conforming or transgendered do when the need to relieve strikes? Some folks take the risk of passing in gender-coded washrooms, while others simply "hold it" until a safe, more gender-neutral space is available. Holding it, however, can cause pain and discomfort as well as health problems such as urinary tract infections. Imagine yourself as a child on a long car ride and being unable to relieve yourself because Mom, Dad, or whoever is driving says there is no time to stop and pee. Now imagine after that long car ride, when you *can* finally pee, that everyone is watching to see *how* you pee and which washroom you use to do it. While Halberstam's (1998, 2002) conceptualization of female masculinity offers insight, particularly for butch lesbians and transfolks, it says little about the identities of masculine females who identify as heterosexual. This is an area for further consideration in queering gender, sex, and sexuality.

If we are participants in the discourses of our gendering, sexing, and sexualizing, then we can understand identity as performance. We can also see how culture and the body are interrelated in identity constructions. Think about the way you act around your friends and then consider the way you "act" at work or perhaps when visiting your grandmother. You may act and dress differently, you may speak differently and use different language, even the subjects that you can talk about may be different but are you different?

You are expected to perform appropriately and to "be" normal. However, definitions and expectations of what is normal shift. Judith Butler (1990) argues that norms shape bodies and that through performances these norms are never repeated in exactly the same way but are themselves changed. The naming of queer identities allows us to recognize such shifts as they emerge. For example, a boy-identified dyke is a youth who identifies as lesbian but not necessarily female; bio-femmes are biologically female and hyperfeminine; a no ho is a transgendered person who does not take hormones; boy-chicks are boy-identified females; trykes are transsexuals who identify as dykes; and andros are androgynously gendered people (Wilkins 2004).

While queer theory seeks to be as inclusive as possible, much of this theorizing is decidedly Western, occurring largely in Western contexts. Although inroads are being made in queer diasporic and transnational studies, queer theory is still embedded in liberalism, which reinforces the Western ideals of liberty and freedom (Patton and Sánchez-Eppler 2000; Hawley 2001; Braziel 2008; Gopinath 2008; Spurlin 2010; Kulpa and Mizielinska 2011). Since queer theory implies theorizing from personal experiences, the focus remains on individuals, which is another tenant of Western thought and which makes collective action for social change more difficult. Finally, relatively little research has been undertaken on the experiences of queer identities beyond North America and Europe.

Third World Feminisms

The meaning of otherness, not of the dominant group and therefore "Other," is founded on the power relationships embedded in such binary terms as Third World/First World, Global South/Global North, the West/the rest, and racialized/white. All of these are contested terms, which reinforce existing relationships of power and privilege. The term "Third World," for example, emerged from the Bandung Conference (1955), which was held to foster economic and cultural cooperation, a new Third Way for development, among newly independent African and Asian states that did not fit neatly into the Cold War power dynamics between the East and the West (Graves 1996). We continue to use these terms variously, recognizing the inequities they represent, to help us grasp the different social, historical, cultural, economic, political, and geographic spaces in which lives are lived and theorizing takes place. Third World feminists claim this title as a symbol of political solidarity with and among women in the Global South. The concepts of Global South and Global North became common among feminist theorists in the 1990s as a way to express locations of inequality. They defined the locations of high incomes and high consumption patterns as the Global North, whereas the Global South was marked by low income and low consumption patterns. These locations are not specifically geographic or particular to specific countries, but rather they are spatial and can be present in any country (Mann 2012).

In theorizing the importance of race and interlocking systems of oppression, feminists of colour in the West, as we saw in the last chapter, have significantly shaped feminist thought. They have failed, however, to grasp how their theorizing about race has positioned racialized people living in the West as the only groups who are targets of racism, which has resulted in a particular kind of identity politics. What about Third World women (and men) living in the Global South? When Western feminists thought about Third World women, they did so as a homogenous Other. Women yes, but not Western, not modern, not liberated, not empowered women. Third World women are often constructed as a homogenous category, which reflects paternalistic Western thinking. Such thought assumed a passive, backward, powerless, and definitely non-Western woman. Under this Western lens, Third World women were seen as always oppressed, sexually and otherwise, by Third World men and their backward cultures. Little consideration was given to how the impact of colonialism might have affected and continued to affect these women and men.

Binary thinking and *us* versus *them* categories reinforce the legacy of colonization, spurring nationalisms and independence movements (Grewal, Inderpal, and Kaplan 1994; McClintock 1995; McClintock, Mufti, and Shohat 1997; Narayan 1997, 1998; Anthias and Yuval-Davis 2005). Criticisms of essentialism, homogenization, and Eurocentrism came from Third World women. In the context of feminist theorizing and international development, Third World refers to both the geopolitical spaces of the Global South and the people who live or are from there. The term has fallen into a mire of criticism as a pejorative term that reinforces the power wielded by the West/Europe/Global North. Feminists such as Chandra Mohanty (1984, 1991, 1995), Lourdes Benería (1992, 2003) and Gita Sen (1987, 2002), among others, have argued that the experiences of Third World women need to be framed within the contexts of women's poverty and illiteracy, oppressive cultural practices, and unequal development between the Global North and the Global South. Their works expose Western-dictated modernization and development models as well as the ongoing processes of (neo) colonialism as sites of Third World women's oppression.

Western models have hypothesized that so-called Third World countries could become developed/modern only *if* they followed the models of economic and resource development set by the West (Rostow 1960). These externally imposed models were developed and implemented by and for wealthy men, with no input from or concern for the women who constitute the majority of the poor globally. These development models maintained their colonial relationships of control by Western interests long after independence was achieved by many nations in the Global South (Harcourt 1994, 2009; Marchand and Parpart 1995; Fraser and Tinker 2004). The oil industry in Nigeria, for example, continues to be dominated by Shell Nigeria, a branch of the Dutch multinational corporation Royal Dutch Shell.

The exploitation and appropriation of resources by the West have resulted in the majority of profit and wealth accumulating in the West and a (neo)colonial legacy of dependency for countries in the Global South (Cardoso and Faletto 1979). This siphoning-off process has worsened the lives of the majority of people in the Global South, and it continues to do so. Poverty, illiteracy, poor health care systems, and weak educational systems have all been influenced by Western dominance and exploitation. Because of women's responsibilities for bearing and raising children, these issues affect women more dramatically than men.

The inequities and oppressions of colonization sparked nationalist and independence movements throughout the Global South following the end of the Second World War. These struggles resulted in social and political unrest, which

Perform 66% of the World's Work
Produce 50% of the Food
But
Earn 10% of the Income
Own 1% of the Property

Perform 34% of
the World's Work
Produce 50% of the Food
But
Earn 90% of the Income
Own 99% of the Property

Statistical source: UNIFEM 2007.

affected women more negatively than men. Even though many countries won their independence and saw the removal of direct colonial control, an indirect external control has been maintained through the international monetary system and multinational corporations. The horrors of colonialism were, and are, extended through neocolonialism—a new kind of colonialism. Independence, decolonization, and neocolonialism marked a new space for postcolonial theory. The boundaries that distinguish Third World from postcolonial feminist theorizing are not always clear and many feminist theorists straddle the two.

Postcolonial Feminist Theory

Postcolonial theory recognizes that the "post" in colonial is symbolic rather than a liberation from the unequal power relations of a colonial past. The histories of imperialism and colonialism cannot be erased; they remain present in neocolonial power structures. Postcolonial theorists recognize that systems of inclusion and exclusion are central to maintaining established power structures. Edward Said called attention to the power of naming in *Orientalism* (1979). He argued that we can only know the West (the Occident) by seeing what it is not—the East, the Orient. In naming the West, (neo)colonial discourses assert Western authority. By naming the Orient, and thereby excluding it from the West, the East is made Other, the unknown and, by extension, the unknowing. To be defined as unknown, as unknowing, disempowers those who are excluded from the West and reifies the supremacy of Western thought.

In the 1980s, feminist scholars in the Global South, particularly those from South Asia, challenged Orientalism's exclusionary thinking, the core of which defined them as unknowing and unknowable (Mohanty 1984, 1991, 2003; Spivak 1988; Grewal and Kaplan 1994; Narayan and Harding 2000; Lewis and Mills 2003). Building on the theories of postmodern and Third World feminisms, postcolonial feminist theory also challenges the idea of grand theories of modernity, imperialism, colonialism, and modernization as universally valid. They contend that these Eurocentric and masculinist theories, which name men as the key actors in the world, invalidate women's contributions, particularly those of women in the Global South. Such assumptions are embedded in the processes of colonialism and neocolonialism, and they are central to the discourses that exclude women.

Postcolonial feminist theory offers a gendered analysis of the past and current circumstances of colonialism and neocolonialism. It exposes the power assumptions embedded in these practices, which maintain global inequalities. Postcolonial feminists pay careful attention to the interconnections of gender, nation, class, caste, race, ethnicity, religion, culture, and sexualities in the contexts of women's lives. At the same time, postcolonial feminist theory recognizes that the particulars of historic moments affect the specifics of women's lives. This means that the experiences of the past such as slavery, for example, cannot be compared with the work relationships of today. They are not the same; they do not take place in the same historical moments or under the same conditions. Postcolonial theory, however, recognizes that the effects of the past remain in the present.

Postcolonial feminist theorists acclaim the voices of those who have been most marginalized as knowing and empowered people. Accordingly, they draw heavily on narratives from those commonly left out of history. Much has been written about conquerors, conquests, the winners of wars, and the "Great Men" who make history. This writing, however, is only a small part of the *his*tory. By taking marginalized women's experiences seriously and listening to women's stories, postcolonial feminist theory sheds light on the details of women's lives, their struggles, and their resistance. Postcolonial feminist theory calls attention to women's resistance to domination and systems of power. The purpose in acknowledging these narratives is to heal epistemic violence and change the world.

Gayatri Spivak (1988) coined the term *epistemic violence* in her essay "Can the Subaltern Speak?" to explain the ways in which Western discourse has constructed non-Western Others as unknowing bodies, in opposition to Western knowing subjects. Epistemic violence is the destruction of non-Western ways of knowing and being. Postcolonial feminists like Spivak are deconstructing the Western-imposed concepts and terms that perpetuate such violence by questioning their foundations. Through the processes of deconstruction, stereotypical depiction of Eastern women as silent, mysterious, and exotic, for example, are exposed as Western fetishizations and as ways to demarcate the powerful masculine West from the disempowered feminine East.

By theorizing from specifics, from narratives, from memories, and from the experiences of those most marginalized, postcolonial feminists reclaim non-Western knowledge and challenge the universalizing processes of Western domination. Highlighting these tensions exposes the increasing

Illustration 6.3: Hmm ... you Western experts, what are we going to do with a washing machine?

inequalities and polarization caused by the globalization of capitalism and Western dominance.

Transnational Feminism

As the world becomes more integrated at the levels of economics, politics, and culture, feminist concerns take on a new global dimension. Accordingly, theories evolve and change, and feminist theorists are participant in these dialogues of, and for, change. They straddle categories of theorizing and cross the borders that attempt to divide Third World/postcolonial/transnational feminist frameworks and theories. Scholars and scholarship are not stagnant; just as globalization changes, so do the theories that explore, explain, and confront it. Postcolonial and transnational feminisms reject linear views of history and unidirectional flows of culture, knowledge, and social change, as well as the hierarchies of North/South (Grewal 2005; Moghadam 2005; Alexander and Mohanty 2010; Nagar and Swarr 2010; Wetherell and Mohanty 2010; Jónasdóttir, Bryson, and Jones 2011; Zinn, Hondagneu-Sotelo, and Messner 2011; Mohanty and Miraglia 2012). War, militarization, climate change, pandemic disease, environmental degradation, human and drug trafficking, human rights, the displacement of people, refugees, migration, diasporas, and poverty are all transnational issues. In the 1990s there was a shift in feminist theorizing from the focus on imperialism and colonization to a focus on globalization and transnationalism. *Transnational* means that issues/people/goods/finances/ideas cross national borders and, therefore, demand a global understanding. Nonetheless, many women's economic aspirations and understandings of success, which are complicated by class divisions and systemic racism (through conscious and unconscious racist thoughts), result in the oppression, exploitation, and domination of other women. Consequently, women's own actions are complicit in colonial and neocolonial projects of imperialism.

In North America, for example, women are continually enticed to buy the latest in fashions (Micheletti, Føllesdal, and Stolle 2006). Every six weeks, new clothing lines are introduced, leading us to believe that last week's chic is now passé. This cycle of buying and the social pressures on women to "look good" result in women spending larger portions of their wages on clothes and accessories (Bartky 1990). Women's wages are already routinely less than men's, so this may mean scrimping and going without other things. This consumerism has transnational consequences. Women around the globe are working in garment factories producing goods for consumption abroad. Multinational corporations with headquarters in the Global North, where profits also accumulate, dominate manufacturing sectors in the Global South. Women who work for these companies commonly work in unsafe and unhealthy environments, often referred to as "sweatshops," for long hours with few or no breaks, and for little pay. Women's demands for ever-cheaper fashions in the Global North, therefore, collude with global capital to exploit and oppress workers in the Global South.

The unquestioned and dependent relationship between North and South identities is well reflected in the binary of mother/nanny. The ideal for many women in the West is to employ a nanny to do the onerous domestic labour of taking care of the home and the children. This aspiration demands the hiring of other women to do the lower-paid jobs of caring, while elite women have the freedom to build their careers. The paradox of this freedom, however, is that it relies on the exploitation of other women, commonly racialized women, and women who are "imported" as foreign workers from the Global South. Their foreign status often means that they experience vulnerability and precarious living conditions. Many nannies, in addition to 8- or 10-hour days, are on call 24 hours a day as needed. They may live in rooms that double as family areas, offering them little privacy or personal space. As live-in caregivers, they may also be subjected to sexual violence and, because of their vulnerable status as foreign workers, have few options through which to seek redress. They are usually tied to their employer for a contracted period and are unable to change jobs without risking their immigration status. Moreover, many of the women who become nannies do so at great personal cost. While they can send money home to support their families, they are forced to allow other people to mother their own children back home, at the same time as they mother the children of economically privileged women in the West (Ehrenreich and Hochschild 2003; Stasiulis and Bakan 2005; Dreby 2006).

Many scholars contend that women in the West are still struggling to decolonize their thinking and practices rather than reinscribing Western imperialism. To *decolonize* our thinking and practices we must recognize how our assumptions are embedded in colonial and neocolonial theories and suppositions, and then we must challenge them. Let's take, for example, the wearing of the hijab. Some Westerners assume that women are forced to wear hijab, and therefore see it as oppressive, backwards, and an expression of patriarchal control over Muslim women. In contrasting the Muslim girl's body to the Western "sporty" girl's body, especially in media representations, the Muslim girl remains a covered body, a silent body, an oppressed body, but also an immobile and physically constrained body that is unable to fully participate in anything or go anywhere (see, for example, Hoodfar 1993; Saadallah 2007; Jiwani 2009).

Yet wearing hijab means different things to different women in different social, geographic, and political contexts. Wearing hijab, a religious symbol and signifier of modesty, is often a choice that Muslim women make for themselves rather than having it imposed on them. It is neither a constraint nor a marker of physical, social, or cultural limitations. It is ironic that many of those same Westerners who criticize hijab have no problem with Western practices such as wearing a G-string or miniskirt, or with breast implants or injecting Botox to remove facial wrinkles. And, what about the newest rage in cosmetic surgery— vaginal rejuvenation or designer vaginas, which assumes that a young, tight, surgically altered vagina is the optimum vagina (see, for example, Davis 2002; Myrick Stocker 2004; Goodman 2011)? Such practices are invariably linked to patriarchal systems of power in which women are both willing and unwilling participants. It is the condemnation of hijab on the one hand and the celebration of Western clothing and cosmetic surgeries and procedures on the other that we need to challenge if we are to decolonize our thinking.

Through this process of decolonizing our Western thinking, we begin to contest the notion that *West is best*! Indeed, what does it mean to be best? Does it mean the ability to maintain domination through both discourse and the direct use of violence? Military and anti-terrorist interventions abound, and civilians, particularly women and children, suffer. The very word "intervention" conjures up a sanitized image of Western justice and rightness. This authority erases the costs of war, especially the human costs. The West spends billions of dollars on the manufacturing of tanks, guns, and bombs; more money is spent on military personnel and the planes and ships that will get them to war zones; and even more funds are invested at home to train the soldiers and provide bases on which they practise manoeuvres. These expenditures result in the destruction of economic systems, infrastructures, the environment, and lives around the globe. Militarization, however, affects women and children in

Illustration 6.4: FIFA says no to hijab.

It was the end for Iranian Women's Soccer at the Olympics in 2012. Officials of FIFA (Fédération Internationale de Football Association) claim that headscarves that cover the head, ears, and neck are a safety risk. But could there be a link between banning hijabs and making women's soccer sexier, and therefore more profitable? Consider Sepp Blatter's, then president of FIFA, suggestion in 2004 to increase the popularity of women's soccer: women should play in more feminine clothes ... skimpier ... tighter shorts ... to create a more female aesthetic. (Christenson and Kelso 2004; Erdbrink 2011)

conflict zones most negatively. It hinders food production and distribution; disrupts social networks and family relationships; adds to women's work of caring for the ailing and injured; destroys people's health care systems; and displaces people from their homes, creating millions of refugees (Riley, Mohanty, and Pratt 2008; Cheldelin and Eliatamby 2011; Wibben 2011).

Such a criticism of Western interventions may seem unpatriotic, particularly as so many troops are giving their lives to the "cause." It is the cause of winning that is at the very root of imperialism. Patriotism, therefore, is part of the colonizing process, because it makes us feel compelled to act in particular ways that support the cause, the purpose of which is to secure the world for capitalism in all its glory and devastation. Women are convinced of their liberation, being able to soldier on the frontlines, equally with men, in active war zones. Having equal access to killing and being killed is not a feminist goal. Moreover, the image of liberated women is commonly contrasted with the poor and oppressed women for whom we are told we are fighting. The picture of an empowered Western woman juxtaposed with a disempowered non-Western woman, as has been displayed in the media, where depictions of veiled women alongside female soldiers or reporters are useful to imperialist goals (Zarkov 2006; Enloe 2010; Mackie 2012). Such representations elicit feelings of virtue on the one hand and pity on the other. It is these thoughts in our heads that we need to decolonize.

Conclusion

In this chapter, we explored postmodern, Third World, queer, postcolonial, and transnational feminist theories. Each of these theories fosters feminist thinking and actions. They expose and challenge neocolonialism and imperialism, as ongoing, oppressive, and exploitative projects of Western dominance. In so doing, they expand our understandings of *who* can know, *what* is known, and *how* knowing resists and produces social change. These theories challenge Western dominance by valuing non-Western and non-conventional knowledge and experiences. Accordingly, we can begin to recognize theory, not as a process that we do in the abstract, but as thinking and actions that we do with purpose in redressing oppressions, exploitation, and inequities. In the next chapter, we will explore methods, tools, and techniques used to collect data for feminists to theorize about.

Questions for Study

1. Why is it necessary to question the bases of modern Western thought? What role does science play in privileging Western thought? How are Western biases reflected in feminist theories? Is Western bias a political issue for feminists? Which feminists and why?
2. What are the components and goals of postmodern feminist theory? What do postmodernist feminist say about objectivity? Why do postmodern feminist theorists using deconstruction? Give two examples of the practice of deconstruction. What are the deficits in postmodern theory?
3. How does language produce knowledge?
4. What does Foucault argue is the result of "disciplining difference"? Give two examples of this process based on your experience.
5. How has phallocentrism excluded women from power and encouraged the different treatment of women?
6. What is the contribution of queer theory to feminist theorizing?
7. How is identity a performance? How can performance transgress norms and expectations? Give some examples of queer identities. How and why are these identities transgressive?
8. How have Western development models weakened, and in many cases destroyed, social, cultural, and political structures in the Global South?

How have Third World feminist theories exposed and addressed Western flaws?

9. What is postcolonial feminist theory? What are its aims? What kinds of questions would postcolonial feminists ask? Where would they look for their answers?

10. What is epistemic violence? How is epistemic violence institutionalized? Why is the concept useful in understanding the experiences of racialized women and marginalized people?

11. What are the aims of transnational feminism?

12. What does decolonizing our thinking and practices entail? Why is this essential to feminisms and feminist theorizing?

Activities and Questions for Discussion

1. In 2011, a young Canadian couple made the decision to keep their new baby's gender a secret until their child could make up its own mind about gender. How would this conflict with social expectations about gender and the idea of gender as performance?

2. Describe your play with others as a child. In what ways was your play gender-specific and in what ways was your play not gender-specific? How did your parents and other adults react and influence your play?

3. Argue how overconsumption of the Global North has created poverty in the Global South. What do you believe are solutions to this multifaceted problem?

4. Performances of gender, sexuality, and transgendered identities have long been subjects for making money in Hollywood-style films. Why is this the case? Review one of the following movies. Think about how gender and sexuality are constructed, learned, and performed by the key characters. How is the script written to conform with or transgress expectations?
   - *Juwanna Mann*
   - *Yentl*
   - *The Crying Game*
   - *Ma Vie en Rose*
   - *My Beautiful Launderette*
   - *White Chicks*
   - *The Associate*
   - *Boys Don't Cry*
   - *She's the Man*
   - *Nuns on the Run*
   - *Just One of the Guys*
   - *TransAmerica*
   - *Kinky Boots*
   - *M. Butterfly*

Facts are theory laden; theories are value laden; values are history laden.
—DONNA HARAWAY, "IN THE BEGINNING WAS THE WORD"

CHAPTER SEVEN

TAKING FEMINISM ON THE ROAD

FEMINIST METHODS

Theory is all very well, but what is the point in theorizing if we have nothing concrete about which to theorize? Where is the evidence? Where is the research? How do we collect it? Feminist research draws on insights from the struggles and lived experiences of women and marginalized people. Feminist perspectives, informed by theory and practice, encourage feminist researchers to ask different questions. It makes sense that the evidence to answer our questions must also come from different places. Feminist research is complex and sometimes, rather than just answering the research questions posed, it leads us to more and different questions.

We will see in this chapter that feminists use both quantitative and qualitative data to increase knowledge about women's lives and the lives of marginalized people. We will examine the assumptions that surround the methods for collecting data. We will explore the reasons for using quantitative evidence, which tends to be viewed as "objective," statistical, verifiable, and testable. We will also explore qualitative evidence, which tends to be viewed in the opposite manner as subjective, intangible, and situated. We will see that some feminists use both quantitative and qualitative data to support their research. We will briefly explore some of the methods used to collect each type of data. Our investigation will push us to question the values attached to data and how those values translate into knowledge about women's lives and the lives of marginalized people.

Recall that situated knowledge is the knowledge that people have of their position in their communities and the world (Haraway 1988). It comes from individual understandings of gender, race, ethnicity, sexuality, ability, class, geopolitical location, nationality, citizenship, religion, and level of education, to name a few. Feminist research uncovers women's and marginalized people's subjugated knowledge. This knowledge is too often erased in mainstream social and scientific research. Feminist researchers recognize the knowledge of subjugated people as *valuable* and *real*. I emphasize these two words, "valuable" and "real," because as we learned in other chapters, the production of knowledge is intrinsically tied to Western narratives of reason, rationality, truth, and science, all of which can preclude the knowledge of marginalized people. The stories of Western thought are about the production of knowledge by those in positions of power—scientists, men, white people, heterosexuals, elites, and the highly educated. Such narratives falsely assume that women, people of colour, gay men, lesbians, queers, the aged, the differently abled, the economically disadvantaged, and the less educated have nothing to contribute to the production of knowledge. These stories are inherently linked to truth claims that are upheld by *scientific methodology* (Harding 1987; Burt and Code 1995; Narayan and Harding 2000; Longino 2002; Denzin and Lincoln 2003).

Ways of Knowing

Scientific methodology determines how research should proceed. *Scientific methods* are the procedures and techniques used to gather facts and test the evidence found. Scientific methods are based on objectivity, empirical evidence (see definition below), observable facts, quantitative laws, and experimentation. Social scientists, such as political scientists, sociologists, anthropologists, criminologists, geographers, linguists, and historians use scientific methods as a way to make sure their research is taken seriously. The assertions of such research are powerful, compelling, and command attention because they are steeped in the narratives of science and positivism. *Positivism* is the belief that the social and natural worlds are both accessible and understandable. This means that it is possible to know everything. This seems a bit daunting, but it is this belief that spurs the never-ending pursuit of knowledge.

Most social scientific methods remain stubbornly positivist. They are informed by *empiricism*, which assumes that the relationship between the observer (the researcher) and the observed (the person or people who are being studied) is without bias. This is referred to as the subject–object relationship. The assumed absence of bias is commonly taken one step further by presuming that there is *no* relationship between the researcher (subject) and the observed (object). These assertions seem like a bit of a stretch. How can there be no relationship between the researcher and the people he/she wants to know about? It is very difficult to keep your distance and to stay "neutral" when people are telling you about their lives and personal experiences. Positivists use methodological techniques to prevent any relationship from developing between the researcher and the participants, such as not discussing their personal experiences or information with participants and not telling the participants their research question. They presume that these techniques can achieve objectivity.

Empiricism requires neutrality. It assumes a value-free environment in which both the observer and observed are liberated from any social, political, or cultural influences and can produce objective knowledge. As you might have guessed from previous chapters, these assertions of neutrality and objectivity are disputed by feminisms. The assumptions of neutrality and objectivity, feminists contend, have led to androcentric and homogenizing approaches to both theory and methodology (hooks 1984; Harding 1986, 1987, 1989, 1993; Burt 1995; Lloyd 2002; Hesse-Biber and Leavy 2012). Feminist thought defines *androcentrism* as a way of knowing and seeing the world from the perspectives of men, maleness, and masculinity. Androcentrism privileges the knowledge, interests, and experiences of men, consequently discounting those of women. Androcentrism assumes a male bias. Androcentrism is sexist. It puts men's lives and bodies at the centre of social and scientific inquiry. Homogenization assumes that men's experiences and bodies can be extended to women. It also assumes that experiences of the West can be superimposed on non-Western bodies in non-Western contexts. Together, androcentric and homogenizing assumptions make white men's lives and bodies the focus of social and scientific inquiry. These assumptions both subjugate and exclude women's and non-Western knowledge.

> ## Just the Facts!
>
> Facts are things thought to be irrefutable and provable. They come with claims of indisputability. They are commonly based on *empirical evidence*, which is information that is discovered through the use of our five senses—sight, hearing, taste, touch, and smell. Since we can determine that something exists and therefore is accessible for others to observe as well, we think of it as a fact.

Feminist Empiricism: The Value of Statistics?

Feminist empiricists who use quantitative methodologies challenge the androcentric and homogenizing assumptions that dictate what gets accepted as scientific and therefore *real* evidence. When women are not taken into account, the results are skewed. Objectivity and presumed neutrality are actually androcentric and therefore embedded in *male bias* because much research begins from the perspectives and bodies of men. Feminist empiricists, however, don't want to throw the

Sexism in Medical Treatment

We might have birth control in the form of a pill, but the side effects of weight gain, headaches, heightened risks of cardiovascular disease as well as the possible increased risks of breast and cervical cancers all remain. And there is still evidence of a medical hierarchy of diseases wherein "men's diseases," those that have clear and detectable symptoms or affect vital organs, take priority in treatment. In contrast, "women's diseases" are viewed as less important often because they present symptoms that are more difficult to diagnose or that cannot easily be attributed to known causes. Diagnoses of fibrositic diseases (rheumatoid arthritis and fibromyalgia), autoimmune diseases (multiple sclerosis), chronic fatigue syndrome, and depressive disorders rank the lowest on the medical hierarchy of diseases. These diseases are found more frequently in women than men. Giving "women's diseases" a lower priority is sexist and it results in unequal medical treatment between women and men. Perhaps asking different questions and using feminist approaches in research and treatment processes could change the outcomes (Wong 2009).

baby out with the bathwater. They insist on the importance of keeping empirical scientific methods, which produce observable, testable, measurable, and quantifiable information. They add to this method questions about women, their ideas, experiences, and bodies. Rather than creating a "female bias" in the research, feminists seek to fill in the gaps in the research about women (Tuana 1989, 1992; Hawkesworth 1989; Nelson 1990).

Feminist empiricists who use quantitative methodologies rely on quantitative laws that assume all evidence can be analyzed mathematically. Quantitative methods assume that through repetition, experimentation, and the manipulation of variables, outcomes can be successfully predicted. This kind of evidence often tells us what to think about things, from how we should vote in an election and what we should think about a particular government policy or program to the type of toothpaste we ought to use. As you know, we are constantly bombarded with commercials that offer factual support: "4 out of 5 dentists choose Crest." Every day we hear the results of public opinion polls claiming that statistical evidence demonstrates this or that, credible within "x" standard deviations. This sounds so scientific that we seldom question the authority and truth of the numbers, how the data was gathered, from whom the data was gathered, what questions the survey asked, how the data and answers were recorded, or what mathematical contortions the data went through. Yet quantitative data is valued and it therefore influences the decisions we make.

Illustration 7.1: Hmm ... I think we need more feminism.

Many feminist scholars rely on quantitative data for their research. As we've seen, quantitative data can be compelling. Its power is derived from the power of science. Feminists who take this approach combine feminist perspectives with scientific methods to gather information that reflects women's everyday lives. This knowledge is inclusive of women, benefits women, and represents women's experiences (Fonow and Cook 1991). For example, conducting large-scale surveys allows masses of information to be sorted and coded for analysis. This information offers researchers knowledge about trends in the data and insights into their research questions. The purpose of the research is to offer some generalizations about those populations of women surveyed. The information gathered and the value of that information varies. The quality of the information depends on, among other things, the following factors:

- the size of the sample population (the number of people surveyed),
- the screening process (how participants get selected or excluded),
- the motivation of participants (whether they are being paid or persuaded in some way to participate),
- the context in which the survey is given (information given to potential participants about the survey or current political environment about the issue under discussion), and
- the survey questions themselves.

These are just some of the things that we might want to consider when evaluating statistics based on quantitative methodologies used by feminist scholars.

Let's consider a hypothetical survey on abortion. If activists wanted to find out what people really think about abortion, conducting a large-scale survey might be an appropriate method to use. On the one hand, a survey's results could offer pro-choice activists the evidence to influence government programs and funding policies that could protect women's reproductive choices, save women's lives, promote women's health, and ensure that children are born into homes where they are wanted. On the other hand, anti-choice groups might also choose to conduct a survey designed to bolster their position. Their purpose would likely be to gather information about the value of life, the harmfulness of abortions, the value of children, and to discover whether tax dollars should be spent on abortion services.

The premise for each survey is strikingly different. Based on the application of scientific methods, however, both groups could assert with some authority that the data they gather is true. Or could they? Let's think about the kinds of questions each group might want to ask. Certainly, the questions that the surveys ask have a direct relationship to the hypothesis posed. A *hypothesis* is a statement taken to be true for the purpose of argument or investigation. The hypothesis for a pro-choice survey would assume that abortion is a woman's choice, whereas the hypothesis for an anti-choice survey would assume that abortion is wrong.

If the purpose of the survey were to support a particular hypothesis, the researchers would formulate their questions along these lines, while being aware of the language used in their questions and how this language might influence the answers. For example, in the pro-choice survey, researchers might use the word "termination" rather than the politically charged and stigmatized term "abortion" to soften the questions. Anti-choice survey questions might use the term "with child" rather than "pregnancy," or they might refer to women as "expectant mothers" to conjure images of mothers nurturing their babies. It might not surprise us that the outcomes of such surveys could differ greatly. When we hear the statistical results from each survey, however, we are not given these details about how the evidence might have been gathered. We are simply asked to put our faith in the numbers. Whether conducted by a feminist researcher or not, it is always imperative to check the methods used in a study before we accept the results offered to us.

I am not suggesting that all statistics are unreliable or inherently biased, nor am I suggesting that quantitative methods be abandoned completely because researchers have produced flawed or biased surveys. I am suggesting that we need to question the methods used to collect the information that we receive rather than automatically accept the results.

PRO-CHOICE SURVEY	ANTI-CHOICE SURVEY
1. Age	1. Age
2. Sex	2. Sex
3. Religion	3. Religion
4. Education	4. Education
5. Cultural background	5. Cultural Background
6. Do you believe in equal pay for women?	6. Do believe God has a purpose for your life?
7. Do you believe in shared responsibility for the home between women and men?	7. Do you think a woman's role is to be a mother?
8. Do you know someone who has had pregnancy complications?	8. How important (on a scale of 1 to 5) are children in your life?
9. Should women have control over their reproductive health?	9. Should women always make room in their lives for children?
10. Do you know someone who has terminated a pregnancy?	10. Do you believe life begins with conception?
11. If you found yourself pregnant and you were economically unable to raise a child at this time, would you consider terminating the pregnancy?	11. Does every life have intrinsic value?
12. If you found yourself pregnant and you were not currently in a relationship, would you consider terminating the pregnancy?	12. Have you heard about a woman who had an abortion and later regretted her decision?
13. If you found yourself pregnant and you felt that a child at this time would interfere with your education or career goals, would you consider terminating the pregnancy?	13. Do you believe that women use abortion as a method of birth control?
14. Do you think that reproductive health should continue to be publicly funded under the current health care system?	14. Do you think that your tax dollars should fund abortions?

Quantitative data and statistics are only as good as the methods used, as this example shows. Clearly each of these surveys is biased. The questions asked lead or prompt the person being surveyed to respond with particular types of answers and attempt to influence those answers. Look at question 14, for example, in each survey. Similar questions are asked, but each is skewed to a particular outcome that is already loaded with assumptions. In the pro-choice survey, the assumptions are (1) reproductive health is already publicly funded; (2) reproductive health includes abortion; and (3) health care should be publicly funded because it already is. In the other survey, the assumptions are (1) I should have control over how my government uses my money; (2) abortion should not be funded with my money; and (3) abortion is wrong.

Feminist researchers who use quantitative methodologies argue that scientific methods must be honed to make them more objective by removing androcentrism and homogenization. This can be accomplished by including women in scientific methods as researchers and subjects of study. Their purpose is to reveal women as conscious subjects of knowledge. This means that their study designs must recognize women as thinking and knowing people, as actors in their own lives rather than simply hostages to interlocking systems of oppression such as patriarchy, (neo)colonialism, racism, sexism, heterosexism, ableism, and classism. Accordingly, feminist researchers who use quantitative methodologies assert that if you want to better appreciate the complexities and diversity of women's lives, you need to ask women. The best people to help us understand marginality are those who are marginalized.

Feminist research exposes oppressions of all kinds and supports the struggles to overcome them. At the core of feminist research are links between theories and practice, between feminisms and activism, and between knowledge and women's lives. But just how feminist researchers get to the evidence—the *methods* used or the techniques for gathering information—is still mired in debate. Many feminist researchers have wondered whether quantitative, statistical evidence, the evidence of social scientific inquiry, can really provide all the answers to all of the questions they wanted to ask. Quantitative methods founded on the biases of positivism continue to reinforce hierarchies between the researcher and participant, where the researcher remains the knower and the participants are objectified. Feminist scholars continue to search for new methods and techniques for gathering different types of evidence that reflect women's experiences, and those of marginalized communities, more appropriately.

Feminist Research as Quality Research—Why Qualitative Research?

Much feminist inquiry leans towards the collection of qualitative data. Qualitative data is descriptive, representative, and situated (hooks 1984; Collins 1991; Harding 1993; Kirby, Greaves, and Reid 2006). Qualitative data is about people, their perspectives, their feelings, and their experiences. It is inherently subjective. In chapter 3 subjective knowledge was defined as knowledge informed by the person who is speaking or observing. In contrast, objective knowledge is considered unbiased, substantiated information and viewed as factual. Because it is subjective, qualitative research is often considered "too touchy-feely" to be taken seriously by researchers who take a positivist stance. However, qualitative evidence is also specifically grounded in the social, cultural, historic, and political contexts of people's lives. It is not simply abstract; it is knowledge that is representative of lived experiences.

Qualitative methods offer valuable techniques for approaching information that is not easily accessed because of its personal nature. Sexual practices, violence, rape, and incest as well as health, work, family, and politics are all experienced personally. Capturing knowledge about the intimate details of people's lives demands a different approach to collecting this information. Feminist researchers often choose qualitative methods because they offer the possibility for accessing such subjective knowledge.

Qualitative methods also allow for flexibility and fluidity in the research process. This means that changes to the research agenda can be made at many stages in the research to allow for new questions and greater input from participants in shaping the research outcomes (Denzin and Lincoln 2003; Kindon, Pain, and Kesby 2007; Denzin, Lincoln, and Smith 2008; Meezan and Martin 2009). It may sound strange that research questions are changeable or that the participants can influence the research. But just imagine conducting primary research in an unfamiliar place, where people's experiences are not similar to yours, where your gender, race, class, sexuality, ability, nationality, and citizenship status are all different from those you want to know about. Would you necessarily have all the right questions from the start? As feminist qualitative researchers, we question our positions, our assumptions, and our biases. Those we want to know about are the best people to ask our questions and, in many cases, they help us formulate our questions.

You might be wondering what kind of feminist research could be enhanced by qualitative methods. Feminists have sought answers to questions like:

- How do gendered expectations and the division between public and private spaces impact women's lives?
- How do women cope with the multiple responsibilities of home, children, paid employment, and caring for sick or ailing parents?
- Are stay-at-home dads good for kids?
- How does staying home to care for children affect men?
- How does violence affect women's lives?
- How does being violent affect men?
- Why do women stay in abusive relationships?
- Do women have choices when it comes to reproductive health?
- How do women make decisions about how many children they bear?
- How does sexuality affect women's lives?
- What does it mean to be gay, lesbian, or bisexual?
- How do racialized people understand and experience racism?
- What empowers people to challenge oppressions?
- How do people resist exploitation?
- How do media images affect girls' and women's understandings of their bodies?

- How do men experience violence in the media?
- Is there a crisis of masculinity?
- How does racism intersect with masculinity?
- What dreams do women have?
- And so many more …

Qualitative methods enhance the research process by allowing feminist researchers to ask questions that place women's and men's lives and the lives of those in their communities at the centre of social inquiry. We might find, however, that our questions are not the right questions. What we thought was happening or what we thought our subjects' lives were like might be wrong. If we are committed to valuing situated knowledge, then we might sometimes need to modify or throw away our original questions because they don't work. Changing the research questions does not mean abandoning the research; it may even mean our research will be better. When feminists do qualitative research, they develop flexibility and practise reflexivity in the various stages of the research process—questioning, talking, listening, observing, documenting, analyzing, and reporting.

Qualitative feminist researchers recognize that there are relationships between researchers and their participants. They acknowledge that there may be power imbalances in these relationships, differences of race, class, sexuality, nationality, religion, education, and in their positions within the research (Fonow and Cook 1991; Denzin and Lincoln 2003; Kindon, Pain, and Kesby 2007; Denzin, Lincoln, and Smith 2008; Meezan and Martin 2009). They accept that differences and maybe even similarities may exist in experiences and perspectives. The recognition of personal biases is not considered an impediment to feminist qualitative research. Many feminists would argue that this is what makes their research not only different but better. Because feminists locate themselves in the research process, critically reflecting on and engaging with their biases, their research can offer both context and authenticity for multiple voices (both the researcher's and the participants'). Accordingly, feminist researchers recognize marginality as a place of authority and women as the knowers of their own lives. They are committed to making space for women's and marginalized people's situated knowledge. This can make a difference in women's lives. It is empowering for women and marginalized people to speak and to tell their stories.

Feminist qualitative researchers recognize the power of voice. They engage in qualitative methods that rely on voices to give meaning to their research questions. They also recognize that voices are vulnerable to appropriation and misuse. Feminist researchers constantly have to question their positions in the research vis-à-vis those about whom they want to know more. They need to acknowledge that their positions of power and privilege—education, class, race, sexuality, ability, and nationality, among other things—influence not only the questions they ask but also the answers they seek (Harding 1987, 1988, 2006). Accordingly a feminist ethics—the feminist principles that guide us—must be instilled in the research process to ensure that voices remain authentic to those speaking rather than being appropriated by the researcher to speak for others.

The plurality of voices cannot easily be reduced to statistical accounts. Statistics are likely to obscure important nuances in collected data. Many feminists argue that statistics don't easily account for many of the *how, why,* and *what* questions that we ask. For these reasons, feminists welcome qualitative methods. Some of the qualitative methods used by feminist researchers include the following: observation, interviews, storytelling, case studies, ethnography, oral history, and narratives. These methods are not necessarily always feminist, however. For the research to meet the rigours of feminist ethics, careful attention must be given to *how* the research is conducted *as* feminist, and the feminist purpose of the research must be made clear. This means that feminist theory influences how we collect, study, analyze, and write about our research.

Experience, Talking, Listening, and Knowing

The qualitative methods or techniques used to uncover everyday experiences involve both talking and listening. These activities can take place in groups or in one-on-one encounters. Let's begin by examining focus groups.

Focus groups are interviews in which multiple participants are tasked with providing information to the researcher in a group setting. These group sessions are called focus groups because the discussion has a focus on a specific issue. The researcher facilitates the discussion to obtain the information she is looking for. Focus groups are commonly organized according to similarities among the participants. Similarities are determined in initial screenings of participants, and could be based on sex, age, race, culture, income level, marital status, sexuality, or beliefs about or experience of the discussion topic. The purpose of grouping participants for the researcher is to create an affinity, a sense of comfort among the participants, which will facilitate the discussion. The researcher will likely record (audio and/or video) the group to allow for further analyses of what is and is not said, how it is said, what language is used, and the context in which it is said (whether it was a response to another participant or to the researcher).

Unlike focus groups, interviews may take place in a one-on-one environment. Again the researcher acts as the facilitator of the discussion by posing questions. As in the case of focus groups, individual interviews may be recorded to allow for more accurate data collection and to facilitate future analysis. The

Thinking Through Positionality in the Research Process—In the U.S.–Mexico Borderlands

I spent three months in the U.S.–Mexico borderland area of Ambos Nogales, the two separate towns of Nogales divided by national borders. My research led me to travel between the uncomfortable divisions between the United States and Mexico, English and Spanish, North and South, "developed" and "developing," theory and lived experience, and whiteness and "Otherness." As a white, middle-class, educated woman, I understood that I was located in between what bell hooks (1984) refers to as the margin and the centre. While I could experience gendered oppression and therefore locate myself on the margin, my many privileges worked against such a location since I was neither poor nor "of colour." As a researcher who wanted to know about the experiences of women living in Ambos Nogales, I had to wrestle with my inclusions as well as my exclusions. Think about this for a moment. While I am included as white, middle-class, and educated in some contexts, I am excluded as a woman in others. In the borderlands, my identity as a woman could include me. However, as white, middle-class, and educated, I was also privileged and thereby excluded. I could always go home. I would one day leave, and I was not of the borderlands. This predicament of simultaneous inclusion and exclusion forced me to consciously examine my positionality in relation to the contexts and lives of the participants I wanted to know about. I applied a feminist ethics and critical self-reflection to make sure that I was not appropriating the stories of those who trusted me to ensure their voices were heard (Bromley 2002).

questions posed for qualitative research are often open-ended. Unlike a written quantitative survey where the expected answer is "yes," "no," or answered on a scale of one to five, open-ended questions allow infinite and detailed responses. The purpose of an open-ended question is to elicit people's experiences of complex issues in their lives, as they understand them. While qualitative interviews offer a wealth of knowledge, they also allow flexibility in the process since the interviewer can ask additional questions to clarify the ideas or experiences that have been presented by the participant. As you can imagine, asking additional questions demands careful listening and interaction on the part of the researcher, requiring empathic engagement with participants who are offering their lived experience as evidence. It is imperative to create a safe interviewing environment, especially when the topic of the interview is a sensitive one, as is frequently the case in feminist research. Researchers must build a trusting relationship with participants. Safety and trust make it possible for the participant to tell their stories without fear or coercion.

Ensuring a safe and trusting environment for participants is supported through the informed consent process. Informed consent means that participants are knowledgeable about the research project; the risks, if any, in participating; and how the information that they give will be used. Once they are told of these particular points, participants are asked to sign their informed consent, documenting their understanding and their permission. The safety of participants is an ethical concern. Universities and research institutions always require approval by an ethics committee prior to conducting *any* human research projects, qualitative or quantitative, to ensure all safeguards are met.

In contrast to structured interviews, where the researcher asks questions, storytelling is unstructured and uninterrupted by the researcher. Listening is the key skill that the researcher brings to the process and the listening is facilitated by the skill of the storyteller. Storytelling has a history as old as humanity itself. It has been used as a way of conveying knowledge from one generation to the next in many different cultures. It is a way of recording history orally. The telling and retelling of the same story presents a continuity of knowledge about the past and maintains an understanding of the past in the present. By committing stories to memory and (re)telling these memories, local, family, and cultural histories are preserved. The stories told are representative of events and experiences as well as morals and beliefs, rather than exactly documenting events or experiences. Researchers use this method to collect knowledge about the past, knowledge that would be lost if not for the telling of stories. It is not the method of collecting stories that makes this research feminist, however. It is the theory used to frame the research—how and why we collect, study, analyze, and write about it—that makes it feminist.

As with storytelling, in the case study method, the researcher has little or no influence over the experiences or events that they are studying. Case studies are used to examine social experiences and events that occur in real-life contexts. Case studies are ideal for studying complex social issues. They commonly present an in-depth analysis of a single event, experience, practice, social condition, artifact, text, or location. Often, case studies involve an examination of these issues over a period of time. This allows the researcher to explore both the changes and continuities that emerge. Consequently, case studies may be descriptive, explanatory, or exploratory. They may also be comparative in nature. Again, it is not the case study method that makes it feminist. What makes the research feminist is (1) the feminist criteria used to select the case(s); (2) the feminist "how" and "why" questions explored through the case study; (3) the framing of the data provided by the case study within a feminist theoretical perspective for analysis; (4) the recognition and incorporation of subjectivity; and (5) critical self-reflexivity.

Our Own Research and the Research of Others: Primary and Secondary Sources

So far we have talked about doing *primary* research. This research requires us to go out and find people to study. This may not be the kind of research that you need to do at the moment. Let's think for a moment about writing a research paper for your course in women's and gender studies or political science or history or sociology. What are the kinds of things that you are curious about? Perhaps you are interested in body image, women's work, transgender issues, reproductive health, and a million other intriguing topics. This is *brainstorming*—a good place to begin building your research paper. Maybe you don't know anything about these topics. This is a common problem when we begin our investigation. However, a quick Google search could give us some basic insights on our topic. Of course, this will have to be followed up with some good old-fashioned library research. Nonetheless, the Internet is still a good place to begin this information-gathering process.

The information or data that we gather in the research process is often divided into two categories: primary sources and secondary sources. *Primary sources* are things that are directly linked to the subject of study. These might include personal accounts of events, narratives of personal experiences, raw survey data, letters, diaries, historical records, legal documents, artwork, and photographs, among others. To be a primary source, the data, document, or information is in its original form and has not yet been analyzed or interpreted by a researcher. A *secondary source* is material that is not in its original form. It has already been analyzed and interpreted for us. Secondary sources might include reports, articles, books, magazines, newspapers, and novels.

Feminist researchers use both primary and secondary sources. We use established research, secondary sources, to extend our knowledge about what has already been done, to find out what other people think about a topic, and to decide whether we buy their arguments. This review of existing literature is what leads researchers to formulate new questions, apply new theories to existing materials, expose the missing links in the research, challenge assumptions in research, and uncover biases. It may also lead some researchers to conduct their own investigations using primary sources.

The processes that researchers use are the same ones that you follow when you are doing research for a class paper. Your curiosity makes you an ideal researcher. Developing your skills and paying careful attention to the complexities of your topic will make you an even better feminist researcher.

Conclusion

In this chapter, we explored scientific methods of positivism and empiricism. We delved into the importance of both quantitative and qualitative methods, as well as revealing some of their shortcomings. For feminist researchers, there is no one tried and true *feminist* method. The method chosen depends on multiple aspects of the research including the research question itself. What makes research feminist is the theory and analysis that is applied to the data collected. In the next chapter, we will make the connections between feminist theorizing and women's movement across the waves.

Questions for Study

1. What are scientific methods? What are the foundations of scientific methods? Feminist empiricists argue that scientific methods can be objective. How do feminist empiricists make their research more objective? How do feminist empiricists attempt to control for, and eliminate, bias?

2. Define and provide examples of positivism and empiricism. Are these feminist issues? Why or why not?

3. What is situated knowledge? Why is situated knowledge important for some feminist researchers? What methods or tools might feminist researchers use to find out about the situated knowledge of research participants? How do feminist scholars design their research to account for and control biases in their data? What kinds of questions might feminists ask that would demand the inclusion of situated knowledge in their research?

4. What makes feminist scholars rely on quantitative methods and data for their research? What makes other feminist scholars rely on qualitative methods and data for their research? Is there any time when combining these methods would be beneficial for feminist researchers? Give examples of when feminists might use each of these methods and when a combination of these methods would be useful.

5. What are the strengths and weaknesses of quantitative methods? Why are statistics sometimes problematic? Give an example.

6. Why are qualitative methods especially well-suited for some feminist research and information gathering? Provide three reasons why they are well-suited and an example for each reason.

7. Why do some feminists contend that bias is not an impediment to their research? When and why is bias sometimes okay in the research process?

8. Why is voice such a central concept in qualitative feminist research? What power does voice have? Give an example.

9. There are four ways to conduct qualitative research: focus groups, structured interviews, unstructured interviews, and narrative. Provide the purpose, value, and technique of each.

10. What are the differences between primary and secondary sources? Why do feminist researchers use both?

Activities and Questions for Discussion

1. Qualitative and quantitative methods differ. However, both can be essential to feminist research. Create a research question for a possible feminist study that would rely on both qualitative and quantitative methods. How would your research question be answered if only quantitative methods were used to collect data? What would be missing from the research? How would your research question be answered if only qualitative methods were used to collect data? What would be missing from the research? How would missing data (based on the method of collection used) affect your research results?

2. Create three interesting feminist research questions that would best be answered by using qualitative research methods. Be careful not to repeat those listed in the chapter.

3. Find out more about your school: How accessible is it to people with disabilities? Is there an equity office? How does your university address discrimination? Is there a safe space program on campus? Are students and faculty aware of its existence? Is there a sexual assault support centre on campus? Is a sexual assault support centre needed on campus? Is there a LGBTQ centre? Are there consequences for those who use the LGBTQ centre? Is there day care on campus? Is there a need for on-campus day care? Who would use it? Does your university have a policy in place to recruit students and faculty from marginalized groups? How effective is this policy? What methods would you use to find answers to each of these questions?

4. "I'm a feminist"—Try claiming the feminist identity by publicly stating to friends and family members: "I'm a feminist" or "I'm taking a women's/gender studies course." What did people say? How did they react? What body language did you notice? Write a short response/reflection paper noting the ensuing reactions or discussions. What theories and assumptions were at play in the responses you received? Were people's responses rational, gendered, or scientific? What theories and assumptions influenced your responses? How was the data collection process flawed?

5. For one week, do a "page capture" for each day of all images found on the Google news home page at http://news.google.com/. Keep a separate file for each day so that you can do a comparison of the images displayed at the end of the week. The purpose is to get a sense of the gendered imagery-at-a-glance. Note under which heading—top stories, world, sports, technology, business, entertainment, and science—the pictures are displayed. At the end of the week, revisit the data that you have collected. What do these collages of images says about women, men, and power? What do they say about how we know and who can know? Is your method of collecting this data scientific? Why or why not? Does it matter?

I know there is strength in the differences between us.
I know there is comfort where we overlap.
—ANI DIFRANCO, "OVERLAP"

CHAPTER EIGHT

IT'S NOT DEAD?

CONNECTING THE DOTS ACROSS THE WAVES OF FEMINISMS

The link between feminist theory and women's movement is not always immediately visible. Nonetheless, doing feminist theory means you have to be grounded in lived experiences. It is this connection to women's lives that gives meaning to feminist theory. Feminist activists have long been struggling to increase the value of women's experiences in order to achieve women's equality and their inclusion at all levels. However, it is through the process of theorizing these activist practices and the lives of women that activism becomes more effective. This means that theory and practice must become praxis. *Praxis* is the bringing together of theory and practice in a synergistic process. Accordingly, each component—theory and practice—combines and interacts to become greater than it could ever be individually. Feminist praxis is a necessary component of the movement to end the oppression, exploitation, and exclusion of women and marginalized people.

In North America, women's movement has been conventionally divided into three distinct eras, which are often referred to as waves. The first wave of women's movement spans the period from the early nineteenth century to 1930, the second wave is the era from the 1960s through to the 1980s, and the third wave is used to describe women's movement from the 1990s onward. The struggles of each movement, however, are not as compartmentalized as these divisions suggest. Nor is the wave metaphor as simplistic as we have been led to believe. In this chapter we will explore the metaphor of waves in describing women's movement. We will examine the principles of the first, second, and third waves of women's movement, their theoretical connections, and their

Illustration 8.1: So, is this theory or practice?

critics. An emphasis will be given to some of the cool and new aspects of third wave feminism—its virtual focus, and its emphasis on DIY (do-it-yourself)—as well as the ongoing and unfinished feminist business of second wave.

Ripples in the Waves

If we think of waves, we might imagine the calm and peaceful lapping of water on a beautiful beach. Or perhaps we envision the undulating rhythm of waves on a quiet lake, stirred by a slight breeze. We might even conjure up images of surfing, riding the waves, followed by the almost inevitable wipeouts and failures. These, however, are not the images that waves of women's movement are meant to summon. Women's movement is and has been much more turbulent and certainly not as mundane. The images of spills and thrills certainly come to mind, and even some setbacks, where there are lost opportunities and even a receding of the waves, like at a low tide. Women's movement, therefore, is much more akin to tsunami-force waves crashing and transforming how we think about the world in which we live. It is unlikely that the turbulence of women's struggles was the motivation for naming women's movement in waves. Nonetheless, women's movement, both then and now, takes place in a tumultuous context. Efforts to bring about social change have been met with significant barriers across the years, and yet women's movement has been successful to varying degrees since it emerged. The wave metaphor can help us understand how feminists in different historical contexts, with distinct political challenges, applying diverse theories, continued to push for social change directed at improving the lives of women, men, and communities. The wave metaphor offers us a sense of feminist continuity.

What is most important to remember in imagining the waves of women's movement is that feminist struggles for change did not end with one historical era and start over again with the next. Each era of struggle is connected to the past and the struggles of past eras are interwoven with ongoing and future feminist struggles. Like waves in the water, women's movement has its high points and its low points, peaks and valleys that are tied together. It is the highs, the breaking point of the wave, where we tend to see women's movement happening. However, this does not mean that women's movement disappears just because there seems to be a dip in the water. It is at these points where women's movement is less visible but certainly not dead. This lull is a point at which women's movement is doing the hard work of rethinking achievements, adjusting to the changes that have been brought about, evaluating the meanings of these changes for women's lives, and examining the failures and errors in their judgments. In times of seeming quietude, women's movement is doing the hard work of strategizing, theorizing, building for future changes, and ensuring that there is no backsliding in the achievements already realized. It is this ongoing connection among and between the waves that needs to be emphasized if we are to recognize the unfinished business of women's movement and continue its momentum.

Another misconception fostered by the wave metaphor is the presumption that women's movement is linear. Linearity leads us to believe that waves are moving in a unified motion and in a singular direction. Again, the simplicity of the wave metaphor misrepresents the complexity and the heterogeneity of women's movement. While the goals of women's movement are to achieve social justice and to eliminate sexism, oppression, and exploitation, there is no single way to achieve these goals. Various groups, defining themselves both as feminist and not, are working towards this end. However, the means used, the strategies taken, the ordering of priorities, the theories applied, and the actions taken vary from group to group and differ across time and space. The divisions among groups tend to undermine much of the continuity that exists across the waves. In particular, the generational divide between second and third wavers pits "older" feminists against "younger" ones.

The wave metaphor tends to emphasize mainstream feminist movement while eclipsing groups of feminists that don't fit comfortably into the imagined mainstream of white, middle-class, heterosexual, able-bodied women's movement. This is especially problematic since women of colour, lesbians, differently abled women, and working-class women, as well as men of all sorts, have contributed significantly to advancing equity and social justice, and to ending sexism, oppression, and exploitation in each of the waves of women's movement. Despite these problems with the wave metaphor, it is still useful to describe the existence of mass feminist movements that ebb and flow, struggle and survive, succeed and sometimes fail in their goals.

Linking Theory and Practice in First and Second Waves

One critically important part of the first wave of women's movement was concerned with issues of political citizenship for women. It is often referred to as the suffrage moment and its activists as suffragists. While enfranchisement points to an important goal of the movement—the vote—political citizenship meant much more for women. First wavers insisted that women should be entitled to own property, to be granted inheritances, to access higher education, and to enter the professions (Bacchi 1983; Backhouse and Flaherty 1992; Deetley and Pettegrew 1997; Moynagh and Forestell 2012). And, in Canada, women campaigned to be declared "persons" under the law (Sharpe and McMahon 2007). Women wanted all the political and citizenship rights already held by the men. All of these rights would ensure that a (white) woman was able to have a certain degree of independence and some economic security, should she find herself without a man. Women's demands, however, did not rest on the assertion of women's equality but on the declaration of women's superiority to men.

Some women's rights activists, often called maternal feminists, believed that because women were mothers, they were inherently moral, emotional, and kind, and were therefore in fact superior to men. They argued that women would bring their attributes of caring, nurturing, and virtue to the political sphere. Reflecting this view, Canadian activist Dr. Augusta Stowe-Gullen famously argued, "When women have a voice in national and international affairs, wars will cease forever" (Bannerman 1977, 284). Women activists would carry brooms to suffrage demonstrations to show that women would clean up the mess of men's politics. Accordingly, they would cure the political and social ills of the day. Some feminists, for example, asserted that alcohol and tobacco use bred poverty and that these vices needed to be contained. Yet some women supported prohibition but not the vote. First wavers' ideological perspectives were influenced by their white middle- and upper-class status, and Christian charity was a motivating factor for much of their social activism. However, most working-class feminists supported temperance because it was an issue that often directly affected their families and communities. Charity in this era was inspired by God's unlimited love and translated into good works and kindnesses towards the less fortunate. The objects of charity were the underclass, the poor, the infirm, widows, and orphans. For privileged women, charity work was a duty. Often they were motivated by pity for the underclass, especially for poor women who suffered from men's debauchery (drinking,

The Persons Case

While clearly Canadian women were indeed people, the British North American Act, a founding document of the Canadian constitution, failed to name women specifically in its definition of persons. This omission was used to deny women legal status and to prevent their election to Parliament or appointment to the Senate. Canada's Famous Five, the key first wavers who fought for women's equality and personhood, were Emily Murphy, Nellie McClung, Louise McKinney, Irene Parlby, and Henrietta Edwards. After losing their fight for women's personhood in the Supreme Court of Canada in 1928, they took the Persons Case to the highest court, the Privy Council in London, England. Luckily for Canadian women, the Famous Five won their appeal and women were declared persons under the law in 1929. While contemporary feminists sometimes devalue this group because of their ties to the widely popular eugenics movement, their achievements for women's political citizenship in Canada cannot be dismissed.*

* Eugenics is the scientific notion that through the "breeding" of genetically superior people a superior human race could evolve. It was a social movement that held wide support during this era. It is with our current knowledge of the horrific genocides perpetrated in Nazi Germany and elsewhere that we are able to re-evaluate and condemn the movement as racist, homophobic, and ableist.

gambling, smoking, and running around on their wives). "Votes for women and chastity for men" was a powerful slogan coined by British suffragette Christabel Pankhurst, which reminds us that it was not just working-class men who engaged in such behaviours but men of all classes. The call for chastity for men was one response to stemming the spread of venereal diseases (VD) at the time (Pankhurst 1913).

The most prominent women in the movement were largely white women of affluence. Often they were the daughters or wives of men of means and therefore had greater opportunities for leisure. And what better activity to fill their leisure hours than the good works of charity and women's suffrage? On the one hand, these women believed they could provide wisdom to and instill their moral values in less fortunate women through their acts of charity. On the other hand, these women's leisure time was often predicated on the hiring and exploitation of poor and working-class women whom they required to care for their children, cook family meals, and clean their homes. My favourite image of this contradiction of empowerment for some at the expense of others comes from the 1964 Walt Disney movie *Mary Poppins*. In the "Sister Suffragette" scene, the divide between the wealthy Mrs. Banks and her household staff is clear. Mrs. Banks offers a song to her staff, heralding the great achievements that the vote for women will bring. She asserts that the vote will ensure the rights of women for generations to come, confirm solidarity among *all* women, expose the problems of male leadership, and mark women's liberation from the shackles of the past. It is particularly interesting that Mrs. Banks' nanny repeatedly attempts to interrupt this sisterhood of solidarity to tell her that the children are missing, and she is leaving her job. However, Mrs. Banks refuses to listen. This clip captures the contradictions of the first wave—the paternalistic approach, the class exclusions, and the imposition of Christian moral standards. It confirms the image of first wavers as privileged white women.

First wave feminists were not simply focused on charity work or achieving the vote for women, however. In the United States, for example, Elizabeth Cady Stanton (1815–1902) was involved in multiple issues. Her involvement in women's movement in the first wave shows the complexity and diversity of women's concerns. Stanton was committed to women's employment, income rights, equitable divorce laws, spousal support, custody rights, family economic security, temperance, and birth control. One of the key organizers of the 1848 Seneca Falls Convention, Stanton was the principal author of the Declaration of Rights and Sentiments signed by sixty-eight women and thirty-two men attending the convention (Stanton 1848). Another feminist first waver, Victoria Woodhull (1838–1927), offers us some insight into the vision for the future of women's movement. She campaigned for sexual freedom, social welfare programs, graduated income tax, and an eight-hour workday, issues that are commonly attributed to second wave feminists (Woodhull 1873).

Nineteenth-century women were also deeply engaged with the problems of the slave trade, slavery, and racial inequality, both in Europe and North America, and these concerns shaped first wave feminism. Many first wavers were women and men of colour who drew their understandings of women's rights from their participation in the anti-slavery and abolitionist movements. They made significant contributions to the first wave of women's movement. For example, Sojourner Truth (1797–1883) was an anti-slavery advocate, a women's rights supporter, and an evangelical preacher. Born a slave in upstate New York, she escaped slavery and was later legally freed. Sojourner Truth became an eminent orator on abolition and suffrage. In her now famous speech, "Ain't I a Woman?" to the Women's Rights Convention in 1851, she challenged the notion of women's inferiority to men and black women's inferiority to white women. She asserted that all women deserved equal rights (Truth 1851, 1867; Washington 2009).

Frederick Douglass (1818–1895) was another important advocate for women's rights who attended the Seneca Falls Convention. Douglass was born a slave in Maryland and escaped slavery in 1838. It was only after the publication of his *Narrative of the Life of Frederick Douglass: An American Slave*, wherein he disclosed his fugitive slave identity, that Douglass was freed. Fearing his arrest, friends purchased Douglass' freedom in 1845 (Douglass 1845). Douglass was an outspoken abolitionist. In his essay "Why I Became a 'Women's Rights Man,'" published in 1882, Douglass exposes the injustices of governments that wage wars, institute injustices, condone oppression, and uphold slavery (Douglass 1882). He wrote that democracy excluded women who have demonstrated both the intelligence and strength of character to right the wrongs of the past. Finally, Douglass asserts that there is no valid argument for men's participation in government that cannot be applied to women as well.

During the aftermath of slavery in the United States, abolitionists struggled to ensure that former enslaved people would be granted the vote. These debates split the women's suffrage movement. Some suffragists protested that black men, former slaves, should not vote before that right was granted to white women, while other suffragists insisted that freedom required the vote for all men. Many abolitionists, including Douglass and Truth, continued to struggle for universal suffrage, but these debates revealed that some women's suffrage activists did not support voting rights for former slaves, men or women (Lind 1994; Terborg-Penn 1998).

Mary Ann Shadd Cary (1823–1893) was another first waver who worked tirelessly on multiple activist fronts, including civil rights, temperance, abolition, racial integration, equal education, and suffrage. Born in the United States, Shadd Cary fled to southern Ontario following the passage of the Fugitive Slave Act (1850), which threatened to enslave former slaves and freeborn blacks, who at the time carried simple documentation—affidavit, letter, or bill of sale—as to their status, which could be easily destroyed and ignored by slave catchers. If captured, there was no recourse as fugitives were not entitled to a hearing or trial under the act (Fugitive Slave Act 1850). In Canada, Shadd Cary worked as a teacher to promote the racial integration of schools and community life. She founded *The Provincial Freeman*, a weekly newspaper, becoming the first woman editor in North America. She used her editorial power to challenge racial discrimination, to promote racial integration, and to encourage blacks to emigrate to Canada. Mary Ann Shadd Cary was a member of the National Women's Suffrage Association and founded the Coloured Women's Progressive Franchise Association in 1880, a forerunner to the National Association of Coloured Women (NACW) (Yee 1997).

There are many more racialized women and men, both known and unknown, who advanced women's rights and were active in their communities during the first wave of women's movement. Few are given prominence in high school textbooks, and fewer still are visible when we imagine those who rode that first wave. Nonetheless, they were there and they made important contributions that brought about significant social change.

Opposition to the first wave of women's movement came from men and women alike. Those who feared change and those who benefited from the status quo were the most vocal. Women in politics, naysayers argued, was un-ladylike;

public affairs were too complicated for women to understand; it would sully women's delicate nature to expose them to evil; and, of course, women needed to be protected. You get the idea: women were likely to get the vapours if they cast their vote. The strength of women's organizing posed a clear threat to patriarchal hierarchies and power structures, such as those within political institutions, and especially within the family.

There were critics among first wavers, who rightly pointed to the essentialism that underpinned the movement. Elizabeth Cady Stanton, for example, argued that the notion of women's essence was romantic nonsense. She urged her sisters in the struggle to reject such gibberish and fight for suffrage as an issue of social justice (Mann 2012). With the benefit of hindsight, second wavers were also critical of the essentialism that pervaded first wave activism (Fuss 1989). What might seem obvious to us today was certainly less clear to the women in the trenches then. The essentialist idea that women were morally superior to men because of their mothering capacity and that they could create a different political environment guided by caring and nurturance was clearly idealistic. The focus on attaining political citizenship by dismantling discriminatory laws and exclusionary social practices was guided by classical liberalism. It was governed by a sense of individualism that conceptualizes good women as a counterbalance to bad men. At the same time, it was asserted that universality among women existed, thereby precluding any recognition of the diversity of women's experiences. While many first wave activists were engaged on multiple fronts for social change (abolition, temperance, and education) and the eradication of women's subordination and oppression, the priority of getting the vote privileged the white affluent women in the movement.

With the successes of prohibition, greater access to higher education, and enfranchisement for women, the 1930s in North America was a period of adjustment. It was a time for rethinking women's achievements, adjusting to new roles, and evaluating the meanings of these changes for women's lives. The Great Depression and the Second World War complicated the adjustment period and women were called to action on a different front. They were on the move out of their homes and into factories in support of the war effort. Who had time to think about examining the successes and failures of the first wave or strategizing, theorizing, and building for future change? The lull in women's movement, however, did not mean that women were satisfied. Debate concerning the differences between women and men continued. And questions as to whether women should be treated equally because they are essentially the same or equitably because they are essentially different from men ensued (Lorber 2010). This battle began to play out in the post-war years, when women were sent back home. Banned from the better-paying skilled factory jobs they occupied during the war years, women's brief independence was shut down when the men came home and wanted their jobs back. Women were forced to resume their traditional roles of mother and wife, and not surprisingly, a baby boom erupted and women were once again up to their elbows in diapers and baby food.

The Myth of Domestic Bliss in the Second Wave

Domestic bliss was far from the reality of most women's lives. The second wave of women's movement was bubbling to the surface. Women began to wonder about the future and what was possible. This time around, women's movement would confront the patriarchal structures that were restricting them—gender roles at home, the sexual division of labour in the workplace, and control over their bodies everywhere. As we saw in chapter 2, in North America civil rights activists were challenging segregation, gay and lesbian activists were demanding their rights, Indian activists were demanding self-determination and peace activists were demanding an end to war, and independence movements gained strength in former European colonies, creating new nations based on new political realities. Women's liberation, as it was called at the time, meant ending women's oppression on every level.

At its heart, the feminist second wave was an equal rights movement. Building on the accomplishments of their foremothers, many second wavers embraced liberalism as their guide for social change. These activists did not want to topple capitalism or derail democracy. Their goal was to reform social and political institutions to ensure women's equality. What these second wavers realized was that the legal rights achieved in the first wave failed to redress the everyday inequalities in women's lives. Eradicating women's oppression demanded the rethinking of women's lived experiences and the formulation of strategies for change. Second wavers came to understand that women's oppression was embedded in cultural practices that reinforced relationships of power, privilege, and patriarchy. They campaigned for the reform of judicial processes and legislation to address women's inequality. Second wave feminists asserted that women experienced inequality through their bodies. Accordingly, these feminists saw women's bodies as both targets of oppression and sites of struggles for change. Many second wavers were also active in trade unions and other labour organizations and focused on issues of workplace equity.

Second wavers focused on challenging traditional gender roles and redressing the unequal power structures in the home. Gendered conventions of femininity dictated that women were exclusively responsible for their homes and children. How could women hold down jobs, let alone achieve careers, if they had their hands full in the domestic sphere? How would women gain economic independence if they didn't have birth control and care for their children while they worked? What about equal pay? If women were doing the same work as men, shouldn't they get paid the same wage? How could women enjoy their (hetero) sexuality if the cost of doing so was pregnancy, job interruptions, and potential job loss? Shouldn't women, who were, after all, reproducing the labour force, be compensated with maternity leave and the ability to return to their jobs afterwards? And what about violence against women? How could women live and work in a world where they were not safe, even in their own homes? All of these questions percolated as second wave feminists set out to change their worlds.

Margaret Sanger, an activist in both the first and second waves and founder of the American Birth Control League (1921), fought for women to gain control over their fertility, to be able to decide if, when, and how many children they would bear. Her commitment to birth control came from her experiences as a nurse and from observing the effects of eighteen pregnancies on her mother's health and well-being. In the late 1930s science had already developed the ability to prevent women's ovulation and therefore conception. The problem, however, was that pharmaceutical companies, universities, and governments were uninterested in funding further research to make birth control affordable and available to women. Margaret Sanger remained at the forefront of the feminists' struggle for birth control. For second wavers, including Sanger, contraceptives would not only give women control over their fertility but also liberate women sexually and economically. If reliable contraceptives were available, sex would no longer necessarily result in pregnancy. The ability to control their reproduction also gave women greater freedom to participate in the labour force. Yet the first birth control "pill," specifically prescribed for contraceptive use rather than to regulate the menstrual cycle, was not available in the United States until 1960 (Goldin and Katz 2002). While it was illegal in Canada to sell, advertise, and distribute contraceptives, some clinics, influenced by the eugenics movement, began dispensing contraception in the 1920s to Aboriginal and poor women. In the 1930s Canadian courts determined that distribution was acceptable if it were in the interests of the public good, which corresponded with political discourse of the time aimed at controlling the fertility of marginalized groups. By 1961, prescriptions for the pill were available to married women. There remained much debate as to whether single women would or should have access to contraception and it was not until 1969 that contraception was decriminalized along with abortion (Sethna 2005).

Still, to create equality in the home, women's unpaid work—cooking, cleaning, laundry, and caring for children—had to be recognized as valuable and necessary. Feminists argued that responsibility for the home and children needed to be shared equally by women and men. If women were to engage in paid employment *and* have total responsibility for the home, equality could not prevail.

The double work day of paid work outside the home and unpaid work within it allowed employers to create a sexual division of labour. According to this division, women were relegated to low-wage unskilled work, whereas men were funnelled into higher-paid skilled jobs. In this way, women continued to be seen as mothers and wives first, and as valued employees second. The segregation of women into *pink-collar* jobs, work designated as female, reinforced patriarchal power structures in which men were on top and women were on the bottom. Moreover, this set-up allowed for power to be played out in particular ways that oppressed women further. Sexual harassment became commonplace and women had to either put up and shut up—or quit. What was a girl to do? Feminists worked to institute affirmative action policies as well as sexual harassment and antidiscrimination laws. Second wavers agitated, marched, and lobbied to reform the system.

Sexual harassment on the job was not the only place where women experienced violence. When women got home from work, they were not necessarily safe. Home could also be another battleground. Women were even more vulnerable to violence at home because it was presumed to be a safe place. Security concerns over "stranger danger" were heard everywhere, yet the very real danger of violence against women in their homes was less often verbalized. In complex ways, women's inequality made violence (physical, psychological, and structural) permissible. Second wavers recognized the importance of creating safe spaces. To address this need, they fought to create shelters for women and children fleeing violence.

Second wave liberal feminist efforts were successful in many ways in reforming the system. Yet critical reflection was called for. Feminist theorists and activists engaged in important dialogues that challenged liberal efforts to work within the system. More radical feminist groups were not prepared to settle for equality eventually trickling down to women through reforms. They wanted a revolution that would transform the broken white supremacist, heterosexist, patriarchal, capitalist system. They demanded genuine democracy and an equal voice for all women. Dialogues, heated discussions, and outright battles ensued among women and within women's movement. The priorities, strategies, and theories guiding the movement were hotly debated. Racialized women, lesbians, and working-class women who had played a less visible, but no less important, role in the movement were no longer willing to remain silent. Some women were active in political parties of the left, aimed at creating socialism either through political reform or protest. Their priorities, strategies, and theoretical positions challenged the monolithic, liberal, white, middle-class, and heterosexual image of the second wave.

One example of this challenge was and continues to be the "sex wars." In chapter 2, we examined the debates around lesbian community, political choices, and lifestyle. Feminists also argued over the impact of pornography on women's lives. Many feminists contended that pornography exploited women and subjected them to violence. Others said that pornography normalized heterosexism, misogyny, and violence against women, extending its negative effects beyond pornography to women everywhere. Other women argued that it was a mistake to empower police and courts to legislate sexual representations, and they pointed to conservative religious groups that also lobbied for the control of pornography, often supporting feminist initiatives. These women wanted to create feminist sexual images that would counter the misogynist mainstream porn.

Heated debate over the effects of prostitution also ensued. On one side, feminists argued that prostitution was not a real choice but was imposed by patriarchal structures that viewed women as consumable and disposable. Accordingly, prostitution victimized the most marginal of women who had little choice and few alternatives. On the other side, feminists argued that prostitution was work like any other work. Prostitution did not define a woman but was an occupation that she performed. Feminists working in the sex trade created prostitute rights organizations. Both of these arguments were made with the goal of ending oppression and exploitation.

While feminists of all stripes struggled with all these tensions and more, within women's movement, they also recognized these struggles as critical to the processes of forwarding women's equality, attaining social justice, and ending oppression. Such dialogues ultimately create better ways of doing feminism over time. After all, as we have seen, critical self-reflection and unpacking privilege are healthy and necessary, if difficult, activities for feminists.

Some of the key strategies and tactics used by second wavers to get their messages across included letter writing, lobbying, mass demonstrations, sit-ins, protests, and marches. Most importantly, they used their bodies to send their messages and the sheer number of bodies participating demonstrated their strength. These were the images that were covered by the front pages of newspapers and headed the evening news. Giving a platform to "celebrity feminists" such as Betty Friedan and Gloria Steinem, the media simultaneously raised the visibility of the second wave while confining it to a few spokespeople whose rise and then fall signalled the rise and fall of the movement itself. The media also played an important role in pitting women against each other and discrediting the movement. On the one hand, the media exposed the lack of uniformity in the movement, while on the other, they challenged its diversity of goals and ridiculed it (McRobbie 2004; Bromley and Ahmad 2006).

Overall, media attention gave more weight to those who opposed women's movement, particularly those who benefited from sexism, racism, and the economic marginalization of women. The media pounced on the growing discontent among marginalized women who opposed the priorities of Western white middle-class heterosexual able-bodied women in the movement. Journalists and reporters repeatedly and forcefully pronounced feminism dead, seemingly bringing women's movement to a halt in public awareness. Tensions and backlash, however, could not stem the growth of feminist consciousness, and this is the complicated environment in which a third wave of feminism emerged.

Everybody Wants To Be a Feminist: Postfeminism and Power Feminism

From the political right to the political left, everybody wants to claim feminism and they can. This assertion, however, raises some interesting questions. For example: Who owns feminism? What defines feminism? And how do feminists claim feminism as their own? Because of its complexities, we must practise critical thinking about who is claiming feminism, from what theoretical perspectives, using what historical knowledge, and for what political purposes. Let's take a look at the implications of some of these questions in the new so-called postfeminist era.

By the late 1990s, the postfeminist era had been born (Staggenborg and Taylor 2005). According to popular media representations, women are assumed to be equal and social institutions are no longer steeped in sexism, racism, ableism, homophobia, or any other systemic inequities. It might seem like feminism is now passé. So 1970s! But why are so many conservative women claiming to be feminists today? Why, for example, would conservative American women like Sarah Palin, Katie Roiphe, Christina Hoff Sommers, and Camille Paglia all claim the position of "power feminism?" These women contend that the second wave's focus on women as "victims" is no longer relevant to the new status and power that women hold in North America (Sorisio 1997; Showden 2009). Some women have certainly benefited from the struggles and gains made by the second wave and clearly this positions *some* women as economically secure and politically powerful. Does benefiting from the accomplishments of feminism make one a feminist? No. Feminism is still about social change to end oppression and actions still speak louder than words. Where are the actions of conservative feminists? Is their rhetoric enough?

If such "feminists" were engaging in innovative political tactics such as that suggested by Janet Howell, a Democratic senator from Virginia, perhaps we might rethink the concept of "power feminism" wielded by those listed above. As Virginia prepared to pass a bill requiring pregnant women to undergo a transvaginal ultrasound prior to having an abortion, Senator Howell added an amendment to require men to undergo a rectal exam and a cardiac stress test prior to getting a prescription like Viagra for erectile dysfunction. Howell argued that a transvaginal ultrasound is unnecessary, invasive, and costly for women having abortions and therefore should be balanced with equally unnecessary, invasive, and costly procedures for men. The irony of Howell's suggestion that "We need some gender equity here" was not lost on feminists. While the amendment narrowly failed in a 21 to 19 vote, 13 men sided with the 6 women supporting Howell's effort for gender parity (IBT 2012).

Some feminists challenge the idea that postfeminism is somehow antifeminist. In British and Australian contexts, the "post" in postfeminism can be understood as a link to rather than a break from feminism. It is intended to provide a space for engaging with and talking about the changing meanings and thinking around feminisms. Comparing the "post" in postfeminism with other critical "posts" such as postmodernism and postcolonialism, these proponents call for an ongoing critical engagement with patriarchy and modernist thinking (Brooks 1997; Braithwaite 2002).

I am reluctant to agree with this representation of postfeminism, in part because it is too easily conflated with popular media representations of feminisms as no longer necessary. The pronouncement of a postfeminist era erases the history of struggle and hard-won feminist gains far too easily. The "post" in the context of feminism is not the same "post" as in postmodern or postcolonial feminist theories. The "post" in these compound words signifies a struggle against the term with which it is paired. So postmodernism posits a challenge to modernism and postcolonialism contests colonialism. Following this line of argument, postfeminism would place feminism in question. I am not suggesting that feminism is perfect, far from it. This is why feminists continue to debate, theorize, and engage in activism. To abandon feminism for its *nouveau* sister postfeminism, however, seems politically shortsighted and may undermine the power of feminist movement. Even if we accept postfeminists' claim to engage with feminisms, patriarchy, and modernism, it seems to me that it muddies the waters to simply define postfeminism as feminist in the current anti-feminist era.

Indeed, the declaration of a postfeminist era erases the history of struggle and hard-won feminist gains far too easily. The shift in thinking marked by postfeminism marks an era when feminisms are presumed to be no longer necessary or useful. This leads to the possibility that we might take the accomplishments of the past for granted. Feminist achievements then become vulnerable to backlash and erosion (Kinahan 2004). In this way, postfeminism simultaneously discounts, appropriates, revises, depoliticizes, and trivializes feminisms. It puts forth the notion that feminism *was* needed at one time and that women benefited; however, feminism is no longer necessary because "we are all equal now."

Many women and men, including the ones reading this book, have certainly benefited from the gains made by first and second wavers. Many things have certainly changed, but not everyone has benefited equally from these changes. What is important to note in this so-called postfeminist environment is the shift from collective feminist politics to individual "feminist" politics— an "I-feminism." If we can claim feminism only when it suits us or is useful to us, then we may lose some of the politics that feminisms offer. This will make the struggle against oppressions, for equality, and for social justice even more difficult (see, for example, Kinser 2004).

Seeing Continuity and Change in Third Wave

Third wave feminism emerges from within this postfeminism era as a space for resistance, subversion, and social change. Like the waves before it, third wave feminism is complicated and contentious. It has no singular definition to explain it, no one theory that informs it, no one space to practice it, and no one method that defines its actions. But this is okay with some third wavers who argue that defining feminism sets unduly tight parameters and runs the risk of leaving some things out. This is also where third wavers meet with much criticism. Their critics suggest that because feminism in the third wave can mean almost anything, it loses its political power. Not so, say third wavers. They argue that the vast diversity and many meanings of feminism among third wave feminists is a strength (Sorisio 1997; Sanders 2004; Renegar and Sowards 2009; Showden 2009).

Third wave is characterized as eclectic, humorous, non-mainstream, accessible, empowering, dynamic, hip and happening, and undefinable. This indefiniteness is critical to third wavers who resist any labels slapped on them, challenging boundaries and defying categories. They push the boundaries of the second wave axiom "the personal is political," and at times they invert it to recognize that the "political is personal," too. Third wavers make feminism their own while at the same time using theories, methods, and activist strategies developed by second wave feminists. They inherit a powerful legacy from the second wave: policies and legislation that recognize minority rights, sexual and reproductive freedoms, employment equity, and affirmative action. Third wave feminists take the critiques of beauty culture, sexual abuse, racism, and unequal power structures made by the second wavers, and complicate them further. Third wavers wrestle with the pleasures and dangers of complicity with the power structures that inform our constructions of race, ethnicity, beauty, the body, (dis)ability, sexuality, sexual practices, pornography, sex work, and consumerism, among others. They recognize this struggle as individual but also acknowledge that their individual struggles with these things are not in isolation from others struggling with similar issues.

The groundwork that makes it possible for third wavers to take on complex and even contradictory positions was laid by previous waves of feminism. In this sense, the third wave is a continuation of women's movement. Several foundational texts —such as *Third Wave Agenda* (1997), *Colonize This!* (2002), *Catching a Wave* (2003), *Third Wave Feminism* (2004), and the Canadian anthology *Turbo Chicks* (2001)—offer a look at the complexities and contradictions of the third wave, its breaks from as well as its links with previous waves. These texts demonstrate the capacity of third wave feminism to adapt to historical changes and confront current concerns at home and abroad. On a theoretical

level, many third wavers draw on four feminist theoretical perspectives: intersectionality, postmodernism, postcolonialism, and queer theory.

Intersectionality (see chapter 4) enables third wavers to embrace empowering, complex, and multiple identities, while recognizing that such positions
may be contradictory. Building on the foundational work of black and anti-
racist feminist theorists (see chapter 5) allows for more complex thinking about
important issues that remain unsolved from the second wave. For example, third
wavers recognize that issues of reproductive rights and employment equity are
complicated by the intersections of gender, race, class, sexuality, ability, and age.
Third wavers criticize second wavers for privileging gender at the expense of
understanding the implications of interlocking systems of oppressions. They de-
centre essentialisms in favour of embodied, experiential, and situated knowledge
to reveal the intersections of oppressions (Fixmer and Wood 2005).

They also recognize the intersections between the global and the local. By
engaging in transnational environmental, anti-capitalist, anti-colonial, and anti-
military activism across borders (physical and virtual), third wavers contribute
to this work. They complicate these struggles by insisting on an intersectional
feminist analysis to expose the everyday lived experiences of environmental
degradation, capitalism, and neocolonialism. In so doing, third wavers are contributing to theory-making and real social change.

Postmodern feminist theory (see chapter 6) enables third wavers to critically question universalizing processes. This encourages third wavers to resist
homogenizing categories and identities. Categories create boundaries and
reinforce systems of inclusion and exclusion. Accordingly, third wavers challenge fixed identities (woman, black, lesbian, working class, dis/able-bodied,
etc.) as *inauthentic* since everybody experiences their identity differently. So
being a woman or man is different for different people. Challenging binaries
of, for example, disabled/abled bodies, third wavers bring into question the
temporality of *able-bodiedness*, the fact that anyone can "become" disabled and
thereby revealing the instability of fixed identities. This work disrupts the notion of the "self" in opposition to the "other," distinctions between "us" and
"them," and the able-bodied in comparison to the differently abled (Wendell
1989; Fawcett 2000; Garland-Thomson 2002). Because women with disabilities
have been less visible in society and in feminist analyses, third wave feminists
offer an intersectional analysis that challenges the exclusion of women with
disabilities as knowing subjects.

By placing *authenticity* in question, third wavers deny the legitimacy of
claims about who is, and what it means to be, a "real" woman or man (and
whether the distinctions are even useful), or that there is a "real" way of being
black, lesbian, gay, queer, racialized, classed, or feminist. Contesting authenticity means questioning who can speak and who can know (Chakraborty 2004).
Many third wavers are willing to take this individualistic position even if it risks

the possibility for collective struggle, and the strength in numbers that feminist movement offers.

For many third wavers, feminist postcolonial theory (see chapter 6) gets us through the problems created by intersectionality, such as divisive identity politics based on race, sexuality, gender, ability, and age, and postmodernism's reliance on deconstruction and relativism as the key to liberation (Springer 2004; Showden 2009). Living in a postcolonial era, a time after colonialism but while neocolonialism continues to oppress people, third wavers recognize that postfeminism does not mean that feminism is dead, but rather that new feminisms are emerging to challenge oppressions, injustices, and inequities (Zobl 2009).

Some of the most important work in the third wave of feminism uses feminist queer theory. These third wavers embrace a sex-positive position in a challenge to the perceived moralizing stance of second wavers. This has allowed third wavers to explore and question their sexuality. They have come to recognize that expressing and performing gender and sexuality can be both empowering and subversive of expected norms (Friedman and Valenti 2008; Glick 2009; Snyder-Hall 2010). Third wavers acknowledge that identities of gender, sexuality, and biological sex are fluid rather than fixed. They embrace transgender politics by rejecting the notion of binary male/female distinctions (Stryker 2004; Green 2006). They reject terms such as "biological" male/female or "genetic" male/female, insisting on the term cisgender instead. Yet this personal gender identity, cisgender, has the potential to challenge narrowly constructed and imposed gender norms, thereby creating more fluid gender identities. In refusing to give biology all the credit for determining sex, queer theorists, such as Riki Wilchins (2004) point out that chicks can have dicks and boys can have vaginas. Gender identity does not determine sexual identity. Moreover, third wavers' sex-positive attitude has also advanced discussions around sex work (Showden 2012). Many third wavers challenge some second wavers' assumptions that all sex workers are victims and that sex work is never a choice (see, for example, Glick 2000). While they acknowledge the dangers of sex work and the possibilities of violence and exploitation, third wavers insist that sex work can also be empowering and a career choice (Showden 2012). Third wavers see difference as empowering, and empowerment is defined as people feeling good about themselves and the choices they make.

Linking Third Wave Methods as Theory

Criticism of third wave abounds. The most common critiques are that third wave's focus on individualism jeopardizes feminist solidarity and women's movement; that it lacks political commitment; that it fails to acknowledge feminist history; that theory building is absent; and finally that it is invisible to most, thereby lending credence to claims that feminism is dead. Third wavers are ready to take on these criticisms and more, especially the claim that they are invisible. To challenge this criticism, let's explore some of the strategies and tactics used by third wavers to get their feminist messages across.

Personal narratives, "performance politics," cultural productions, and cybertechnologies characterize third wave strategies (Mitchell 2001; Woodhull 2004; Whitfield 2006; Staggenborg and Taylor 2005; Snyder 2008; Zobl 2009). Some of the old ways of doing feminisms fail to meet the needs of third wavers' sense of independence, individuality, creativity, or the desire to subvert and resist systems of oppression. Third wave tactics need to be recognized as valid and valuable strategies. Second waver tactics such as letter writing, lobbying, mass demonstrations, sit-ins, protests, and marches need to be adapted and updated to meet the challenges of a third wave feminist movement.

Third wavers are active and activist. They are engaging with feminist issues as they define them. They are challenging oppression and creating social change. It may not be as visible to the mainstream as second wave mass demonstrations or marches but the third wave is alive. Mainstream media and second wavers who criticize third wavers for a lack of engagement need to acknowledge new looks and different spaces for feminist activism. The preferred strategies for third wavers' DIY (Do-It-Yourself) productions include writing personal narratives, performance, zines and ezines, culture jamming, blogging, social networking, squats, and flash mobs. And many new spaces for feminist activism are virtual. DIY strategies are empowering because they place individuals at the centre of production, as authorities in their own lives.

While these strategies are not entirely new, they certainly are different, and the venues where they appear as well as the technologies they employ are new. This means that the way in which feminist messages are transmitted and received is new. Although third wave feminism is seldom on the front pages of the news unless there's an opportunity to make a full frontal anti-feminist attack, it remains active and present if you know where to look and really want to see it. Of critical importance to third wave feminisms is the use of individual bodies to resist and subvert normative expectations of sex, gender, and sexuality. User-friendly web-based technologies and widespread access to the Internet are instrumental for the mass dissemination of third wave thought. These changes have reinvigorated the women's and feminist movement, as we will see in chapter 10.

Conclusion

In this chapter, we explored the first, second, and third waves of women's and feminist movement. The purpose was to acknowledge the important issues confronting each wave and the historical contexts in which their struggles occurred.

There are both continuities and divergences between the waves, lessons to be learned, new goals to be set, and even missed opportunities. Acknowledging women's movement, its achievements and its failings, encourages us to continue in feminist struggles, in all their complexities and manifestations, new and old. It is vital to recognize women's movement, which has produced tremendous social change and bettered the lives of women and marginalized people. In the next chapter, we will examine men and masculinities to demonstrate how feminisms benefit men, too.

Questions for Study

1. What is praxis? Why is praxis important for feminists?
2. Why is the metaphor of "waves" representative of women's movement? What are the limitations of the waves metaphor? Can you think of a better metaphor?
3. What were the issues that first wave feminists tackled? Who supported these initiatives and why? Who opposed first wave feminism and why? What did critics say about the first wave? How successful were first wavers in achieving social change? Give specific examples.
4. Why was there a seeming lull in women's movement in the 1930s and 1940s? What happened to all the feminists? What did feminists do during these years?
5. What were the key issues in the second wave of women's movement? Who supported these second wave goals? Who opposed second wave feminism, and why? What did critics say about the second wave? How successful were second wavers in achieving social change? Give specific examples.
6. What is the sexual division of labour? How was the sexual division of labour created? What are the negative consequences of a sexual division of labour? Does a sexual division of labour still exist? Give specific examples.
7. What are the major changes and characteristics that differentiate the second wave from the first wave of women's movement?
8. What are the characteristics of the third wave of women's movement? What issues raised by second wavers continue to be important for third wavers? What's new about the third wave?
9. What is postfeminism? Is postfeminism the same thing as third wave feminism? Why or why not?
10. How does intergenerational bickering, between "old" and "young" feminists, influence women's movement? How can this negativity be overcome?
11. What is the role of the media, both promoting and challenging feminisms, in the second and third waves of women's movement? Why is there such a big effort to claim "feminism is dead"?

Activities and Questions for Discussion

1. Use the Internet to create biographies for one feminist from each of the three waves. How do these feminists define key issues of concern, strategies, and tactics for their activism? How are they connected and how do they differ?

2. Attend a social justice, feminist, or women-centred activist event. Was this event feminist? How was it feminist or not? In what wave does this group fit? Write a brief reflection about the event.

3. Abortion is a touchy subject for everyone. Whether you have an opinion or are ambivalent, when it comes to personal experience, abortion decisions are difficult even for the most committed of pro-choice activists. And what about anti-choice activists, do they sometimes have abortions, too? When Democratic Representative Jackie Speier told Congress the story of her abortion during the Planned Parenthood funding debate in February 2011, it was considered both shocking and brave (Grimm 2011). Maya Dusenbery, a contributor to *Feministing* (www.feministing.com), says that she continues speaking publicly about her abortion as "a consciously political act. In the hopes that someday other women will be able to do so and it won't be political." What do you think about abortion? Search the Internet to find stories about women's experiences of abortion. Consider carefully the sources of these stories. What are the key factors in making the decision to abort or not? Do the decisions appear to be well thought through? How do the politics surrounding abortion influence women's decisions? Is the personal also political? Do you have a story to tell? Check out some of these sites:
    - Feminist Women's Health Center, http://www.fwhc.org/abortion/index.htm
    - I had an Abortion, http://www.experienceproject.com/
    - http://www.prochoiceactionnetwork-canada.org/articles/anti-tales.shtml
    - http://feministing.com/
    - http://www.rhrealitycheck.org/blog/2010/11/04/i-abortion-tweeting

If the world were a logical place, men would ride sidesaddle.
—RITA MAE BROWN, 1983

CHAPTER NINE

DON'T MEN COUNT, TOO?
FEMINISMS AND MASCULINITIES

As a feminist, I know it is important to think about men and masculinities. However, to write about them with a sense of authority is a challenge. This is not because I have no understanding of the issues, debates, and research—I do. Men are important in my life; they are my family members, my friends, and my colleagues. Still I struggle. Perhaps this struggle is related to my identity as a "woman" and all that it encompasses. With all the achievements of feminist movement and my own commitment as a feminist, I have still been socialized to defer to men as knowers, to continue reinforcing gendered hierarchies, and to reify patriarchy and male privilege. I am a product of my socialization—my sex, class, race, sexuality, and ability—even as I resist it. As a woman, I have been socialized to see myself as less—less powerful, less knowledgeable, less capable, and less deserving. I know that this is not true but I still question my legitimacy. This is not *because* of the particular men in my life but because of the dominant position that men as a group hold within patriarchal society. It is because of the power and privilege that masculinity promises and femininity dismisses. However, male power and privilege are not assured for *all* men, either. Race, class, sexuality, ability, and social constructions of masculinities also influence men's positions of power and privilege. Feminist thinking offers ways to challenge patriarchy and redress unequal gendered power relations.

If feminism is about social justice—the elimination of all forms of oppressions and exploitations and the realization of gender equality—then women cannot be the sole focus of any feminist movement. Men's experiences of manhood and understandings of masculinity must also be examined. Feminist and pro-feminist men must be welcomed as valuable contributors to ending patriarchy, sexism, racism, classism, homophobia, ableism, ageism, and transphobia. They also participate in the struggles against capitalist exploitation, environmental degradation, and militarization. Men have long been supporters and participants in women's movement. In the 1960s, when the civil rights, women's liberation, gay and lesbian liberation, and peace and anti-war movements emerged, men were also actively engaged in social justice movements. In the 1970s many men began to (re)formulate their positions and question the complexities, contexts, and consequences of masculinity, patriarchy, and male privilege using feminist lenses. By the mid-1980s, research on masculinities had exploded in the areas of constructions of masculinities; the multiplicities of masculinities; gay masculinities; raced and ethnic masculinities; located masculinities; and men and feminisms. This critical thinking happened in academic spaces, in men's movements, and in the lives of individual men.

Over the past forty years, extensive research in the areas of men's and masculinities studies has made significant contributions to understanding what it means to be a man in North America and around the world (Connell 2002; Connell and Messerschmidt 2005; Hearn and Kimmel 2006). As we saw in chapter 3, science has had an overwhelming influence on how we know and what we think about the world. Science lends legitimacy to theories; however, as noted biologist Anne Fausto-Sterling (1981) reminds us, science does not equal fact. Science takes facts and adds ideology and politics to the mix to create a particular story.

In the study of human behaviour, science is often relied on to explain gendered behaviours as biologically determined. Science has naturalized masculinity and femininity as the behaviours of men and women. So when we hear on TV or read in a magazine that men are biologically "hard-wired" to cheat on their partners, do better at math, gawk at pretty women, or not ask for directions, we tend to believe it as scientifically true. We have all experienced at least one man exhibiting these behaviours. But does this mean that biology determines masculinity?

Is the possession of testosterone, XY chromosomes, and a penis enough to define a man? And what about female masculinities? In this chapter, we will explore some of the radical thinking about masculinities, men, and men's lives in patriarchal society. We will gain an understanding of how feminisms have created space for men (and women) to confront hegemonic masculinity, misogyny, and homophobia; to rethink gender inequalities and hierarchies in politics, at work, and in the home; to (re)examine the relationships between masculinities and sexuality; and to explore the complexities of racialized, classed, and gay masculinities.

What Do We Know about Masculinities?

Much of what we know about men and masculinities, we learn from popular culture—sports, video gaming, movies, television, music, and music videos.

These media tell us how boys and men should act, look, and think. Boys and young men are taught what it means to be a "real man" from watching and emulating other men, in their lives and in popular culture. Especially influential are male professional athletes, entrepreneurs, celebrities, politicians, soldiers, police*men*, and criminals. These models of masculinity provide boys and young men with a gauge against which to measure their own masculinities. While the women in men's lives—as mothers, sisters, wives, peers, colleagues, friends, and sexual partners—have an influence on how masculinities are constructed, performed, and embodied, masculinity theorists contend that other boys and men are important sources for the affirmation or denial of masculinity. Accordingly, boys and men of all ages look for confirmation of their masculinity from *homosocial* networks, male networks that exclude women (Meuser 2004; Holmgrena and Hearn 2009). In this sense, masculinity is socially constructed by and for men in patriarchal society.

Most people think they have a clear image of what masculinity is. But do they really? As we learned in chapter 1, the stereotypical image of masculinity is constructed as aggressive, physically strong, dominant, authoritative, independent, detached, rational, objective, reasonable, and sexually proficient. Boys and men learn to conform to these stereotypical ideals. These popular ideas about masculinity seem to be fixed and unchanging. They are constructed in opposition to femininity: to be masculine is *not* to be feminine. This is a somewhat unhelpful definition, and it's one that has, as we will see, facilitated backlash allegations of a masculinity crisis. Before we go into crisis mode, let's explore some of the dominant images of masculinity.

"MAN UP" AND OTHER CALLS TO MASCULINITY

The dominant form of masculinity has endured in Western culture through four classic images—the hero, the warrior, the sports star, and the entrepreneur. These images can be found everywhere, from fairy tales and popular culture to "scientific" accounts of reproduction.

The icon of hero, at its root, invokes an image of the victor. Heroes are honourable, trustworthy, and respected. Like Robin Hood, who stole from the rich to give to the poor, heroes are intelligent, easily outwitting their opponents; they are skilled with weapons and their bodies. They are virile, always rewarded, and they are revered by friends and foes alike. This image is decidedly gendered. The masculine hero requires a feminine counterpart. He must have someone to protect and to save, whereas the heroine, at least traditionally, has been protected and saved. For Robin Hood, his masculinity and heroism are dually affirmed in *saving* Maid Marian and *providing* for the poor. Consider the fairy tale of Cinderella and her life of toil at the hands of her wicked stepmother and stepsisters. It is the handsome prince in this story who saves Cinderella from her wretched servitude. Through the act of saving Cinderella, the prince's masculinity is confirmed, while the clichéd damsel-in-distress, Cinderella, is hyperfeminized as weak and dependent. Modern incarnations of the hero are found in Hollywood movie characters such as James Bond, Rocky, Batman, and Captain Jack Sparrow of the *Pirates of the Caribbean* movies. These films and their leading men provide norms, rules, and scripts for embodying and performing masculinity as well as femininity. By defining masculine as not feminine, the rules for women are also made clear.

Another iconic representation of masculinity is the warrior. The warrior has clear connections to the hero. He is the *protector* of women, children, and nations. The feminine, we are told, is ever in need of the warrior's *protection*. The classic binary of masculinity/femininity is reproduced in the protector/protected dichotomy. The warrior protector in this formula is strong, invulnerable, aggressive, powerful, threatening, and violent. His job is not only to protect and defend his territory but also to conquer foreign territories, defeat the enemy, and dominate others. The warrior icon has multiple purposes in affirming men's masterful roles in history. The warrior's story legitimizes the processes of conquest (of women, nations, and the environment); colonization (of nations, cultures, resources, and people); and globalization (of markets, technologies, and cultures). Control of, and domination over, are the central features of these histories. It is "real men" who make history happen. In these histories, women and marginalized people, the "feminine," remain largely invisible.

The sports hero is the third icon of masculinity. He is athletic, active, skilled, powerful, muscular, successful, handsome, and virile. As a professional athlete, he is rich and famous, casting him as every woman's ideal and the ultimate aspiration of every man. Boys are schooled in the culture of sports early on in life. They are taught to play hard, to be competitive, and to measure their success against the team captains, star players, and coaching cues. Starting in Little League, followed by high school and hopefully college or university, and ultimately finishing in the professional ranks, many boys view sports stardom as the pinnacle of masculinity. Boys and young men in North America grow up wanting to be like hockey star Sidney Crosby, basketball legend Michael Jordan, soccer great David Beckham, or superstar NFL wide receiver Jerry Rice. Even if most men never become professional hockey, basketball, soccer, or football players, they can assume some of the rewards that flow to these players by watching, celebrating, and debating about favourite teams and athletes. Vicariously, boys and men affirm their masculinity through these processes (Nikolas and Duncan 2006; Anderson 2009; Woodward 2011).

It is also important to note that some sport legends are known not only for their athletic abilities but also for their alleged bad behaviour. Some examples are NFL hall of famer Lawrence Taylor, who was charged with third-degree rape of a sixteen-year-old girl in 2010 (Zinner and Schweber 2010); NBA star Kobe

Bryant, who was accused of rape in 2003 (CNN 2003); and, boxing great Mike Tyson, who was convicted of rape in 1992, but only served three years of the six-year sentence (Shipp 1992). These athletes are both revered and denounced. They are admired as wealthy superstar athletes and they have sought protection in their superstar status and wealth when they faced allegations of violence against women. Although this is not the behaviour that most men would align with in confirming their masculinity, violence against women does seem to be a problem for many male athletes. A quick search online provides a multitude of sites documenting male college and high school athletes who have been alleged to have committed rape or who have been charged with and convicted of rape.

The entrepreneur is the final iconic representation of masculinity. He is successful, intelligent, hardworking, aggressive, and knowledgeable. He is the ultimate provider, since he provides jobs to workers and boosts local and national economies. He is also a highly competitive, smart, well-educated, tough-minded, strategic, risk-taking, and often a ruthless, cut-throat deal-maker. He wields power and accumulates wealth, which he readily displays through his designer suits, fast cars, ostentatious homes, and perhaps his "trophy wives." Luck and unearned privilege, he assumes, play no part in his achieving wealth and status; these are the natural rewards of his masculinity. He deserves his rewards and, therefore, he seizes them. Real estate mogul Donald Trump quickly comes to mind as the embodiment of this model of masculinity.

Remember that each of these representations—hero, warrior, sports star, and entrepreneur—is an iconic image. Their archetypal characteristics are seldom wholly achieved by any one man. Yet we can likely identify some of their characteristics in the men that we know and maybe even find these characteristics in ourselves. These models of masculinity construct ideals of masculinity that are reproduced in popular culture's fictive characters, celebrities, and in real life by boys and men.

Emily Martin's anthropological study of the biology of human reproduction, for example, found that scientific accounts are shaped by cultural codes of masculinity and femininity. She found that descriptions in scientific textbooks of biological processes were invested in stereotypical definitions of maleness and femaleness. These narratives defined sperm as valuable, strong, and aggressive, and eggs as disposable, passive, and vulnerable. Replicating the hero icon, in biology textbooks, the sperm is depicted as saving the "damsel-in-distress." According to these narratives, the egg simply waits for her hero the sperm to make her useful by fertilizing her; otherwise, her value is lost and she is expelled at the end of the monthly cycle. The personifying of the egg and sperm is also told in the myth of the warrior sperm that actively and aggressively swims in enemy territory to penetrate and capture the passive, lazy egg. While these stories should elicit some laughter, they are also telling of the cultural myths and scientific myths that reinforce dominant forms of masculinity and femininity (Martin 1991).

HEGEMONIC MASCULINITY

The dominant model of masculinity is widely referred to as hegemonic masculinity (Connell 1985). In North America, *hegemonic masculinity* is defined as white, middle-class, heterosexual, and able-bodied. It is not necessarily the most common form of masculinity found in the everyday lives of boys and men in North America and many men may not meet that ideal; however, hegemonic masculinity remains an idealized mythical status.

Hegemonic masculinity is not the only model of masculinity. A plurality of masculinities exist, rooted in different contexts, experiences, and social, political, cultural, and geographic locations. Yet hegemonic masculinity continues to shape gendered orders and hierarchies of masculinities. A *gendered order* is a system that establishes and attaches value to particular gendered patterns, such as masculinity, femininity, or androgyny (Connell 2002). Within this gendered order, hierarchies of masculinities are formed where certain masculinities are more socially valued and where they wield more power and authority than others. This order is embedded in historical institutions and social, cultural, political, and economic structures rather than in individual identities. Under the current gendered order, men, as a group, reap significant benefits in comparison to women as a group. However, the costs for some men are also quite high. *Hypermasculinity* is an exaggerated sense of hegemonic masculinity and the performance of aggression, virility, and courage. Indian psychologist Ashis Nandy (1983) coined this term in his analysis of Indian nationalist movements. He noted that Indian elites were mimicking and exaggerating the affectations of their male imperialist colonizers. In this sense, there is also a racial dimension to the term. In the contemporary context, hypermasculinity has been linked to higher injury levels in car accidents for young men than young women. This is verified by higher insurance rates for young men under the age of thirty. Hypermasculinity has also been linked to such phenomena as road rage and street racing. These situations are often a response to a presumed threat to a man's masculinity. Accordingly, some men feel compelled to respond to the threat by engaging in risky demonstrations of hypermasculinity. This behaviour is also present in other everyday situations—someone hitting on a guy or his date, put-downs on the job, racial slurs, and gay taunts. In such cases there is a clear jostling for position within hierarchies of masculinities by both the attacker and the target. The responses to such threats take various forms, depending on the context of the situation and those involved. These defensive performances suggest that masculinity is a vulnerable identity, one in constant need of affirmation. Commenting on this masculine conundrum and paraphrasing Shakespeare, feminist Germaine Greer noted: "The tragedy of machismo ... is that a man is never quite man enough" (cited in Cohen 2009, 306).

Illustration 9.1:
Hegemonic masculinity.

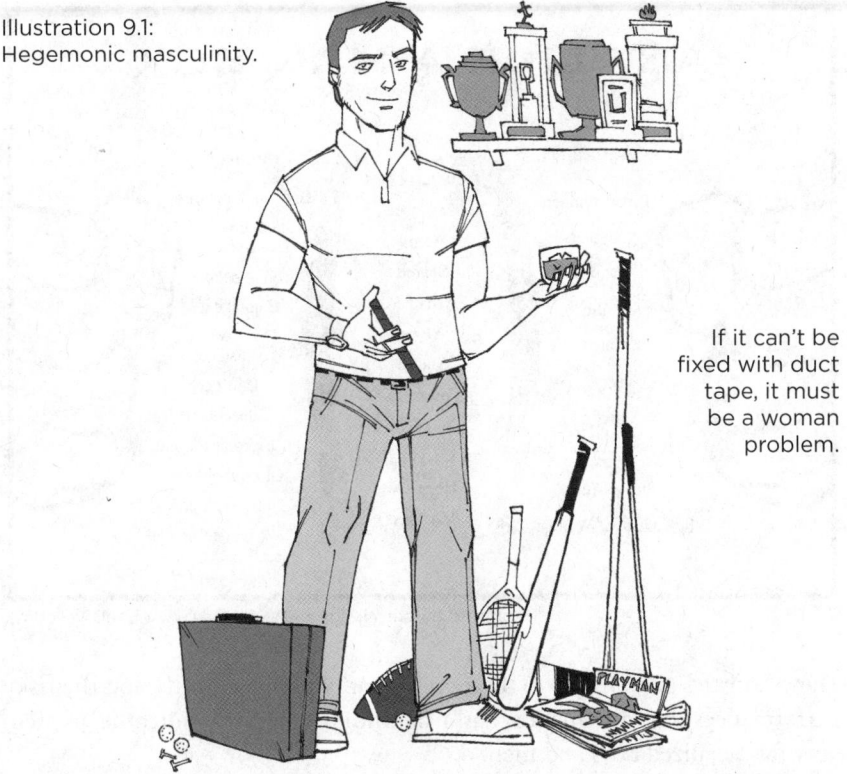

If it can't be fixed with duct tape, it must be a woman problem.

Hegemonic masculinity can also be linked to patterns of poor health and premature mortality among men. Internalized assumptions about toughness, independence, and invulnerability can lead to poor diet, drug and alcohol abuse, and not seeing a doctor on a regular basis. Hypermasculinity can also be linked to high levels of violence and victimization. While male violence against women is widely discussed, male-on-male violence, which accounts for the majority of reported incidences of violence, is less often talked about critically. Nor are the resulting high levels of imprisonment for men, particularly racialized men, discussed. In 2009, Correctional Services Canada reported that a disproportionate number of male prisoners are Aboriginal, compared to the national population. Aboriginal men account for 17.3 per cent of the prison population and only 2.7 per cent of the Canadian population (Correctional Services Canada 2010). In the United States, black and Latino men account for a larger portion of the prison population. According to a 2010 Pew Research Center report, while 1 in every 87 white males ages 18 to 64 is incarcerated, the number for similarly aged Hispanic males is 1 in 36, and for black men it is 1 in 12. The report further states that, among black men currently serving time, 37 per cent are high school dropouts who are between 20 and 34 years of age. This is three times the rate of white male prisoners in the same demographic.

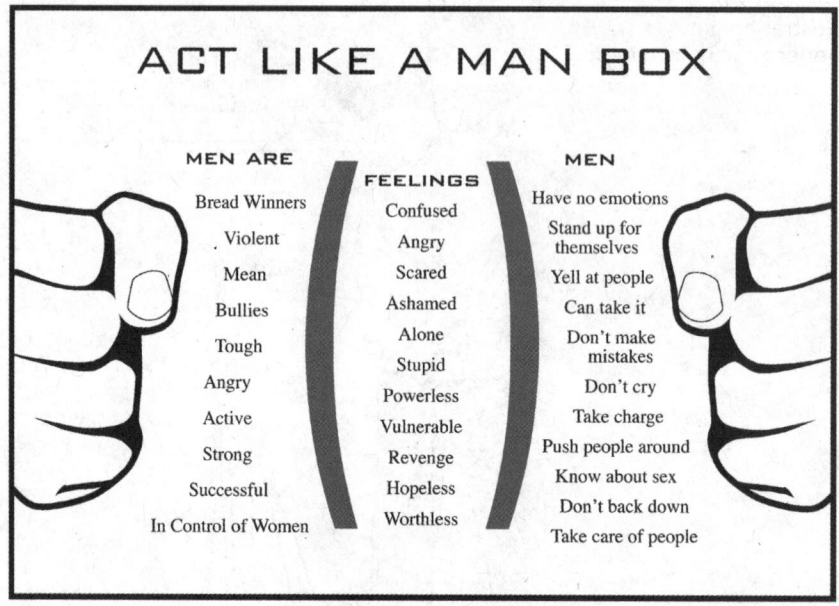

Reprinted by permission of Paul Kivel (www.paulkivel.com).

These statistics give weight to the notion that hypermasculinity, and the risky performances that it demands, has a significantly negative outcome, particularly for racialized boys and men.

CONSEQUENCES OF SEXISM AND GENDERED LANGUAGE

The power of hegemonic masculinity is widespread. Its influence, however, is seldom critically exposed. This results in invisibility. We hear it and see it every day, but we seldom call it out as sexism. Let's examine popular cultural vernaculars, which are decidedly gendered and freely peppered with sexism.

In sports, war, business, and popular culture, language is used to ensure that boys and men perform and embody the physicality of masculinity. For example, everyday comments on boys' and men's masculinity include some of the following: "Man up," which challenges boys and men to be tough and not to act like a "pussy"; "Suck it up," used to encourage boys and men to continue playing when they are hurt and be more like hockey players who are admired when they continue to play even after a concussion with potentially serious consequences; "Dude, you throw like a girl," which attempts to demoralize or stigmatize a player on a sports team or any other team; and "Grow a pair," which presumably refers to male genitalia and confirms that "real men" are biological and that biology dictates strength and toughness.

If we think about war and the language that is used to describe allies and enemies, there is certainly a hierarchy imposed. But is the language gendered?

Heading Off Road Rage

I recall a time I was driving with my dad. We were a bit lost and I made a quick change of lane and inadvertently cut off the driver behind me. Oooops!

The car instantly pulled around our car and came to a stop in front of us. A rather big, burly fellow jumped out and menacingly stomped towards us. I remember my dad saying, "This guy better not mess with us. I'll take care of him." Instantly, I was filled with fear. I was sure a fight was moments away and I knew that my dad was no match for this bruiser.

I begged him to let me "talk my way out of this." Reluctantly, and under the protest of male bravado, he did. I rolled down my window and immediately apologized for my error. I told the guy I was from out of town and I was lost. His posture immediately changed from ominous to gracious. He said, "Hey, we all make mistakes," and then courteously told us how to get to our destination. My dad and I laughed about the situation for the rest of the night. Each of us was thankful that "nothing" had happened.

Let's return to the iconic warrior image. The sex of the warrior is unquestionably male. Although today, women are active participants in the military, we are still more likely to think of soldiers as men. Take G.I. Joe for example. He is the doll that little boys play with, but he represents much more. He is also "the man" that boys want to be. He is a soldier, brave, patriotic, and righteous in his acts of aggression and violence. He is "locked 'n loaded" and ready to "pull the trigger." These are the underlying images that reinforce the belief that "might is right." Since biological females cannot "penetrate," the language of conquest and invasion are also gendered masculine terms.

The language of war is also heard from bars to boardrooms. The comedic saying "them's fightin' words" quickly comes to mind when a proverbial "pissing contest" among men occurs. The pissing contest is a male phenomenon, where, so I'm told, little boys challenge each other to see who can squirt the farthest. Clearly, the winner is indeed "the man." In such contests, the phallus is both implicitly and explicitly measured and laid bare in the process. The threat, or perceived threat, to masculinity, is socially and culturally constructed as a demand to duel.

My story about my dad and me in "Heading Off Road Rage" is a good example of a masculine call to "duel." While nothing violent happened in the end, there was an ever-present possibility of a challenge, or duel, of masculinities unfolding. According to the National Highway Traffic Safety Administration (NHTSA) in the United States, road rage is defined as "an assault with a motor vehicle or other dangerous weapon by the operator or passenger(s) of another motor vehicle or an assault precipitated by an incident that occurred on a roadway" (NHTSA 2000). Road rage and its prevention, however, can be understood in gendered terms. Currently, men are still more likely to react aggressively when driving than are women. So, in the situation with my dad, perhaps it helped that I was "just" a woman. Most of us have heard the sexist jokes about bad women drivers, or the offhanded comment that "it must be a woman" when someone (whose sex/gender is unknown) makes a driving error. Maybe when the "tough guy" saw that I was a woman and heard that I was lost, he realized that this was a chance to affirm his masculinity—to act like a hero and direct us to our destination—instead of defending it. Perhaps my taking the blame allowed him to see himself as superior and me as inferior and weak. Because my father did not intervene, he too might have been seen as weak and this may have "diminished" his masculinity in his eyes and in the eyes of the other driver. However, the retelling of the story that night allowed my dad and me to reconceptualize his masculinity as superior for acting rationally and intelligently and not like a hooligan. This story illustrates how masculine/feminine dichotomies are ever-present and helps us see how fluid and subject to change they are at any given moment.

Language and behaviour reflect dominant cultural patterns and can frame our experience. Let's return to businesses and the boardroom where battle metaphors persist. Organizational structures, hierarchies of dominance, and positions of power play key roles in the workplace. The purpose is to ensure that everything runs "like a well-oiled machine," where men are the presumed mechanics applying the oil to guarantee "military precision." The language of warfare is evident in a host of common business phrases: sales targets, marshalling resources, attacking the project, digging deep, in the trenches, minimize the collateral damage, strategizing, the war room, pick your battles, penetrate the market, and trade wars. And how many of us have felt "under the gun" to complete a project? Because war is still understood as a predominantly male space, when this language is applied to the workplace, it reinforces images of winning and losing, the inclusion of men and the exclusion of women.

Sports metaphors are equally common in business terms and expressions, for example, stepping up to the plate, Monday morning quarterbacking, levelling the playing field, time out, keeping a score card, blocking the play, tackling the issues, running interference, carrying the ball, the bases are loaded, and throwing a curve ball. These catchphrases can be found in presentations, meetings, motivational talks, management books, and business courses.

Men and masculinities are implicated in other common expressions as well. For example, *man*power, *man*ager, work*man*, *man*ning the phones, *man*-made, fresh*man*, and *brother*hood have their roots in maleness. At this point, you may be thinking, "Wow, I use some of these expressions and I am not just talking about men or trying to exclude women." The point here is *not* to adhere to a formula of "political correctness" but to recognize how language reflects dominant cultural patterns and frames our experiences. Let's consider replacing the word "man" in some of these expressions with the word "white," to see if notions of race influence how we understand the implications of language (Kleinman 2007). Instead of *man*power, how would *white* power sound? And, instead of *man*made, how would *white* made resonate? What about fresh*white* instead of fresh*man*? Let's try replacing work*man* with work*white*. How would we understand our movie and comic book heroes named Super*white*, Bat*white* or Spider*white*?

Although these terms sound ridiculous, we can see how terms and concepts are embedded in power structures, and, in these examples, racist power structures. The absurdity is in the *un*naturalness of the words, but this also exposes the unquestioned normalcy of sexism in the English language. Sexist words feel comfortable to us. Consequently, we can begin to identify the exclusionary processes that using male-based terms and masculine concepts have for women. We can also begin to recognize, consciously or not, how language masks masculine, white, heterosexual, classed, and able-bodied privilege.

Gender neutrality is not only assumed in language, it is presumed almost everywhere. Consequently, gendered expectations continue to influence how decisions are made in many situations. Recent research shows that gender is always present. In an American study of musical auditions, for example, it was found that female musicians fared better when the auditions were conducted without the evaluator seeing the candidates. This ensured that only the candidate's musicality would be judged, rather than allowing conscious or unconscious assumptions about visual characteristics to seep into the decision-making process. The research found that female musicians fared far better under conditions that eliminated the possibility for gender bias (Goldin and Rouse 2000).

THE BREADWINNER/HOMEMAKER DIVIDE

The iconic image of men as breadwinners who bring home the money to their homemaker partner has serious gender implications. First, it assumes that not only are men the ones who are responsible for making money but also that they are charged with ensuring the family's economic security. The second assumption is that their partnerships are heterosexual. This scenario quickly falls apart in the context of multiple and diverse family configurations—blended families, lesbian and gay families, single-parent families (by choice or not).

But what does the breadwinner image say about masculinity? It tells us that "real men" make money, they have important jobs, and they are good providers. This picture of masculinity stands in stark distinction to the reality

Illustration 9.2: Number two. Yes, definitely number two.

that most two-parent families face: the necessity of two-income earners and an economy that no longer supports the highly paid professional and unionized jobs of single-income earners. If men's capacity to provide is woven into their sense of masculinity, how do men experience their masculinity when they lose their jobs? This is a much more common experience than we would like to think in the current economic environment. Since men's masculine identity is intimately tied to their careers, many men experience not only economic crisis but also personal crisis when they are unemployed. Job loss commonly results in increased vulnerability. In contrast to their previous independence, the unemployed may become dependent on family, friends, or the government to provide for basic needs. Vulnerability and dependence are socially constructed as feminine characteristics; therefore, when men find themselves in such predicaments, their masculinity is threatened.

Few women, in contrast, interpret their femininity through their careers. Yes, women's careers can be an important component of their identity as individuals, but their jobs are not a measure of their femininity. Few women, therefore, would experience job loss as negating their femininity. Because the feminine is *not* socially constructed as provider, femininity is not threatened by unemployment, even though many women are the primary providers for their families. Femininity is affirmed elsewhere, particularly in the home and in relationships with family and friends where the characteristics of caring can be freely displayed.

INTERSECTIONALITY AND NON-HEGEMONIC MASCULINITIES—CLASS, RACE, AND SEXUALITY

It is overly simplistic to identify hegemonic masculinity as a single model to which all men subscribe. Masculinities are complex and in constant processes of change. It is inadequate, then, to assume that hegemonic masculinity imposes rigid gender hierarchies where women and other(ed) masculinities are subjects of domination and subordination. At the same time, it is impossible to specifically define non-hegemonic masculinities according to race, class, sexuality, or ability. To do so would create caricatures of masculinity and impose stereotypical understandings of what it means to be a black man, a Latino man, an Asian man, a working-class man, a gay man, a man with a disability, or indeed any man.

Drawing on feminist intersectional analysis (see chapter 4), the complexities of masculinities can be better understood. It is important, therefore, to recognize that masculinities, like femininities, are informed by the interrelationships of class, race, sexuality, age, and ability. The intersections of these identity markers shape the configurations, performances, and embodiments of masculinities. Moreover, the multiplicity of masculinities are performed and embodied differently in various local, regional, and global spaces. Ideas about masculinity, therefore, reflect specific social and cultural experiences, messages, and practices in complex ways.

Changing economic conditions significantly influence constructions of masculinity, as previously stated, for example, under conditions of unemployment. However, status of employment is not the only factor affecting masculinity. Employment opportunities, the actual jobs that are available to men throughout North America, have changed. Rapidly disappearing are the better-paying jobs guaranteed by unionization and work in the manufacturing sector. Instead, we are confronted with a shift to a working class that is largely located in service industries. As a result of this shift, Linda McDowell (2005) argues, there has been a feminization of the workforce. This is not the replacement of men with women as the term often assumes. Rather, it is a change in the context of what jobs men hold and the ways in which they perform this work.

In some cultural spaces, such as ritzy Italian and French restaurants, posh steakhouses, or exclusive men's clubs, men have always worked as servers and attendants. In these settings, masculinity was not diminished by service work; it was, in fact, affirmed because only men were permitted to perform such jobs in these particular spaces. In the current economic environment, however, men, especially young men, are increasingly pushed into service sector employment.

In retail sales, the fast food sector, call centres, messenger services, coffee outlets, and restaurants, hegemonic masculinity is under threat. Employment in these sectors is commonly low-paid, insecure, "unskilled," "flexible," part-time, and contract (rather than permanent). These are the same vulnerable positions and precarious conditions that women have long complained about.

For men, service work demands a reconfiguration of masculinity. No longer are the tenets of hegemonic masculinity acceptable guidelines. In these environments, men's ways of "doing masculinity" must necessarily shift. No longer are the rough, tough, independent traits of the working-class man valued, although they were always mythical "ideals." Employment in the service sector constitutes a different image of working-class men. Service work demands the performance and embodiment of the so-called feminine characteristics of empathy, caring, docility, and deference. Moreover, working in the service sector requires the embodiment of socially constructed "desirable" aesthetics, including age, race/ethnicity, body types, hairstyles, and clothing, as well as gestures, mannerisms, and scripts. All of these requirements are the *unwritten* rules that govern exchanges among employers, service providers, and consumers to ensure profitability.

> **Brainteaser**
>
> A patient is brought into the emergency room.
>
> The surgeon says, "I can't operate on this patient: he's my son."
>
> The surgeon is not the patient's father. Why can't the surgeon operate?

An intersectional approach to understanding configurations, performances, and embodiments of masculinity demands an analysis of "race." Recall in chapter 4, that race is a socially constructed concept. Nonetheless, studies show that race influences constructions of masculinity (Hunter and Idden 1994; Collins 2004; hooks 2004; Gerami 2005; Gutmann and Vigoya 2005; Taga 2005; Gutmann 2007; Hurtado and Sinha 2008; Balaji 2011; Liang et al. 2011; Mutluer 2011). Again, let's not take the position that *all* black, Latino, or Asian men fit particular configurations of masculinity; nor do they perform or embody their masculinity as a racial group. There is no rigid black masculinity, Latino masculinity, or Asian masculinity. However, stereotypes about these various masculinities persist.

Black men, some scholars argue, are feared by others in white-supremacist societies (Collins 2004; hooks 2004; Ferber 2007). Racism, therefore, affects how black men can experience their masculinity. Many black men often contain and control their masculine performances in ways that might be understood as conforming to hegemonic masculinity. However, in qualitative studies, where black men voice their ideas about manhood, it is clear that black men had other ideas about what shaped their values and behaviours. Family, community, and spirituality were all telling influences on black men's sense of masculinity (Lease et al. 2010). Commonly noted attributes of being a man were having self-respect, resourcefulness, direction, taking responsibility, good parenting, providing for family, and demonstrating kindness and caring. These attributes contrast blatantly with racist stereotypes of black men as violent, uncivilized, uneducated, criminals, and deadbeat dads. Young urban black men are commonly labelled as "gangstas" and "players." These images abound in music videos and on "reality" crime TV shows that depict the supposed criminality of black men. While individual black men are not necessarily viewed in these ways, because of racism, black men as a group are often homogenized by racist stereotypes.

Racism plays a significant role in black men's lives. Negative stereotypes about black masculinity continue to overdetermine the lives of black men. Widespread unemployment, for example, contrasts starkly with the perceived potential for easy money and wealth from illegal activities and lures many young black men to life-threatening performances of masculinity. The appeal of gang activities, street violence, drug use, and hypersexuality (risky sexual behaviour and multiple partners) as a means for affirming black masculinity are reinforced by patriarchal capitalism, where money-making and risk-taking behaviours are rewarded. Such behaviours demand strength, toughness, independence, and virility, the very elements that hegemonic masculinity asserts.

Illustration 9.3: Is this what a "real" man is supposed to look like?

Yet they play out quite differently in the lives of many black men who are excluded from white male privilege because of racism. While the stereotypes prevail, the majority of black men affirm their masculinity through the everyday channels of career, education, family, and community activities.

Stereotypically, Latino men's masculinity is socially constructed as *macho* (Gutmann and Vigoya 2005; Gutmann 2007; Liang et al. 2011). To be a Latino man is to perform and embody *machismo*, which is defined as aggressive, strong, dominant, and virile. Sound familiar? It, too, parallels the definition of hegemonic masculinity, except for the white part. *Macho* is a caricature of Latino man, however. It is the character portrayed by Hollywood and on TV as "outlaw," drug dealer, and gang banger. The scripts are limited to those who father many children, degrade and violate women, and recklessly abuse drugs and alcohol. These images of hypermasculinity, like those imposed on black men, are perilous for those who attempt to perform and embody them. Importantly, like black men, Latino men do not readily conform to such stereotypes.

To understand more fully how Latino men define their masculinity, *caballerismo* provides a necessary counterbalance to representations of *machismo*. *Caballerismo* emphasizes the social construction of Latino masculinity as embracing honour, dignity, respect for others, caring, and family (Liang et al. 2011). Consequently, when asked to define their manhood, research shows that Latino men often do so in positive relational, ethical, and counter-hegemonic ways. Yet racialization based on light or dark skin tones and notions of "indigeneity" or whiteness also influence their understandings of themselves as men. Race, together with class, are interwoven with gender to complicate Latino men's experience of patriarchal privilege. Various "stigmatized" social identities—working class, black, Latino, Asian, gay, or differently abled—can hinder access to education, careers, and interpersonal relationships.

Racially and ethnically specific masculine stereotypes regrettably endure. Images of Muslim terrorist, Asian martial artist, and the Italian gangster or "Guido" come to mind. "Guido" is a racist term used to depict Italian men as working-class, crass, uneducated, and unintelligent. Yet, it has been re-popularized by MTV's reality series *Jersey Shore*, which adds hypersexualization to the stereotype. Each of these images serves a purpose in patriarchal white-supremacist capitalist North America. They maintain gendered orders, systems of inclusion and exclusion, and hierarchies of masculinities, where hegemonic masculinity is understood as white, middle class, heterosexual, and able-bodied.

Interestingly, homosexuality, the ultimate "othered" masculinity, is central to constructions of hegemonic masculinity. In the dynamics of gendered orders, homosexuality is positioned as a threat to both masculinity and heterosexuality. Male-focused homophobia, the fear of homosexual men, constructs homosexuality as a negation of masculinity. Accordingly, gay men are defined as effeminate. Here we can see how exclusionary and subordinating processes emerge from such binary thinking.

Michael Kimmel (1997), for example, suggests that to be a man in North America is to be homophobic because of the *perceived* threat that homosexuality poses to "real men." In North America, while men who have sex with other men experience oppression, they nonetheless also experience some of the advantages of male privilege. Men in general benefit economically from sexism. R.W. Connell (2005) argues that because of patriarchal privilege, even effeminate gay men have an advantage over many women. Moreover, homosexuality does not definitively rule out masculinity.

Research has historically focused on the *etiology*, the study of causes for or origins of homosexuality rather than gender relations and power. Accordingly, homosexuality has been medicalized as a disease or pathology, analyzed as sociologically deviant from "normality," and constructed as a "lifestyle" or "culture," which scripts sexual performances. Research along these lines has ignored questions about gender relations and understandings of masculinity. In more recent research, qualitative studies have sought to address these questions. They found that masculinities are not formed in isolation, but in relation to other masculinities and to femininities. Let's explore how gay men might understand masculinity.

Given the relational construction of masculinity, it might not be surprising to find that gay men understand their manhood as shaped by gendered stereotypes of masculinity and femininity. In describing masculinity, Sánchez et al. (2009) found that among gay men, stereotypically masculine attributes were described as being unemotional, controlling, and good under pressure as well as being interested in sports, cars, and outdoor activities. In addition to these characteristics, some gay men added the ability to "pass" or act straight, as part of the definition of masculinity. More interestingly, some gay men added that being comfortable and secure with one's sexuality was an important indicator of masculinity. Gay masculinity was also positioned in opposition to a feminine persona, affirming a gender hierarchy. Supposedly feminine mannerisms—limp wrists, high voice, flamboyant dress, and swishy walk—all preclude the possibility of passing as heterosexual or embodying masculinity. The power embedded in hierarchies of masculinity and gendered orders, may force many gay men to embody and perform hegemonic masculinity, even when it feels uncomfortable. However, other gay men reject such performances as pointless since hegemonic masculinity absolutely excludes homosexuality.

Many men who have sex with other men do not define themselves as homosexual. Many of these men on the "down low" distinguish sex with other men as just sex, rather than a defining characteristic of their sexuality or their masculinity (King and Hunter 2004). This can be understood as a way of maintaining gendered orders. It can also reflect very different views about sexuality, where sexual conduct and identity are not tied together, so a man may have sex with men but not regard that act as a principle fact of his identity. In raw terms, men who are penetrators can conceptualize their sexual acts as masculine, whereas those who are penetrated may not assume the same privilege. In this case, masculinity might be understood as conforming to heteronormativity, where heterosexuality is the norm against which all sexuality is measured. However, there are multiple meanings associated with sexual practices and men who have sex with men need not identify as gay. Sexuality is much more fluid than the rigid categories of straight and gay. There are multiple ways of being sexual with other people. So, for some men who have sex with men, the gay identity may not capture who they are or even what they do sexually.

The multiplicities of non-hegemonic masculinities, confirms that masculinity is not as rigid as we might think. Masculinity theorists such as Connell

(1992, 1995, 1997, 2005), Kimmel (1997, 2008), Hearn (2004, 2006), and others, contend that hegemonic and non-hegemonic masculinities are always in transition. In no small part, feminisms have influenced the ways in which we understand the complexities of masculinities and directed their transformations. Feminist theories of power, gender, (in)equality, and intersectionality have informed men's lives as well as women's. Many men embrace feminism as a vehicle for social change, not just to support women but also in recognition that feminism benefits men, too.

Men "Doing" Feminism: Being Feminists

For men, embracing feminism provides new ways of seeing the world and themselves. It allows for different types of thinking. Feminism provides men with a lens to see hegemonic masculinity as an unattainable caricature of manhood. It releases men from the never-ending struggle, and ultimately inevitable failure, to measure up as "real men." Since feminisms challenge gender orders, identifying as feminist gives men permission to prioritize family, fatherhood, and personal relationships, places where men can feel confident, capable, and fulfilled. Feminism gives men permission to share the responsibility for financial security with their partners and break free from the male breadwinner model. For many men, these changes have a positive effect on their mental and physical well-being.

There is some debate as to whether men can be feminists or whether they need to qualify their status as male feminists or pro-feminist men. This debate over labelling, however, is much less important than men "doing" feminism. Because doing feminism affects every part of one's life—at home, at work, and in the community—men who embrace feminism are allies in the struggles to end oppression. Men have proven to be excellent allies and activists in the fights to end violence against women, homophobic violence, and racist violence. Women's movement activists cannot be naïve in thinking that social change will happen without men's full participation.

Men have an important part to play, for example, in ending violence against women. Violence against women is overwhelmingly committed by men, or rather *some* men. Yet, as Michael Kaufman (2008) contends, men as a group hold a great deal of power—over social discourse, political policies, jurisprudence, and policing—and in large part they have been silent, which has allowed the violence against women to continue unchecked. An important challenge to this silence is the White Ribbon Campaign, which originated in Canada in 1991 when a group of men decided to take responsibility in urging men to speak out against violence against women (Kaufman 2008). The wearing of a white ribbon symbolizes the pledge to never commit or condone violence against women. White Ribbon Campaigns and organizations are now present around the world in Africa, Asia, Europe, Latin America, Australia, and the U.S. Men's voices in ending violence against women are a powerful tool for changing the ways men act and perhaps challenging the ways in which masculinity is constructed as violent. There is concern among feminist activists, however, that there could be a privileging of men's voices and men's groups in the struggle, which could result in the funnelling of funds away from supporting feminist frontline supports for women and children who are victimized by violence.

Many men, especially young men, are feminists, male feminists, and pro-feminist men—supporting anti-male violence, anti-discrimination laws, pay equity in the workplace, affordable and accessible childcare programs, and the redistribution of responsibilities and work in the home. To these men, feminism is common sense. For them, being a feminist and doing feminism is a commitment to being a real man.

Conclusion

Remember that brainteaser earlier in the chapter? A patient is brought into the emergency room. The surgeon says, "I can't operate on this patient: he's my son." The surgeon is not the patient's father. Why can't the surgeon operate? The answer to the brainteaser is the surgeon is the patient's mother. Did you get it right? This brainteaser works because of the pervasiveness of sexism. In this case, the assumption is that all surgeons are male. The socially constructed and institutionalized expectations about men and women, masculinity and femininity, make the answer so difficult to guess.

As we have seen in this chapter, when issues of race, class, ability, and sexuality are added to expectations about men and masculinity, feminisms and feminist theory are useful ways to challenge these expectations. Theorizing men's experiences of manhood and understandings of masculinity are critical for social change. If feminism is about social change and justice—the elimination of all forms of oppressions and exploitations and the realization of gender equality—then women cannot be the sole focus of any feminist movement. Feminist and pro-feminist men have much to offer in challenging patriarchy, sexism, racism, classism, homophobia, ableism, ageism, and transphobia. In the next chapter, we will explore feminist activist tactics and strategies. And we will see that feminists do have a sense of humour.

Questions for Study

1. What is hegemonic masculinity? What characteristics are associated with hegemonic masculinity? Why is hegemonic masculinity so powerful? Is hegemonic masculinity a reality for most men? Why or why

not? What does the failure to achieve hegemonic masculinity mean for some men? How does hegemonic masculinity influence definitions of other forms of masculinity? Can other forms of masculinity shift understandings of hegemonic masculinity?

2. How do gendered orders guide our understanding of masculinity and femininity? What are gendered hierarchies? How are gendered hierarchies infused with power? What are the foundations for gendered hierarchy? How are these hierarchies maintained and enforced? Give some examples.

3. There are four iconic stereotypes of masculinity discussed in this chapter. Describe the masculine attributes of each. How does each representation of masculinity influence the ideas and behaviours of boys and men? What is the relationship of each image to women? How do these images also represent particular reflections of femininity?

4. What are the characteristics of hypermasculinity? What are the consequences of embodying hypermasculinity? Give examples.

5. Language is gendered. How is language used to ensure that boys and men perform and embody the physicality of masculinity? Using assumed gender-neutral and universal terms in referring to people can be sexist. How, and why, is sexism invisibly embedded in the English language? Give examples.

6. How can road rage be understood in gendered terms? How are particular social constructions of masculinity implicated in road rage and other forms of violence? Give some examples.

7. How has qualitative research countered popular negative stereotypes about working-class, black, Latino, gay and other masculinities? How are systemic racism and heteronormativity revealed through this research process?

8. How is work/employment implicated in the social construction of masculinities and masculine identities, for example, in ideas about the breadwinner, businessman, trade union worker, waiter/server, and the unemployed?

9. What is *machismo*? How is the concept of *machismo* for Latino men counterbalanced by the idea of *caballerismo*? Is this counterbalancing important? Why or why not?

10. What problems arise from focusing on the etiology or cause of homosexuality in understanding men and masculinity? According to recent research, how might gay men understand their masculinity differently from heterosexual men? Do such understandings reinforce or contest gendered hierarchies?

11. What is the benefit for men in doing feminism? Is there a role for men to play in feminist and women's movement? How can men participate more fully in feminist and women's movement?

Activities and Questions for Discussion

1. Consider how the portrayal of the four male stereotypes—hero, warrior, sports hero, entrepreneur—are replicated and transgressed in a popular TV show or movie. Consider whether the replications or transgressions are more true to life in your experience? Give examples.

2. Get a copy of the sports section from your local newspaper. Find a major article about a men's sporting event. How is gendered language used to portray masculinity in the article? How is the masculinity of the audience confirmed or denied?

3. In this chapter, there is an example of the author and her dad in a car, where her dad embodied stereotypically masculine identity. Write a short vignette about an experience that you had with a male friend or a family member who exhibited stereotypically masculine behaviour. What happened? Did you recognize the behaviour at the time? Did you try to subvert it? How did it work out?

Never doubt that a small group of thoughtful committed people can change the world. Indeed, it is the only thing that ever has.

—MARGARET MEAD

CHAPTER TEN

THE STRATEGIES THAT EMPOWER US

FEMINIST ACTIVISM

Feminists today have entered a new era of thinking about and doing feminism. We continue to struggle and succeed, but we are still committed to ending oppression and advancing social justice. As feminists, we need to continue to ask new questions and develop new strategies to meet our goals. We must learn from our past, rethinking past actions and strategies, so that we don't have to reinvent the wheel every time a new challenge emerges. Re-examining what we think and how we know about our world is critical. These are not easy tasks. Sometimes we fall back into antagonistic habits that reinforce differences and divisions among feminists. We already know that feminists can be divided by theories and methods, by issues and priorities, by generational differences, and by splits between activists and academics.

What's All the Fighting About?

Differences among feminists need not stop us from realizing our goals. Differences can be assets. They bring new ideas and refreshing ways of doing feminism to the fore. They challenge us to revisit past experiences and revise past strategies. Too often, we focus on our divisions. Over-emphasizing these can make even the most dedicated among us throw up our hands in frustration. When we focus on the divisions, we fail to see the continuity in women's movement.

Now, don't mistake the idea of continuity with sameness. Sameness implies that nothing changes and that the past is indistinguishable from the present. How can we expect feminisms to be the same in different historical, social, and geopolitical spaces? How can we expect feminisms to remain the same when nothing else does? We don't even stay the same as individuals. We learn and change, resist and accept, struggle and overcome throughout our lives. How can women's movement not also change? Change, however, does not mean that continuity doesn't exist. Continuity in women's movement recognizes the permanence of feminisms and the connections among and between feminists, even when they are challenging each other. Continuity also acknowledges differences in particular struggles across the waves of women's movement.

Continuity in women's movement, however, might be missed if we only see difference. History, if we look carefully, can give us some insights into strategies and tactics for change. It can encourage us to see the past in the present, which can give us greater strength to mount our challenges, voice our new (and old) ideas and launch initiatives for change in new ways. Second and third wavers need this strength in the current postfeminist/anti-feminist environment, an environment where "we"—people of all races, genders, sexualities, classes, and experiences—are already assumed to be equal. We cannot allow backlash to impose such assumptions on us. Nor can we allow a generational divide to open up where none need exist, between "older" second wave feminists and "younger" third wavers. There is a great deal of work to do if we are to meet our goals of ending oppression and achieving social justice, and this means there's lots of room for everybody to participate. We need to focus our energies on solidarity and building coalitions, rather than dismissing, undermining, or delegitimizing those who take different paths, use different strategies, or set different priorities. To paraphrase African American lawyer and feminist activist Flo Kennedy (1916–2000), it's all about the numbers and one lion is certainly less menacing than 500 mice (Kennedy 1976).

In this chapter we will explore some of the strategies and tactics feminist activists have used to realize their goals. We will explore some of the initiatives of the groups W.I.T.C.H., Guerrilla Girls, Raging Grannies, Riot Grrrls, Radical Cheerleaders, and RebElles to expose some of the continuities that exist across the waves even in the face of seemingly unbridgeable divides. In trying to make sense of feminist activism, we will need to rethink the divides, re-examine our feminist histories, and redefine continuity.

Turning Everything on Its Head

In chapter 8 we learned that third wavers rely on the strategies of personal narratives, performance politics, cultural productions, and cybertechnologies to get their messages out. They value independence, individuality, and creativity in subverting and resisting systems of oppression and established norms. Third wavers adopt a politics of hybridity—postmodern theories of identity that acknowledge paradoxes, conflicts, multiplicity, and messiness—as critiques of the essentialism and exclusions they sometimes attribute to second wave feminisms. Many third wavers distance themselves from the second wave, particularly the caricature of monolithic, white, middle-class, heterosexual, liberal, gloomy, and prudish women (Henry 2004; Purvis 2004; Gillis and Munford 2004; Gillis, Howie, and Munford 2007). And who wouldn't, if this were the reality? This outright rejection is a bit shortsighted because third wavers also adopt and extend ideas forwarded by second wave women of colour, lesbians, and Third World feminists, as well as building on the theories offered by feminist postmodernism, transnational feminism, and queer theory. By expanding these ideas and building on the theories of the second wave, third wavers show there is continuity in critical thinking and theorizing across the waves. At the same time, third wavers engage in a critique of the gaps and failings, the essentialisms and exclusions of second wave thinking.

Third wavers reject the idea that the identity of "woman" alone can rally support for social justice. Further, they contend that feminism is not just about "women's issues." Instead, third wavers insist that their movement seeks freedom for all those who are oppressed. Their activist politics relies on coalition building among individuals and groups that recognize the need for global justice. In this sense, political coalitions are based on what activists want to achieve rather than who they are. This strategy is politically powerful for women's movement since it encourages broad-based alliances centred on issues rather than on identity politics. As we saw in previous chapters, alliances across social justice issues, such as civil rights, gay rights, the labour movement, and the peace movement were important for second wave feminists, as was the abolition of slavery and temperance for first wavers. Coalition building, then, is not new to women's movement.

Eenie Meenie Miney Moe, Which Wave Are We In and How Do We Know?

Discussions about waves of women's movement are not new. Some people even argue that we are already in a fourth wave. There is no clear indication of this transition or consensus that a transition has occurred among feminist scholars. Nonetheless, some feminists suggest that the "fourth wave" of women's movement is defined by a renewed feminist rights agenda and concern for the environment by teens and those in their early twenties who are starting to engage in women's movement and feminist thinking (Whittier 2006; Seely 2007; Wrye 2009; Diamond 2009). This wave is strongly influenced by transnational feminisms and the globalization of local women's concerns. However, these concerns are not easily separated from those raised in previous waves.

Feminist activists have always been present in social justice struggles. As new concerns and issues emerge, we will be there, too.

Third wavers, for example, are still engaged in the struggles for legal, political, and social equality that were initiated by previous waves. However, they are also concerned with sexual health, eating disorders, body image, hybrid identities, sex work, sex trafficking, ecology, and economic globalization. In some ways, these issues are not new—take for example, Susie Orbach's *Fat Is a Feminist Issue* (1978), Angela Davis's *Women, Race and Class* (1981), or Cherrie Moraga and Gloria Anzaldúa's *This Bridge Called My Back: Writings by Radical Women of Color* (1981). Existing critical feminist theories concerning sexism, racism, sexuality, class, colonization, and imperialism are still useful in addressing the concerns for third wavers.

As an activist tactic, third wavers are engaged in writing from an individual perspective. Personal narratives are empowering because they allow third wavers to voice their ideas, describe their experiences, engage in critical self-reflection, and practice feminisms ("the personal is political"). Eating disorders, for example, can be examined using feminist analysis of sexism and gendered identities of masculinity and femininity as well as challenging consumer culture and the idealization of thin bodies. Our analysis might examine how patriarchal ideals of femininity and embodiment—thinness in this case—intersect with notions of race, class, and sexuality as well as the commodification and objectification of women's bodies, to confront eating disorders, to challenge fatphobia, and to resist conventions of femininity. Using personal narratives to reflect on the experiences of eating disorders by those living with them, especially when linked to theory, as suggested here, is an important third wave initiative (Orr 1997; Siegal 1997; Garrison 2000; Springer 2002; Henry 2004; Kinser 2004; Mann and Huffman 2005; Bobel 2006; Snyder 2008).

Third wave strategies can differ from some of those employed by second wavers. It is also important, however, to recognize that some of the perceived differences are not as distinct as we might at first think. Personal narratives are stories offered by third wavers to document their experiences and to suggest points for theorizing. These initiatives are not entirely new. Feminists have always used writing to speak about their experiences and to challenge conventions. Some have even done so using pseudonyms or pen names because women's writing was trivialized, discounted, and remained unpublished. This was the case for Mary Anne Evans, who famously published her work under the name George Eliot, and for the Brontë sisters, Charlotte, Emily and Anne, who adopted the masculine monikers Currer, Ellis, and Acton Bell. We might also reflect a little further on the vast literary contributions that women writers such as Virginia Woolf, Toni Morrison, Margaret Atwood, and Bessie Head have made to feminist thought through their writings. These authors must not be artificially divorced from feminist activism.

The third wave's emphasis on personal narratives is also reminiscent of the storytelling that has been a central component of past feminist activism, particularly the consciousness-raising initiatives of the 1960s and 1970s era of the second wave. It was through these initiatives—gathering women together to relate the stories of their lives and their experiences of oppression—that the complexities of women's lives were exposed and the intersectional oppressions of gender, race, sexuality, and class became clearer. From these experiences, second wave feminist theorists carved out space for challenging the dominance of scientific research and for insisting on qualitative feminist methods as valuable ways of knowing, as we discussed in chapter 7.

Third wavers suggest that, through the telling of stories, there is *potential* to theorize about experiences. This has been demonstrated in a multitude of feminist academic and community-based research initiatives that have used feminist theories to advance social justice issues. Yet the insistence by some third wavers that each narrative is unique, that one can only speak about themselves and their particular experiences, and that one cannot speak about anyone else's experience makes such theorizing difficult. Although resistance and subversion are personally empowering for those writing their stories, it is critical for third wavers to make clear the role of theory in these narratives if we are to empower anybody beyond the individual writer.

Many second wave strategies are adapted and updated to meet the new challenges and contexts of a third wave women's movement. One of the critiques that third wavers launched at second wavers was that they were too serious. Second wavers, they contend, don't realize that, to quote pop singer Cyndi Lauper, "girls just want to have fun." Play has been especially useful to third wavers in their activist interventions. However, second wavers were not without their moments of humour. Take for example, the 1968 protests of the Miss America pageant in Atlantic City. Feminist protestors staged a parody on pageantry, where women were displayed and evaluated like livestock at an auction.

Second wavers used "guerrilla theatre," a term coined in the late 1960s to describe popular performances in public spaces that challenged political and cultural norms to make their message clear. On the Boardwalk in Atlantic City, activists disrupted the pageant by parading and crowning a live sheep and auctioning off a Miss America dummy to the highest bidder. In so doing, they were challenging women's enslavement to beauty regimes and standards. Adding to the guerrilla theatre spectacle, protesters rid themselves of the "tools of female torture" by pitching high-heeled shoes, girdles, and curlers into a "freedom trash can" (Brownmiller 1999; Carlson 2004). Although no actual bra-burning ensued, this is where the urban myth was born.

Humour also played an important role in the 1968–1971 W.I.T.C.H. movement (Women's International Terrorist Conspiracy from Hell). It began in 1968

Illustration 10.1: At the 1968 Miss America protest in Atlantic City, the participants were diverse, and they weren't sheepish when it came to feminist concerns.

on Halloween, when a group of women dressed like cartoon witches entered a Chase Manhattan Bank and placed a "hex" on Wall Street. The group used *zaps*, a term to describe protest using guerilla theatre tactics and humour to contest the policies of big business and government agencies. The performance of spells and chants by the coven generated shock value to draw attention to concerns about the insidious relationship between capitalism, banks, and the Vietnam War. One of the founders, American feminist Robin Morgan, claimed success, suggesting that the Dow Jones stock market index fell the following day as a result of their zap. W.I.T.C.H. member Florika, an artist, occasional sex worker, and drug user, engaged in *culture jamming*, a term yet to be coined, by creating collages featuring graphic depictions of the relationship between capitalism and American imperialism. For example, she created a collage placing Vietnamese women in Chanel No. 5 advertisements to expose the American imperialism of the Vietnam War. The group's final zap occurred at the 1969 bridal fair being held at Madison Square Garden in New York City. The zap was a protest to expose the link between capitalism and women's oppression. Raising placards displaying Confront The Whoremongers, W.I.T.C.H. exposed the exploitation of women's romantic dreams of the perfect wedding day in the name of profit (Carlson 2004; Brownmiller 1999).

Culture Jamming

Culture jamming, a term coined by the band Negativland in 1984, is a form of activism that challenges dominant cultural messages by exposing the myths about power, consumerism, militarization, sex, race, gender, sexuality, ability, and age, which advertisers use to sell their products and the media employ to maintain the status quo (Dery 1993). It is a mode of guerrilla communication that resists and subverts popular culture by hijacking billboards, refiguring and reframing company logos, and creating alternative advertisements as well as engaging in performance art, graffiti, and hacktivism (cybersquatting and flaming). *Adbusters* magazine is one of the best-known publications producing counter-cultural messages that satirize existing advertisements to challenge the naturalness of their messages, such as "Drinking alcohol is sexy" or "Buying a nice car will get you a hot chick!" Culture jams are created artistically, using humour, irony, and satire. They reference the practice of radio jamming, which dates back to the Second World War, when radio operators attempted to disrupt the transmission of messages to enemy planes, submarines, and missiles with noise or to misdirect the enemy with false messages. Culture jamming is intended to open people's eyes to the extent to which the media control what we think.

Illustration 10.2: An end to the tools of torture.

The Guerrilla Girls are another important group that emerged in the second wave. Founded in 1985, they dubbed themselves the feminist "conscience of culture." Using humour and wearing their trademark gorilla masks to ensure anonymity, they provide information, provoke discussion, and show that feminists can be funny even when they are struggling with the serious issues of sexism, racism, classism, and misogyny. Guerrilla Girls challenge the social construction of women's bodies, control over women's bodies, and the ways in which women's bodies are (mis)used to convey sexist messages. The group originated in New York where their protests focused on the institutionalized sexism and male dominance reigning in the art world (Carlson 2004). In 1989, the Guerrilla Girls designed an advertisement for its campaign to bring attention to the low number of women artists featured in museum collections, which provocatively read: "Do women have to get nude to get into the Met. Museum? Less than 5% of artists in the Modern Art sections are women, but 85% of the nudes are female" (Guerrilla Girls 1989).

The Guerrilla Girls use bodies, physically and artistically, as canvases to graphically contest the exclusion of women artists in major galleries and to address cultural concerns. Donning gorilla masks to draw attention to the issues, paralleling the hideousness of the mask with the beauty of real women's bodies, the group performs and challenges what it means to be a woman and what it means to be a feminist. Guerrilla Girls' art commonly is confrontational and exposes the ridiculousness of sexist and backlash culture.

In 2001, for example, the Guerrilla Girls targeted the Oscars with a sticker campaign to expose the Academy of Motion Picture Arts and Sciences' failure to nominate women directors. The following year they launched the "Anatomically Correct Oscar" billboard. In 2006, the Guerrilla Girls collaborated with the group Movies Directed by Women to place a billboard outside the Kodak Theatre where the Oscars are held each year. The billboard graphically pictured a "female" gorilla dressed in a pink evening gown with chains around her wrists that read, "Unchain the women directors! Women directed only 7% of the top 200 films of 2005. No woman has ever won the Oscar. Only 3 have been nominated" (Guerrilla Girls 2006). Their activism and art demonstrate that feminists can be funny even when they are struggling with the serious issues such as sexism, racism, classism, and misogyny. The tactics and strategies employed by the group suggest continuity across the waves. Since Guerrilla Girls remain active, their longevity suggests a straddling of the second/third wave divide.

Not just young women are engaged in activism. In 1987 the Raging Grannies were founded as a group of aged 50+ women who were fed up with taking a backseat in politics. Clad in funny-looking "old lady" attire—old-fashioned dresses, floppy hats full of flowers, frilly aprons, and knitted shawls—they have protested against everything, from militarism and nuclear energy, to environmental degradation, sexism, and education policies, and they have staged their protests at military bases, legislatures, corporate headquarters, and in the streets. Originating in Victoria, British Columbia, Canada, the Raging Grannies now boast more than sixty groups throughout Canada, the United States, Greece, India, and Israel. Granny activist tactics use humour to draw attention to issues of importance. They create amusing and satirical lyrics to convey their messages and have used popular tunes to entertain and inform crowds (Roy 2004; Narushima 2004; Acker and Brightwell 2004; Sawchuk 2009).

The granny identity is subversive, especially when used in protest, allowing older women to claim public space with their bodies. These older women could easily be dismissed as parodies of passive "little old ladies." Their seemingly

Illustration 10.3: Guerrilla Girls Poster, 1991
http://www.guerrillagirls.com/posters/mia.shtml

harmless, apolitical granny image has earned them official respect as well as access to places where others might be barred. For example, when six Ottawa Grannies attempted to deliver coal for then prime minister Jean Chrétien's Christmas stocking on December 12, 1997, a police officer helped one granny over a barrier securing the residence, only to be embarrassed later when he was instructed to arrest the interloper. All six Raging Grannies were arrested for trespassing. When the case came to trial two years later, the judge reprimanded the Crown Attorney for his overzealousness and dismissed it, stating that it was a waste of taxpayers' money (Granny Pat 2011).

The Raging Grannies are not passive little old ladies; they are energetic, active, political, and knowledgeable about social and political issues. According to a secret 1999 report, the Royal Canadian Mounted Police (RCMP) considered the Raging Grannies a potential threat and an anti-Canadian force (Acker and Brightwell 2004). The United States has also raised concerns about the security risk that the Grannies pose to the war on terror (Sawchuk 2009). Granny protests are multiple and memorable. For example, protesting uranium mining, the Victoria, BC, chapter of Grannies stormed government hearings armed with laundry baskets full of underwear that they argued were "briefs" they wanted to present to the officials (Acker and Brightwell 2004). Grannies in Victoria, BC; Tucson, AZ; and New York, NY have protested against militarization by swarming Armed Forces Recruitment Offices offering to enlist (Acker and Brightwell 2004; Roy 2007; Sawchuk 2009). They baffled recruiters who were by law unable to ask the Grannies their age and therefore were forced to process their applications. Their protest stalled the recruitment process and served as political commentary on the costs of war to young people. When the GST (Goods and Services Tax) was imposed in Canada, the Raging Grannies performed a bit of street theatre. They held a "GSTea Party," a parody of the Boston Tea Party of 1773, by pouring tea into local waterways to express opposition to the GST, which is a regressive tax that affects the poor and elderly most severely. Raging Grannies have also organized protests they called "Closets Are for Brooms" to expose and challenge homophobia in government policies (Roy 2002, 2004; Narushima 2004).

Together, these groups suggest a diversity of second wave feminist activists groups, tactics, and interventions that are smart, informed, creative, and humorous. Clearly not all second wavers are the Debbie Downers of feminism that they have been branded.

Third wavers are building on some of these second wave tactics and enacting new ones in new spaces. What is especially new in this third wave of feminisms is the significance of individual bodies, pop culture, and the Internet. Third wavers recognize that subversion and resistance, especially to sex and gender norms, can be exercised individually. Accordingly, individual bodies become sites of expression and activism. Third wavers are transmitting their ideas and challenges for social change through personal style (clothing, hair, piercings, and body art) and ways of being (gestures and performances). They are rejecting "standards" of all kinds and conveying their politics of multiplicity. While first and second wavers placed their bodies on the line en masse in feminist struggles at demonstrations, marches, and sit-ins, they were usually able to resume "normal" in the aftermath of such events. In contrast, third wavers privilege individual acts of embodied politics, often displaying their bodies dramatically and in subversive resistance for twenty-four hours a day, seven days a week.

Third wavers offer both the production and critique of pop culture as ways of challenging norms as well as altering social expectations and values. Third wavers perform, enact, and produce feminisms through zine, ezines, narratives, poetry, music, art, graffiti, video, dance, and street and guerrilla theatre. Riot Grrrl, which many feminists point to as signifying a transition to third wave feminism, emerged as a grass-roots movement in the 1990s to challenge sexism, male dominance, and the exclusion of women in the punk rock music scene. Their take-charge attitude and DIY (Do-It-Yourself) feminist strategies (see chapter 8) have greatly influenced third wavers' cultural productions and the idea that you can learn by doing. And with doing comes theorizing! Kathleen Hannah's *Riot Grrrl Manifesto* published in 1991 in the *Bikini Kill, Zine 2*, for example, draws on intersectional analysis. It calls for an end to the

Illustration 10.4: Raging Grannies

"bullshit" of racism, ableism, ageism, classism, thinism, sexism, and heterosexism, recognizing how these sites of oppression are interconnected. It calls for a revolution that dares women to not just simply dream but to become the revolution. Riot Grrrl was also concerned with second wave feminist issues such as reproductive rights, domestic violence, rape, and body image. Their intersectional analysis of these issues offers further evidence of continuity across the waves (see, for example, Garrison 2000; Turner 2001; Kinser 2004; Gillis 2004).

Zines, Ezines, & Blogs

Zines are small-scale, do-it-yourself, cheaply produced, "booklet-esque" publications. They are created in cut and paste, artistic and comic formats and offer personal narratives, poetry, and information about feminist issues. They are created and distributed locally. By taking control of all aspects of production, from inception to final product, third wavers are empowered by doing feminism. More recently, with the wider access to the Internet and simplified website production technologies, zines have made it to the web as ezines. Not only have feminist ezines made it to the web but they are also proliferating there! Another web-based cultural production that many third wavers see becoming the next strategy for empowerment is blogging, which uses the Internet to create spaces for many women and marginalized people (although the Internet is not universally accessible) to write their stories.

Third wavers claim that pop culture is transforming social culture and undermining political institutions. Some even suggest that popular television programs such as *Will and Grace*, *Queer Eye for the Straight Guy*, *Queer as Folk*, and *The L Word* can influence government policies and legislation. They argue that, as homosexuality and queerness have gained greater social acceptance, government policies and legislation will eventually be enacted to catch up to these changing social norms. However, this idea may be too optimistic since there have been significant challenges to normalizing homosexuality and queerness (Farrar and Warner 2006; Showden 2009). For the past fifteen years, the U.S. government has been defending the constitutionality of the federal Defense of Marriage Act (1996), which defines marriage as between one man and one woman. In February 2011, President Obama declared that his administration would no longer defend the Act as constitutional, paving the way to strike down the law (Ambinder 2011). Perhaps this is an indication that a changing social landscape can influence legislation; however, the slowness of change suggests that third wavers must engage in strategic political actions in addition to individual political acts, since gay marriage remains banned in thirty states and only legal in five.

The Radical Cheerleaders are another important third wave activist group. Formed in 1996 in Florida, their political protest strategies used cheering and dance to convey their messages. Like the Raging Grannies' subversion of the little old lady identity, the Radical Cheerleaders co-opted the identity of cheerleader, typically defined as feminine, conventionally sexy, polite, well-behaved, and disciplined. Instead, the Radical Cheerleaders create anarchic cheers, choreographed to dance moves and infused with cheerleading tricks to effectively combine performance and protest. Their messages are brash, aggressive, and feminist, making their routines into spectacles. Dubbing themselves "activists with pom-poms," the Radical Cheerleaders challenge, resist, and subvert norms of gender, race, class, and sexuality (Thompson 2003; Farrar and Warner 2006). Their protests confront traditional expectations about gender, women's place in politics, and ways of being in public. Wearing sexy and provocative costumes, occupying public space, shouting rowdily, and often using profanity challenges gender and feminine conventions as well as the cheerleader identity. The twin purposes of empowerment and protest are critical to the process. As one of the original Radical Cheerleaders Jeanne Vaccaro asserts, "It's a safe space to feel feminine and badass" (Vaccaro 2005, 44). Their comedic cheers engage their audiences in politics in an approachable way that engages critical thinking. Not surprisingly, groups of Radical Cheerleaders have been established throughout North America as well as in Europe.

There are many more third wave activist groups of note. Blood Sisters (active between 1996 and 2004), for example, brought feminism to the forefront by linking ecology and women's health. This Montreal-based group exposed

Illustration 10.5: No justice, here's a piece of my mind/No justice, here's a piece of my behind/No justice, piece it together and you'll find/Radical Cheerleaders on the frontlines.
http://zinedistro.org/zines/56/classic-city-chaos/by/an-unknown-author

the toxic effects, for both women's bodies and landfill sites, of commercially produced menstrual products containing bleach and other chemicals. They contested the capitalist exploitation of the environment and control over women's bodies. The rallying call to action for Blood Sisters was "Protect your Pussy!" Through the production of zines, bathroom graffiti, performance, workshops and the Internet, they informed women of alternatives such as creating or buying reusable/washable pads and reusable menstrual cups such as the Diva Cup, which is made from medical-grade silicone, and the Keeper, which is made from natural gum rubber.

There seems to be no end to the diversity of feminist activist groups or actions. Feminists are engaged on multiple levels and are engaging with important issues. For example, RebELLEs is a pan-Canadian young feminist collective, which boasts a membership of diverse women of all backgrounds, ages, races, abilities, ethnicities, origins, sexualities, identities, and classes. They produced a Manifesto at a conference in Montreal in 2008 to identify their concerns, mobilize action, and raise consciousness. RebELLEs recognizes the need for global feminist solidarity to challenge global economic forces and to confront local and national government and business policies that exploit, oppress, and harm women around the world. They expose militarization, war, and genocide as gendered experiences, where sexual exploitation and rape have become common weapons. They contest economic globalization and free trade as contributing to women's social, economic, and cultural insecurity. RebELLEs acknowledges that many of the issues raised by second wavers have yet to be resolved. They contribute to feminist dialogue, theorizing, and actions by expanding on these issues and engaging in an intersectional analysis. To ensure that they are taken seriously, RebELLEs members are organizing, they are informing, and they are protesting (ReBELLEs 2012).

Conclusion

Feminist activism remains a central component of feminist and social justice movements. Linking theory and practice continues to create new and innovative feminist praxis with every wave. Nonetheless, acknowledging continuity across the waves is critical in understanding and strengthening feminisms. As individuals and groups, at local and global levels, on the streets and on the World Wide Web, feminisms are being proclaimed everywhere. As third wavers remind us, feminism is not dead. It lives and continues to struggle. In the next chapter, we will explore some important issues that feminists are still struggling to change.

Questions for Study

1. Why is looking at the history of feminist and women's movement important for building feminisms and social change today?
2. How have narratives been important to both second and third wavers? How can narratives be used to theorize about feminisms and feminist experience?
3. What are the activist issues that link the second and third wave? What are the activist issues that divide them? How are they different? And why?
4. What are some examples of humour used in the second and third waves? Why do you think humour is effective for advancing feminist

and women's movement? How does humour counter stereotypes and backlash about feminists and feminisms?

5. How have the Raging Grannies made activism ageless? How have the Raging Grannies blurred the lines between second and third wave activism and issues?

6. What activist tactics do third wavers borrow from second wavers? What are some of the new third wave tactics for activism? Is the personal still political for third wavers? How and why?

7. How can alternative media such as zines, blogs, non-mainstream magazines, and TV programs and Internet sites transform popular culture and undermine political institutions? Discuss and give examples of change.

Activities and Questions for Discussion

1. Practise culture jamming. Find an advertisement from a men's or women's magazine. How are gender, race, sexuality, class, ability depicted? What is the original message of the advertisement? What are the promises made by the advertisement you chose? Subvert this message by creating a counter-advertisement that challenges the sexism, racism, and classism, and other power structures in the original advertisement. Add text and alternative images to culture jam this advertisement. How are you changing the meaning of the advertisement? What are you saying about this product?

2. Participate in an act to change the world. What can you do to change the world or your small bit of it? How would you do it? Where would you do it? How would you tell people about it? How would you encourage them to do it, too? Do it!

When I dare to be powerful, to use my strength in the service of my vision, then it becomes less important whether I am afraid.
—AUDRE LORDE, *THE CANCER JOURNALS*

CHAPTER ELEVEN

STILL STRUGGLING
MAKING CHANGE

Just when we thought we had equality, reality sets in. While feminism has been struggling for equality for well over a century, we have yet to meet this goal. When we look at the world in which we live, we know that we cannot abandon our struggles. We must continue to fight for social change to end exploitation and oppression in all its various forms. In this chapter, we will look at some of the ongoing struggles in which feminists are engaged. We will explore what is at stake in the struggle for equality and social justice in the areas of paid and unpaid work, gendered violence, and reproductive rights. While these are not the only areas where feminists are active, they have remained central to women's movement since the beginning. Let's first explore how equality fits somewhat uncomfortably with these feminist goals.

Equality Under Fire

There is much debate among feminists and activists in women's movement as to whether equality is even the best way to frame our goals. What does equality mean? Does it mean that women are equal to men? On the face of it, this seems to be the right way to approach things. On closer examination, however, questions begin to arise, such as, Which men do women want to be equal with? Are all men already equal? Are women a homogenous group and therefore potentially equal? Do all women have the same needs and wants? And, how do these needs and wants compare to men's? These are just a few questions that we need to address.

One of the problems that arises in "equality" debates is the literal interpretation of the word. Equality is assumed to mean equal. And equal is simply

Defining Equality at the 1995 United Nation's Fourth World Conference on Women in Beijing

Equality means "removing all obstacles to women's active participation in all spheres of public and private life through a full and equal share in economic, social, cultural, and political decision making ... [And] that the principle of shared power and responsibility should be established between women and men at home, in the workplace and in the wider national and international communities." (United Nations 1995)

assumed to mean "the same." An apple and an orange are both equally valuable fruits, but they are not the same. Similarly, no one is arguing that women and men are exactly the same—well, perhaps those who seek to maintain the status quo of inequality are—but feminists are saying that women and men are equally valuable. For feminists, the key to attaining equality among men and women lies in the notions of valuing people and valuing differences. Throughout this book we have seen that our differences cannot be simply ranked according to a hierarchical system of value based on gender, race, age, sexuality, ability, or social, cultural, or economic status. Rigorous intersectional analyses (see chapter 4) are necessary to understand why many feminist goals remain outside our reach. This analysis alone, however, will not result in the much-needed social changes envisioned by feminists without concerted feminist activism. So, how do we argue with the reality of differences among us and at the same time bring about equality?

Is Difference a Barrier to Equality?

Physiologically, the differences between women and men are evident. Men as a group are on average taller, stronger, and weigh more than women. This does not mean that some women are not taller, stronger, and heavier than some men. Historically, "scientific evidence" dictated that biological sex was fixed and immutable, as well as a clear marker of sexual orientation. Science, or as we now think of it, pseudo-science, has helped to construct rigid divisions between women and men that have reinforced difference rather than facilitated equality.

Often the distinction between the sexes is based on reproductive capacity. This is an important difference between men and women and has led to perceived and real inequalities among the sexes. Remember that difference should not automatically create a hierarchy of value.

Women and men both have a place in human reproduction. As we saw in chapter 9, men's sperm has been cast by "scientific" storytelling as more valuable than women's eggs. Childbearing has been long used to control women's bodies, their mobility, and access to work. In North America, pregnancy has been interpreted variously as an indicator of weakness, as an illness, and even as evidence of a woman's promiscuity. Of course when a man "knocks up" a woman, he is perceived as "the man." Successfully impregnating a woman reinforces the stereotypically masculine characteristics of virility and sexual prowess.

Reproduction is the root of much inequality between women and men. It is the basis of the artificial division between public and private spheres, where the private is constituted by the home and public is everywhere else. The very real, and starkly different, consequences of pregnancy for women and men are significant. Historically, for example, pregnancy was used to deny women employment as teachers, one of the few available career choices for women at the time. In the nineteenth and early part of the twentieth centuries, pregnancy, even for married women, was grounds for dismissal from a teaching post. Such decisions by state boards and ministries of education were supposedly an attempt to protect children (Goldin 1988; Blount 2000; Israel 2002; Cavanagh 2005). They thought that children seeing a pregnant woman would inevitably lead to questions about where, what, and how such things happened. The assumption was that children would be corrupted by their exposure to a pregnant woman, as if they would not see pregnant women outside the classroom and ask the same questions. In the past, if you were an unmarried woman who became pregnant, your job wouldn't last for long.

Today, it is unlikely that you will be fired for becoming pregnant; well, except, perhaps, if you teach at a private school. While you might think we've come a long way, and we have with national and international laws barring discrimination on the basis of sex, recent cases in the United States where unmarried pregnant women were fired from private schools should make us reconsider women's presumed equality (see, for example, Greenberg 1998; Bakst and Phelem 2010; Schumacher 2005). In most cases, those doing the firing are religious-based schools, where sex outside of marriage is considered a sin. But, if not for the appearance of a protruding belly, how would they know if an unmarried teacher were having sex? And, of course, we would never know if the unmarried teacher was a man.

Inequality in the Workplace

It is still possible that, if you are a woman and disclose that you plan on having children in the future, you might just not get that job for which you were interviewed. A woman's skills, high academic achievements, and outstanding past employment record may not be enough to distract a future boss from the implications of repeated maternity leaves, holding the job while the woman "bonds" with her child, and a future of leaving early, coming in late, or missing work altogether when the child is sick. We might rightly think that this is sexist. But proving that this is the reason that a woman doesn't get a job is another matter.

At work, we assume that women and men will be treated equally. We are told that there is no glass ceiling. The *glass ceiling* is a term coined by feminists to explain the invisible structures that hold women back in their careers. The glass ceiling reflects the strengths of patriarchy and the "old boys networks" in the corporate world that continue to exclude women from management and the executive ranks as well as in politics and governmental positions. In 2011, for example, 2 per cent of chief executive officers (CEO) of Fortune 500 companies were women. This means that just twelve women could claim CEO status among the most influential corporations (CNN 2011). Of the 192 member states of the United Nations, only nineteen countries were headed by woman presidents or prime ministers in 2011 (Harris 2010). However, the glass ceiling is not the only thing holding women back.

A woman who gets hired and then has a child will, in all likelihood, be overlooked for promotions and special projects because she is seen as a mother first and an employee second. Employers, however, do not view male workers in this way, regardless of their parental status. There is little redress when you are the target. Women, as a group and individually, suffer "the reproductive tax" once they have a child. This is not a tax levied by government, but rather downward pressure applied by employers on women's wages. Working women with children are likely to see their wages rise more slowly and receive worse job evaluations, and therefore earn lower wages than women without children (Correll, Benard, and Paik 2007; Mukhopadhyay and Singh 2007; Bakst and Phelem 2010). Working fathers, however, are unlikely to be penalized for having children because their role as fathers is socially constructed as secondary to that of mothers.

Employers still expect that few fathers will be forced to leave work early, miss a meeting, or not come in at all because their child is sick. Caring for children is still perceived as "women's work" and patriarchal privilege releases men from this stigma. When fathers do care for their children, they are often rewarded because they are seen as an anomaly rather than sharing equally in parenting. In this example, sexism operates to value the exact same activity differently, depending on whether a mother or father is performing it.

While it is possible to share parental leave, men are less likely to take this option because, as we saw in chapter 9, they are viewed as the breadwinners, career-focused and on track for success. What does this say about women who have children and women who don't? Do we assume that women who choose to bear and raise children are uninterested in their careers? Or do we think the opposite, that women who don't have children are too focused on their careers? Do we assume that women who don't have children *choose* not to do so? Or do we think that they are "unmotherly" or selfish? Women seem to be damned if they do and damned if they don't. Social constructions around concepts of the ideal mother, father, and employee all seem to favour men over women, so what does this mean for equality?

Then there is the *pink collar ghetto*, which allocates particular jobs to women. Pink collar jobs are predominantly in the "caring" and "service" sectors. This is where women's perceived feminine characteristics of nurturing, giving, and docility, together with their "natural talents" for cooking, cleaning, and looking after others can best be used. At least this is how employers have interpreted women's paid employment. Accordingly, the majority of women workers continue to be employed in the areas of nursing, teaching, childcare, elder care, food services, retail sales, and business administration (reception, secretarial, and accounting positions) (U.S. Department of Labor 2010; McMullen et al. 2010). These areas of the economy have traditionally been paid less, viewed as unskilled, and often lack employment benefits such as health insurance and pension plans. These jobs are also likely to be more "flexible," which means they are easily compartmentalized into part-time hours that suit the employers' needs. Flexibility has often been interpreted as meeting women's needs to balance work with family responsibilities. However, working part-time while children are at school is unlikely to meet the economic needs of the majority of women, particularly single mothers, who work in these sectors, because these jobs are commonly lower paid and lack employment benefits.

In contrast to the pink collar ghettos, where work is premised on women's *reproductive labour* in the home, some women are working in blue collar jobs that are associated with men's *productive work* outside of the home. As we have seen in past chapters, binary thinking—in this case reproductive versus productive work—reinforces unequal power and the valuing of one type of work over another. Because men have traditionally performed blue collar work, this work is higher paid and perceived as skilled labour. This means that blue collar jobs where men have dominated the labour force—for example, as construction workers, gas fitters, masons, and factory workers—have been better paid than pink collar jobs. As you might imagine, women who work in blue collar jobs can face sexism in the form of on-the-job pranks and sexist jokes by co-workers and supervisors alike that make it clear women are not wanted; to hyper-surveillance of women's work, which questions women's skills; to denying women promotions and leadership positions. Still, women are successfully taking on blue collar jobs and challenging these barriers.

What about Pay (In)Equity?

In 1963, the United States passed the Equal Pay Act (EPA) to redress the discriminatory wages of women working full-time. The following year, Title VII of the Civil Rights Act added to this legislation by prohibiting discrimination on the basis of race, colour, religion, sex, or national origin by employers. At this time, women earned just $0.59 for each dollar earned by a man. In 2007, American women made $0.78 for every dollar earned by men. The gender pay gap is compounded by the racialization of the labour force. African American women earn just $0.69 and Latinas are even worse off, earning only $0.59 to a man's dollar (NOW 2011).

In Canada in 2006, women fared a bit worse than their American sisters, with women earning on average $0.71 for every dollar earned by men (although comparisons are difficult since these countries use different methods of calculating earnings) (Kapel 2011). While women are graduating in greater numbers than men at high school, college, and university, the gender pay gap persists. A university-educated woman will make only 68 per cent of a university-educated man's wage, significantly increasing the gender wage gap from just ten years ago when it was 75 per cent (CLC 2006). Only Korea, Japan, and Germany had higher gender pay gaps than Canada among OECD (Organisation for Economic Co-operation and Development) countries in 2010 (QMI 2010). Racialized women, according to Statistics Canada, earn just $0.65 compared to men (CLC 2006). Immigrant women fare even worse, earning only $0.56 when compared to Canadian-born women in 2005 (Collin and Jensen 2009).

Factors that maintain gender pay gaps are not based on differences in skills or abilities, the difficulty or importance of jobs undertaken, or even education levels. The reasons for gender pay differences are rooted in patriarchal social constructions of gendered roles and the ways in which men's productive work has been valued and women's reproductive work has been devalued. This division of labour is no longer valid. The economic environment has changed significantly, requiring families to earn two incomes to make ends meet. Men can no longer expect, or be expected, to be the sole income earners and providers for their families. Yet women continue to bear the majority of the responsibility for homes and children, as we saw in chapters 5 and 8. This is not to say that men do not participate in household chores and sometimes take on the caring role of stay-at-home dad, but the social construction of womanhood continues to hold women responsible for caring work in the home. In North America we still live in an environment in which social, cultural, economic, and political barriers to gender equality are thoroughly entrenched. This makes it difficult for women to attain equality.

The Global Care Chain

Globalization, defined as the increased mobility of finances, ideas, technologies, communications, and people, adds another layer to the gendered division of labour in the home. The difficulty in balancing home and work life has resulted in an acceleration of paid domestic labour. The demand for affordable domestic labour to aid in childcare, elder care, and housekeeping duties has increased significantly as dual-income earning families have become the norm in the Global North. This demand has resulted in both a feminization and racialization of reproductive work. Racialized women, who may have limited education and who are economically disadvantaged, are assumed to make "ideal" domestic workers for homes located in the Global North.

Globalization makes the commodification of reproductive labour possible. High demand for workers in the North, coupled with economic need in the Global South, has resulted in an increased transfer of workers in South to North migration. The legal status of immigrants and guest workers is precarious, tied to employment programs, and even to individual employers. The rise of the "nanny phenomenon," importing women from poor to rich countries, makes the outsourcing of mother-work possible. Many of the women who migrate to North America are also mothers, who must often leave their own children behind in someone else's care in order to care for the children of more affluent families in another country. While the remittances (money sent back home) are critical to the survival of their families, the emotional costs of transnational motherhood are high (Hondagneu-Sotelo and Avila 1997; Bernhard, Landolt, and Goldring 2005; Arat-Koc 2006; Nicholson 2006). *Transnational motherhood* is the concept of mothering children located in one country from another.

For these women, the emotional costs of separation from their families are often coupled with exploitation, fear, and sexual violence in the homes in which they are employed. Often bound by immigration policies to live in the homes of their employers, their working and living conditions are unregulated and subject to their employer's whim. Privacy is often compromised when domestic workers are forced to share rooms with children or to sleep in designated family spaces such as dens or common areas. Long hours, sometimes twenty-four-hour on-call situations, are not uncommon, and days off are often undesignated. Some domestic workers are sexually harassed and assaulted. Their precarious immigration status makes reporting abuse and seeking help less likely. Feminist theorists and activists have long worked to expose and confront the interconnected sites of oppression that exacerbate the possibilities of such exploitative relationships.

Men too are engaged in migration from South to North in the global care chain. In areas of domestic responsibilities traditionally designated male—gardening, home repair, and maintenance—there is an increased demand for cheap labour. There has also been a masculinization of some reproductive work, particularly in elder care. Where lifting and moving are important components of the job, male workers are often preferred. In the case of elder care, male caregivers challenge the gendered notions of caring. This transition in defining and gendering reproductive work is facilitated by rising numbers of male caregivers, especially those who are racialized and/or immigrants. Accordingly, the hierarchy of masculinities (discussed in chapter 9) is reinforced, where hegemonic masculinity—white, heterosexual, affluent—can readily be confirmed.

The Global Production Chain

Many women, particularly immigrant women, work from their homes while simultaneously caring for their children and managing household responsibilities. Increasingly, *homeworkers* in Canada and the United States are used by industries to reduce manufacturing costs by contracting out work. In the garment industry, for example, homeworkers are contracted to produce clothes and paid by the piece for completed products rather than earning an hourly wage. The result is commonly a lower than minimum wage hourly rate for homeworkers. Under contracting out, workers are responsible for all overhead costs required to complete their work, including the purchase of industrial sewing machines, electricity, and thread. Because labour laws do not protect homeworkers, they often work in makeshift and overcrowded spaces with inadequate lighting that can lead to eye strain and poor ventilation, which results in the inhalation of high levels of textile dust and fabric particles. Long hours are the norm of the industry and children are often tasked with helping their mothers in the production process to meet tight deadlines and increase productivity levels. The links are clear between homeworkers in Canada and the United States to global production in the garment industries.

International Measures for Women's Equality: CEDAW

In 1979 the United Nations adopted the Convention on the Elimination of All Forms of Discrimination against Women (CEDAW). The purpose of CEDAW was to reaffirm the fundamental human rights, dignity, and worth of every person and the equal rights of men and women, entrenched in the Preamble to the Charter of the United Nations (1945), the Universal Declaration of Human Rights (1948), the International Covenant on Economic, Social and Cultural Rights (1966), and the International Covenant on Civil and Political Rights (1966). You might wonder why there was a need for CEDAW since these other conventions were already in place. The Commission on the Status of

Dirty Laundry or Clean Clothes?

Over the past thirty years, clothing manufacturers in Canada and the United States have relied on a global production system. Manufacturers are able to cut production costs from 30 to 80 per cent by shifting production offshore to countries where labour costs are significantly less (Dana, Hamilton, and Pauwels 2007; Morris and Barnes 2009). Manufacturers in North America may design and perhaps cut the garments here, but they buy the fabrics and assemble the products abroad in Mexico, Bangladesh, Malaysia, China, and other countries. Homeworkers in Canada and the United States then complete the rest of the manufacturing process close to North American retail markets. Multinational corporations rake in huge profits, in the process subjecting workers to unregulated and appalling conditions (Borowy, Gordon, and Lebans 2004).

The Clean Clothes Campaign was launched in Europe in 1989 to support the rights of workers in the global garment and sportswear industries. The campaign works to educate and mobilize consumers, lobby governments, and support workers' fights for better working conditions. Members of the Clean Clothes Campaign include trade unions and non-governmental organizations (NGOs) who support women's rights, consumer advocacy, and poverty reduction. Campaigns for fair wages and better working conditions for homeworkers in Canada and the United States partner with the Clean Clothes Campaign (http://www.cleanclothes.org/). In Canada the Maquila Solidarity Network (MSN), for example, has worked since 1994 to create better working conditions and quality of life for workers in global apparel supply chains. Another example is the Global Exchange, which is located in the United States but works for social, environmental, and economic justice internationally. Global Exchange campaigns expose the human rights abuses inherent in sweatshop labour relations. The next time you buy clothes, consider the conditions under which they were made. Ask the retail manager whether homeworkers were used in the manufacturing process. Consider whether the clothes you buy are clean or whether they mask corporate dirty laundry. (Maquila Solidarity Network, http://en.maquilasolidarity.org/; Global Exchange, http://www.globalexchange.org/)

Women (CSW) contended that the homogenous category "human rights" was male-defined and therefore failed to ensure the protection and promotion of women's rights. The CSW further argued that the UN conventions were incomplete because they failed to address systemic discrimination against women. Both Canada and the United States became signatories of CEDAW in 1980. While Canada ratified CEDAW in 1981, the United States has still not ratified it despite broad-based government, NGO, and public support.

The problem with ratifying CEDAW for the United States may just come down to money and business interests, which apparently outweigh the equality rights of women. For example, if the U.S. were to ratify CEDAW, systematic changes would be necessary to ensure the following:

- The advancement of women's equality in the political, social, economic, and cultural fields (Article 3);
- Equal educational opportunity for women, including job training, which may undercut structural barriers that exclude women from certain sectors or higher-skilled positions (Article 10);
- The right to equal remuneration, including benefits, and to equal treatment in respect of work of equal value, as well as equality of treatment in the evaluation of the quality of work (Article 11); and
- The right to social security, particularly in cases of retirement, unemployment, sickness, invalidity, old age, and other incapacity to work, as well as the right to paid leave (Article 11). (United Nations 1979)

Canadian women have not fared any better by ratifying CEDAW, due to lack of enforcement. To date there are no mechanisms for monitoring or ensuring Canada's compliance with CEDAW and other UN treaty obligations. For example, evidence of Canada's violations of CEDAW can be found in women's higher rates of poverty when compared to men. Aboriginal women, immigrant women, and women with disabilities are more likely to be poor than other women (Articles 2 and 3). Poverty and economic inequality restrict women's enjoyment of their civil and political rights. Noting Canada's slow progress on pay equity, in 2003 the CEDAW Committee urged the Canadian government to accelerate the implementation of equal pay for work of equal value. Instead of moving forward with its international treaty commitment to pay equity, the Canadian government adopted the Public Sector Equitable Compensation Act (PSECA) in March 2009.

The PSECA weakens the existing federal Pay Equity Act, entrenching existing gender wage gaps among public sector workers. The legislation removes the right to seek redress for pay equity violations through the Canadian Human Rights Act. Moreover, pay equity can now be bargained away at the negotiating tables where employers and unions seek the best deal possible. In other words, women's pay inequities can be exchanged for an incremental increase for all union members. This might sound pretty good, since everybody gets an increase, but everybody's increase is not the same. If men earn more than women, for example, then a 2 per cent wage increase disproportionately benefits men. In fact, the gender wage gap increases because women then receive a 2 per cent increase of a lower wage. Moreover, the wage increase for everybody is at the expense of women who are already unequally paid for work of equal value. If workers are not unionized, wage increases get negotiated individually, which can result in greater disparities *between* women and men due to patriarchy and male privilege and *among* women due to race, sexual orientation, ability, age, language skills, religion, or national origin.

Globally, women on average continue to have lower levels of education, poorer health status, less income, and lesser access to resources and decision-making in comparison to men. Women are critical participants in family income generation, food production, and community development, all the while remaining disproportionately responsible for their homes and families. Moreover, women experience gender-based violence, violence specifically because they are women, in ways that men do not. Feminists contend, therefore, that any violence against any woman impedes women's equality everywhere.

CEDAW was silent on violence against women. It was not until 1993 that the UN adopted the Declaration on the Elimination of Violence against Women. The Declaration defined violence against women as "[a]ny act of gender-based violence that results in, or is likely to result in, physical, sexual or psychological harm or suffering to women, including threats of such acts ... in public or in private life."

Violence against Women and Gendered Violence

Violence against women is a major barrier to women's equality globally. Women's unequal access to resources, political representation, social and economic benefits, and power combine to intensify both the effects and practices of violence against women. Violence is gendered, which means that the violence that is frequently committed against women and girls happens because they are female. *Gendered violence* takes into account the complexities of intersectional sites of oppression as violence and therefore takes many forms:

- *Physical*: hitting, pushing, battery, sexual assault, sexual harassment, rape, and murder;
- *Psychological*: emotional abuse, sexism, discrimination in all its multiple forms, harassment, intimidation, victim-blaming, and internalization of oppressive stereotypes; and
- *Structural*: patriarchy, racism, heterosexism, capitalism, (neo)colonialism, Eurocentrism, public/private divides, political exclusions, militarization, social exclusions, poverty, economic segregations, sexual division of labour, job discrimination, cultural structures, inadequate health care systems, absence of reproductive choice, etc.

Gendered violence dominates the lives of many women globally. The problem of gendered violence is more complicated than what we see on the news, read about in the newspaper, or hear about from friends and family members. Another woman sexually harassed at work; another woman date raped; another woman killed by her partner or ex-partner; another woman assaulted by police; another woman seeking refugee status to escape genital circumcision; another woman stoned to death; another woman trafficked for prostitution; another woman raped in a war zone; or another woman killed in the name of "family honour." Gendered violence, however, is not simply about individual incidents of violence. It is about the cumulative, interconnected, and targeted violence and threats of violence that women and girls experience. This is what feminist Liz Kelly (1988) termed as a *continuum of violence*. The continuum of violence ensures that women and girls are ever conscious of the possibility of violence directed toward them. This knowledge affects everything that they do, how they act, what they say, where they go, and what they wear. Recall the Slutwalk protests discussed in chapter 5, as a powerful and playful attempt to challenge the prevailing *rape culture* and violence directed toward women.

Think about how sexual assaults or the even more seemingly mundane acts of "date rape" are portrayed in the media or handled by police investigators. Questions about what *she* was wearing, why *she* was there, why *she* was unaccompanied, what did *she* do, and what are *her* past sexual practices are often posed in an attempt to blame the woman. Yet feminist theorists, front line service workers, and anti-violence activists make it clear that sexual assault is not about sex. Sexual assault is about violence and power. They try to expose the structures that authorize gendered violence: patriarchy, white supremacy, heterosexism, (neo) colonialism and capitalism. These structures are embedded in social, historical, economic, and political systems that defy rigorous questioning.

Is it any wonder that in the United States, more than 60 per cent of sexual assaults are not reported (Rennison 2002)? Or that in Canada, estimates of unreported sexual assault could be as high as 90 per cent (CRIAW 2011)? According to the World Health Organization, estimates of unreported assaults range from 55 per cent to 95 per cent globally. Shame, humiliation, stigmatization, and fear of reprisals or being labelled a liar are all factors in the decision whether or not to report sexual assaults.

Yes, men too can be raped. Approximately 14 per cent of reported rapes are committed against men in the United States (Tjaden and Thoennes 2006). This number may not reflect reality, since men's reluctance to report rape parallels the factors that affect women's decisions—shame, humiliation, stigmatization, and fear of reprisals or not being believed. Trans and gay bashing also constitute gendered violence.

According to UNIFEM, violence against women and girls is a global pandemic. A shocking 60 per cent of women experience physical or sexual violence at the hands of men in their lifetime, and most often the perpetrators are loved ones—husbands, intimate partners, family members—and people known to those victimized. But it's not just about one woman; it is about the prevalence of gendered violence, which has become so normalized that we stop paying attention. Violence, therefore, becomes invisible, expected, and at times, even accepted. The tragic costs of the normalization of violence are significant.

Conservative estimates of the costs of domestic violence in Canada are approximately U.S.$1.16 billion, and U.S.$5.8 billion in the United States (UNIFEM 2010). These numbers only account for the direct economic costs of violence against women, such as medical care, shelter stays, lost wages, and work interruption. However, the indirect economic and social costs are even greater when we take into account the long-term and related effects of violence, such as women's emotional well-being, isolation, depression, personal security, and women's incapacity to participate in regular activities and/or inability to care for themselves and their children. According to the United Nations, gendered violence hampers productivity, reduces human capital, and undermines economic growth. The physical, social, and psychological costs of violence against women, for the women themselves and their children, however, are immeasurable.

Gendered violence is also prevalent in the areas of reproductive health, reproductive rights, and reproductive choice. Globally, gendered violence occurs when women are forcibly sterilized, forced to conceive, used for the testing of contraceptives by pharmaceutical companies, subjected to poor quality or dangerous contraceptives, denied access to contraceptives, denied reproductive health education, denied the means to prevent the transmission of STIs and HIV/AIDS, and/or denied accessible, legal, and safe abortions.

International Measures for Women's Equality: Sexual and Reproductive Rights

The 1994 International Conference on Population and Development (ICPD) in Cairo set the goal of universal global access to sexual and reproductive health services by 2015. The following year, the United Nations Fourth World Conference on Women in Beijing confirmed this goal as a means for gender equality. Without reproductive freedom, including the right to accessible, safe, legal abortion, women will never achieve equality with men.

International conventions confirm the intimate relationship between reproductive rights and women's equality. Remember that equality means equality in value and power. International development policies and programs (international aid and loans) have been implemented to support social, economic, and political development in the Global South. International development ostensibly seeks to eradicate the worst forms of inequality, including

Just the Facts: Violence Against Women

- In the United States, intimate partners are responsible for one-third of the women murdered each year. A woman is raped every six minutes and a woman is battered every fifteen seconds.
- In Canada, 51 per cent of women have experienced at least one incident of physical or sexual violence since the age of sixteen.
- In South Africa, every six hours, a woman is killed by her intimate partner.
- In India, in 2007 alone, twenty-two women were killed each day in dowry-related murders.
- In Guatemala, on average, two women are murdered every day.
- Globally, women and girls account for 80 per cent of the estimated 800,000 people trafficked annually across international borders.
- 79 per cent of women and girls who are trafficked are subjected to sexual exploitation. (UNIFEM 2010)

poverty, homelessness, access to resources, poor health, and the spread of disease, among others. Nonetheless, international policies are trapped in ideological dilemmas. In particular, international development remains stuck in ideological debates about international trade, sustainability, self-determination, the environment, and population growth. These are all important issues; however, we will focus here on population growth.

Overpopulation has long been a concern for the Global North. The problem has been ideologically defined as occurring in the Global South, where populations are commonly young, women tend to have many children, and therefore the potential for population growth is significant. In contrast, populations in the Global North are aging, women tend to have fewer children, and therefore the population is barely growing at all. It is significant to note that this definition of "the problem" of overpopulation pits North against South, reinforcing neocolonial power relations of dominance and control. Recall how epistemology, how we know what we know (chapter 3), and theories (chapters 5 and 6) influence the questions we ask and the answers we get. Not surprisingly, the ways in which concerns about population growth get framed influence the direction of policies and programs.

The most extreme example of population control is the One Child Policy introduced in China in 1979. The implications of the One Child Policy are significantly gendered. The cultural privileging of boys over girls, where families

Missing and Murdered Aboriginal Women and Girls

Research conducted by the Native Women's Association of Canada has documented the disappearances and murders of more than 582 Aboriginal women and girls in Canada. This research, named in solidarity, Sisters in Spirit (SIS), investigates the root causes of violence against Aboriginal women and girls. SIS exposes both the violence—of racism, sexism, economics, and neocolonialism, among others—in the lives of Aboriginal women and girls, and the institutionalized violence embedded in policies, legislation, policing, and systems of support such as healthcare. (Amnesty International 2004; Jiwani and Young 2006; Harper 2006; NWAC 2011)

value a male heir, has resulted in an onslaught of female infanticide and sex-selective abortions. The effects of the policy are now being felt in China, where men vastly outnumber women. For men desiring traditional heterosexual relationships, the demographic imbalances make it difficult. Factors such as education, wealth, and social status advantage some men over others as prospective marriage partners. In India, too, girl children are devalued. In rural areas, where land and resources are key to economic well-being, where property rights pass from fathers to sons, and where married daughters become part of their husbands' families, girl children are seen as unnecessary economic burdens on their families.

Moreover, loans and international aid, necessary for social and economic development in the Global South, are often tied to population control policies. Such conditions exacerbate the privileging of boys over girls in many countries. In an attempt to mask "population control" policies directed at the Global South, notions of "birth control" have been transformed into "family planning" and "fertility control" into "reproductive rights." Accordingly, family planning and reproductive rights can easily be slotted into international development initiatives for women and children's health. However, some key elements are missing from these initiatives. One of the most important is access to safe and legal abortion.

Since 1959, the United States has linked population control to national security. By the mid-1960s, the U.S. had adopted population control policy as a condition for receiving U.S. aid. In 1973, Congress passed the Helms Amendment banning the use of funds from the U.S. Agency for International Development (USAID) for abortion-related activities, which included abortion counselling, information, advocacy, or clinical services. The most well known of U.S. policies, cutting funding for abortion-related activities, is the 1984 Mexico City Policy. This policy denied funding to non-U.S. NGOs engaged directly or indirectly with abortion-related activities. In 1991, Congress attempted to reverse the Mexico City restrictions, but without the two-thirds majority of votes in Congress, which were needed to override then president George Bush Sr.'s veto, the Mexico City Policy remained standing (Locin 1991; Gertzog 2004). It was not until 1993 that then president Clinton rescinded the Mexico City Policy; however, the Helms Amendment remained in force barring USAID for abortion-related activities. Between 1995 and 1999, bitter negotiations over foreign aid funding continued in Congress (Crane and Dusenberry 2004). And in 1999, President Clinton was forced to partially reinstate the Mexico City Policy in exchange for the payment of U.S. arrears to the United Nations (Crane and Dusenberry 2004; Chollet and Orr 2001). Accordingly, U.S. funds could not be used for abortion-related activities. In 2001, the Mexico City Policy was fully reinstated by then president George W. Bush Jr., and again rescinded by President Obama in 2009. In June 2011, Congress passed the Pence Amendment to defund Planned Parenthood, America's largest provider of abortion-related activities, and its affiliate, the International Planned Parenthood Federation, the world's largest global service provider and leading advocate of sexual and reproductive health and rights (Eckholm 2011).

Canada's Conservative government under Prime Minister Stephen Harper has also contributed to the assault on reproductive rights and access to abortion-related activities. As the president of the 2010 G8 Summit, held in Muskoka, Ontario, Canada announced the Muskoka Initiative on Maternal, Newborn and Child Health, its international development initiative in maternal and child health as a means for the G8 to meet the UN Millennium Goal: to improve maternal health by reducing maternal deaths by three-quarters and achieving universal access to sexual and reproductive health care by 2015. Investments in maternal and child health care are necessary, but the failure to include access to abortion-related activities as part of the Canadian initiative means that women's equality and their sexual and reproductive rights continue to be denied globally.

According to the World Health Organization, every year as many as 398,000 women die from complications related to pregnancy and childbirth, which amounts to more than 1,000 women every day (WHO 2012). The majority of these preventable deaths occur in the Global South. An additional 78,000 women die every year as a result of unsafe abortions, or more than 200 women every day. An estimated 20 million unsafe abortions occur each year, which account for 13 per cent of maternal mortality rates (WHO 2008; Center for Reproductive Rights 2003, 2011). According to the Center for Reproductive Rights, 95 per cent of unsafe abortions occur in the Global South, where up to

50 per cent of hospital budgets are diverted to treating "pregnancy complications": the euphemism used to refer to botched abortions. Long-term health problems such as chronic pelvic pain, pelvic inflammatory disease, tubal blockage, infertility, ectopic pregnancy, and poor outcomes in subsequent pregnancies can result from unsafe abortions.

Reproductive Rights Means Reproductive Choice

Reproductive rights are not only a concern in the Global South. They are critical to women in the Global North. It is important to think through the consequences of denying women their reproductive rights. It is also important to recognize that pro-choice does not mean pro-abortion, or that abortion should be used instead of birth control. Pro-choice policies are about ensuring women's rights to choose. A woman can decide that abortion is not something that she would choose for herself, but still be pro-choice and support other women's rights to choose for themselves.

Canadian women's reproductive rights and access to abortion, for the moment, remain intact. Stephen Harper's Conservative government has "promised" not to introduce legislation restricting access to abortion. However, this promise can easily be circumvented through the introduction of a Private Member Bill. This was attempted in 2008 in a proposed amendment to the Criminal Code of Canada. Bill C-484, the Unborn Victims of Crime Act, would have made the injury or death of a fetus a crime. Ostensibly, the bill was intended to protect pregnant women from violence, but the legislation would have granted separate legal status to the fetus. Under Canadian law, the fetus has no legal status and therefore no right to life. If passed, Bill C-484 would have been a step closer to denying women reproductive rights in Canada and recriminalizing abortion. Without majority support in Parliament or in the Senate, the bill failed. With a new Conservative majority elected in 2011, strong anti-abortion forces among them, and the ability of the government to appoint anti-choice representatives to the Senate, access to abortion for Canadian women is under threat.

In the United States abortion is, at the moment, also legal. Since the Supreme Court decision in *Roe v. Wade* in 1973, first trimester abortions have been legal. The decision, however, gave states the authority to restrict access to abortion in the second trimester and to prohibit access during the third trimester. Recall from chapter 2 that prior to *Roe v. Wade*, an estimate of 200,000 to 1.2 million illegal abortions were performed each year in the U.S., causing the deaths of as many as 5,000 to 10,000 women each year. Yet in the current political environment, anti-choice forces are attempting to eradicate a woman's right to choose. The Pence Amendment, to defund Planned Parenthood, was not the first assault. Individual states have also enacted legislation to limit and/ or eliminate access to abortion.

Since 1976, the Hyde Amendment has prohibited the funding of abortion through Medicaid, except in cases where the woman's life was endangered by carrying the pregnancy to term. Additional exceptions were later added to allow funding for abortions in the cases of rape and incest. This means that while abortion is legal in the first trimester, regardless of the reason, poor women are less likely to have access because funding is not available. The result for these women, forced to carry a pregnancy to term, and likely to raise the child, is that their economic status will decline even further. Finances, geography, and age are key factors limiting a woman's right to choose.

Many states have used the provisions in *Roe v. Wade* to deny a woman's right to choose by legislating mandatory waiting periods, mandatory parental consent and involvement, and restrictions on providers. In South Dakota, where there is only one abortion provider, regulations covering abortion are the most onerous in the country. In 2011, South Dakota legislated a seventy-two-hour mandatory waiting period following medical consultation and compulsory screening at a "Pregnancy Help Center." Since 2006, South Dakota has required a twenty-four-hour wait period for first trimester abortions, with an additional requirement that a woman must be given the opportunity to view a sonogram. Her decision to view the sonogram or not is then made part of her permanent medical record. The same legislation banned second and third trimester abortion except in cases where the mother's life was endangered. An amendment was added in 2007, to allow for abortion in cases of rape or incest, provided that the woman reports the rape within fifty days of the crime. Incest survivors must report the crime and reveal the identity of the perpetrators. Planned Parenthood, supported by the American Civil Liberties Union (ACLU), filed suit against the state of South Dakota, in *PPMNS v. State of South Dakota,* arguing that the law infringes on a woman's right to choose by mandating not only attendance at a Pregnancy Help Center but also that doctors discuss all of the so-called risk factors of the procedure, regardless of how questionable, outdated, or refuted by the medical community they may be. In the U.S. District of South Dakota Court ruling, Chief Judge Karen Schreier strongly sided with Planned Parenthood, stating that the process of divulging personal criteria for a woman's decision to undergo an abortion to a stranger at a Pregnancy Help Center is degrading. The process is designed to make the woman feel she has made the "wrong" decision, has not "thought" about her decision, and is "not intelligent enough" to make the decisions with the advice of her doctor. Chief Judge Schreier concluded that Pregnancy Help Centers were hostile environments that violate a woman's right "to avoid unwelcome speech" (U.S. District Court of South Dakota 2011). Such legislation is designed to intimidate and dissuade women from exercising their constitutional right to choose under *Roe v. Wade.* Similar legislation has been introduced in Ohio, Indiana, Georgia, Tennessee, Utah, and Kentucky.

The consequences of reducing access to safe, legal abortion are devastating. Some women try douching with caustic products such as bleach to induce a miscarriage, seriously burning the vaginal area, making treatment both painful and difficult. Yet stories about unsafe abortions continue to surface. In 2006, faced with an unwanted pregnancy, a teenaged couple in Michigan sought information from a "Crisis Pregnancy Center" about legal abortion and state-required parental consent provisions. Armed with misinformation, with his girlfriend's consent, the young man repeatedly hit her abdomen, causing a miscarriage. Similarly, with misinformation from a doctor's office, a teenaged boy in Texas, with his girlfriend's consent, stomped on his girlfriend's stomach, which resulted in the stillbirth of twins. The young man is currently serving a life sentence for fetal homicide. In 2007, in Massachusetts, an eighteen-year-old woman attempted to end an unwanted pregnancy by ingesting an ulcer medication containing Misoprostol. Although Misoprostol is legal in the U.S., she was charged with procuring an improper miscarriage and faces up to seven years in prison and the possibility of being charged with manslaughter (Deeb-Sossa and Kane 2009). The culture wars over abortion have resulted in a slippery slope where pregnant women can be charged with fetal homicide. In thirty-eight states in the U.S., fetal homicide laws have been enacted to protect women and their unborn children from third party attacks, as in the Michigan and Texas cases above. However, the legislation is also increasingly being used to prosecute women who miscarry, have stillbirths, or whose child dies shortly after its birth, as in the Massachusetts case. National Advocates for Pregnant Women estimate that there have been up to 300 women arrested under fetal homicide laws (Di Nicola 2011; Pilkington 2011).

In recent years, attempts have been made to move beyond the abortion debate and towards a concept of reproductive justice. Reproductive justice, as a movement, recognizes that "choice" is always constrained by the social, political, economic, and very personal contexts of women's lives. However, choice is more severely constrained for racialized women, poor women, and women with disabilities. Andrea Smith, for example, argues that in the U.S. the pregnancies of women of colour and poor women are increasingly criminalized. This complicated debate rests in part on the pro-life stance that "because the foetus is a life, abortion should be criminalized" (Smith 2005, 121). Criminalization of abortion, Smith contends, supports the criminalization of other social issues—poverty and race—and places racialized and poor women under greater surveillance. Moreover, criminalization of abortion has not been proven to reduce the number of abortions performed or the desire to have an abortion.

In Canada, the battle for reproductive justice is increasingly played out on university campuses. In recent years, attempts to undermine reproductive rights have increased. Organizations such as the Canadian Centre for Bio-Ethical Reform (CCBR) have infiltrated campuses nationwide with the campaigns

"Echoes of the Holocaust" and the "Genocide Prevention Project," which use graphic imagery to equate abortion with genocide. For those who have had abortions, it equates them unconditionally with Nazis. Furthermore, images are intended to invoke our concerns over racism by comparing abortion to the Holocaust and the lynchings of African Americans in the U.S. South (Kirby 2010). Alarmed by the violence of such anti-choice groups, pro-choice activism has expanded on many university campuses. However, this has diverted resources away from promoting reproductive rights to blocking campus access to anti-choice extremists. It has also shifted the debate away from reproductive rights, women's bodily integrity and choice, to challenging hate speech both on campus and in the courts. Some pro-choice activists also worry that such inflammatory images could be used to incite violence and accelerate legal restrictions on abortion. Indeed, such legislation is already in the works.

In 2008, for example, the Unborn Victims of Crime Act (Bill C-484) was tabled in Parliament to amend the Criminal Code of Canada to allow a separate homicide charge for the fetus when a pregnant woman is attacked. In essence, this bill could give the fetus personhood status under the law. Pro-choice activists argued that the bill was an unconstitutional infringement on women's rights, women's legal access to abortion, and could criminalize pregnant women's behaviour "if perceived as a threat to their fetuses." Also in 2008, the Conservative Party passed Resolution P-207, which made it their policy to support legislation protecting fetal rights (Arthur 2009). Another example is Canada's Conservative government's decision in 2010 not to fund groups that support or provide abortions in developing countries. So, while Canada took the lead on the Muskoka Initiative on Maternal, Newborn and Child Health at the 2010 G8 Summit, contributing $1.1 billion to the Muskoka Initiative as well as renewing previously established funding for similar initiatives for a total of $2.85 billion over five years (Government of Canada 2011), it did so at the expense of women's reproductive rights in the Global South. Many have argued that Canada's policy initiative is hypocritical since it denies women in the South rights available to Canadian women. Yet, as we can see from recent political interventions, Canadian women's reproductive rights also are under siege.

Reproductive Rights beyond the Right to Choose

Reproductive rights go beyond the right to choose when and whether to have children or not. Reproductive rights include access to basic health care, including the prevention, diagnosis, and treatment of HIV/AIDS, sexually transmitted infections (STIs), and infertility.

The global AIDS crisis continues to devastate families, communities, and countries. In 2009, 33.3 million people around the world were living with HIV/AIDS. It is the leading cause of death in sub-Saharan Africa, where 80 per cent of all women in the world with HIV live, and it is the fourth leading cause of death globally (UNAIDS 2010). The transmission of HIV is gendered, particularly since women are disproportionately affected. The feminization of the HIV/AIDS pandemic is rooted in social and economic inequalities. Unequal power relations, unequal access to education, violence, the threat of violence against women, the inability of women to negotiate safer sexual relations, as well as the greater biological vulnerability of women and girls, all place them at a higher risk of infection from the virus and other STIs.

Too often, women and girls have little capacity to negotiate safer sex. Cultural social constructions of femininity as sexually submissive, loyal, and virginal, together with unequal gendered power relations between heterosexual partners, remain strong barriers to using condoms. Women who attempt to negotiate the use of condoms with their partners are often threatened with or experience violence. Men may assume that their female partner has been unfaithful and see the request as an affront to their masculinity or an assault on their "property." The opposite could also be the case. Men may see the negotiation as her accusing him of being unfaithful. In either case, because of gendered power relations, violence can result. Greater efforts to promote universal access to HIV prevention, treatment, and support services for women and girls are necessary. UNAIDS suggests that more must be done to address and eliminate the stigma and discrimination associated with HIV/AIDS. They found in 2010 that 90 per cent of country activity plans included such programs. However, fewer than 50 per cent of those countries budgeted for the costs associated with programs to reduce stigma and discrimination. Furthermore, less than one quarter of country activity plans specifically engaged men who have sex with men, transgender people, IV drug users, sex workers, or prisoners, leaving out many vulnerable populations (UNAIDS 2010). These must be combined with educational programs to engage boys and men in changing their behaviours and understandings of gender inequity, sexual relations, and violence.

Social constructions of masculinity can encourage boys and men to engage in risky behaviours such as excessive alcohol use, multiple and concurrent sexual partnerships, unprotected sex, and drug use. These activities increase the risk of acquiring and transmitting HIV and other STIs. Men who have sex with men continue to bear a high risk of HIV infection, especially in sub-Saharan Africa where homophobia and the criminalization of homosexuality make such sexual activities especially clandestine. In gay communities in the Global North, where HIV awareness and prevention programs have been successful, phenomena such as barebacking, bug chasing, and gift giving have emerged in the HIV subculture. These terms dismiss condom use with claims that "safer sex is not real sex, it's pretend sex" and reconstruct HIV as a desirable subcultural status (Triunfol 2003; Ayling and Mewse 2011; Dean 2011).

Reproductive rights extend beyond prevention and treatment of HIV/ AIDS and STIs; they must include remedies to infertility. *Assistive reproductive technologies* (ARTs) as a response to infertility have gained much support since the birth of the first in vitro fertilization (IVF) baby in 1978. ARTs are methods of conception that involve manipulation of both eggs and sperm. Of all the ARTs, IVF is the most common procedure. The IVF process stimulates egg production through hormone treatments. The ripened eggs are then retrieved from the ovaries and fertilized with the semen in a laboratory. The fertilized embryos are then transferred into the uterus for implantation. ARTs are expensive, averaging from $10,000 to $15,000 for egg retrieval, and upwards of $150,000 in medical costs for a successful delivery. The success rates for IVF are just 25 per cent (Beckman and Harvey 2005). The high costs of ARTs place them beyond the reach of most women in North America. An alternative to ARTs is the much more affordable intrauterine insemination (IUI), often referred to as artificial insemination (AI), which inserts sperm directly into the uterus. This procedure costs from $500 to $2,500. Both IUI and IVF allow for a third-party carrier or surrogate (Beckman and Harvey 2005; Chuck and Yan 2009). This process is rife with legal and ethical concerns.

Of particular concern is the rising interest in international reproductive outsourcing. In 2007 *The New York Times'* article "Birth without the Bother?" drew attention to the possibility of international surrogacy. India was described as an ideal location to "rent-a-womb," especially when compared to costs of doing so in the U.S. (Kristof 2007). The entire process, including airfare, accommodations, surrogate fees, and medical costs could be as low as $25,000 (Baily 2011). In India, where surrogacy is legal, the surrogate fee can be equivalent to ten to fifteen years of income for the carrier (Grinberg 2012). Outsourcing *labour*, whether for production or reproduction, is embedded in unequal power relations, where women's bodies are subjected to exploitation. Contracts between surrogates and "clients" reveal unequal economic status and stark differences in educational levels, particularly with large numbers of illiterate surrogates in the Global South, as well as racial and neocolonial power dynamics. Legal issues around immigration and citizenship status for the newborn may also arise (Banerjee and Basu 2009; Pande 2010; Bailey 2011; Mohammad 2011; Jaiswal 2012).

Conclusions

This chapter gives us a better understanding of how feminist struggles for equality, paid and unpaid work, and reproductive rights as well as the fight to end violence against women are global concerns. These issues were framed by critical feminist thinking. Critical feminist theories have moved us beyond the focus on North American women to more complicated, intersectional, postcolonial, and transnational approaches to social change. These feminisms give us lenses for understanding the interconnectedness of feminists' struggles globally.

Feminist movements offer powerful spaces for women to work in concert with men to bring about social change that will benefit everybody. Feminisms allow us to ask different questions, to look at everything differently, and to find answers in different places. Feminisms are visionary and they are global. Feminisms allow us to imagine a world where sexism, oppression, exploitation, and inequality based on difference have been eradicated. They allow us to see that what happens in one place can affect people in other places. Feminisms encourage us to think through our ideas and our actions, to recognize our positions of privilege, to question how we might effect social change and to make it happen.

Questions for Study

1. What is equality? How is equality defined in feminist terms? How is it defined by the UN? What would it mean for women to be equal to men? Why is equality with men a problematic concept? What are some of the tactics for bringing about greater equality?
2. Global production chains, food chains, and care chains were discussed in this chapter. What are they and how do they work? How does globalization facilitate these global connections between those in the Global North and those in the Global South? How are work experiences gendered in these global chains? How do differences in wages accelerate global movements of goods and people between northern and southern countries/economies? Do these transfers/movements occur in one direction or are they multidirectional? Give examples for each case.
3. What is CEDAW? What are the goals of CEDAW? What are some of its shortcomings?
4. What is gendered violence? What are the multiple types of gendered violence? How is gendered violence raced and sexed? What are the effects of gendered violence? Can men experience gendered violence? Give an example of gendered violence in each of the following places: at work, at school, at home, on the street, in public policy, in law, and in conflict zones.
5. A woman's right to choose has a long history in feminist and women's movement. *Roe v. Wade,* for example, legislated a woman's right to choose in the United States. How has this right been inhibited by political actions and initiatives such as the Mexico City Policy, the Pence Amendment, the Hyde Amendment, and the defunding of Planned Parenthood? What are some of the implications for young women and men who want to terminate a pregnancy in the U.S.? What are the implications for socially and economically marginalized women and men who want to terminate a pregnancy in the U.S.? How is women's

reproductive health affected by these policies and initiatives in the Global South?

6. How do reproductive rights go beyond the right to choose? Do these rights differ based on economic and/or geographic location? Give specific examples.

Activities and Questions for Discussion

1. Many women and men experience sexual harassment on the job. From your own experience, and from talking to a few of your male and female friends, find out what kinds of sexual harassment have occurred. Make a list and discuss the gendered, sexed, raced, and classed aspects of these experiences and discuss them in a small discussion group. How would you theorize these experiences in feminist terms? What theories might you use and why? Make sure you keep all your "sources" anonymous.

2. In Hong Kong, for example, some domestic workers have been required to sleep on a shelf above the washer and dryer or in other inappropriate sleeping spaces. Some have to spend their only half day off in parking garages due to local municipal rulings forbidding them from being in parks and other public spaces. How do these examples make you feel about the outsourcing of mother-work? What challenges does outsourcing present for feminist activists on both sides of the Global North/South divide?

3. How is the violence experienced by Aboriginal women and girls more complicated than simply an issue of sex or patriarchy? For example, why is it that the mainstream media provides little coverage of violence against Aboriginal women and girls? Why is it that the public remains largely unaware of the circumstances of Aboriginal peoples in general, and women and children in particular? What are some activist solutions for getting the word out about the experiences of violence against Aboriginal women and girls?

4. Form an informal group to discuss the following questions: Can you be pro-choice and not pro-abortion? Explain what this might mean? How can choosing *not* to have an abortion still be a pro-choice decision? If you are against abortion for yourself, can you still be pro-choice for others?

5. What has feminism done for you? Reflect on your life at home, at work, in school, and with friends. How has feminism affected you in these various contexts? Are you a feminist? Why or why not?

WORKS CITED AND SUGGESTED READINGS

Introduction

Rich, Adrienne. 1977. *"Claiming an Education." Keynote delivered at the Douglass College Commencement on September 6, 1977. Originally published in the magazine.* The Common Woman.

Chapter 1 Don't Call Me That! Feminism and Other "F-words"

Cook, Sharon Anne. 1995. *"Through Sunshine and Shadow": The Woman's Christian Temperance Union, Evangelicalism, and Reform in Ontario, 1874–1930.* Montreal: McGill-Queen's University Press.
Fastenberg, Dan. 2010. "Five Questions for Several of FORTUNE's 50 Most Powerful Women: Susan Chambers." *Time.com.* November 18. Accessed January 23, 2011. http://www.time.com/time/specials/packages/article/0,28804,2031904_2031902_2031897,00.html.
Hogeland, Lisa. 1994. "Fear of Feminism: Why Young Women Get the Willies." *Ms.* 5 (3): 18–21.
hooks, bell. 2000. *Feminism Is for Everybody: Passionate Politics.* Cambridge, MA: South End Press.
Lorber, Judith. 1994. "The Social Construction of Gender." In *Paradoxes of Gender,* 13–36. New Haven: Yale University Press.
Parker, Alison M. 1997. *Purifying America: Women, Cultural Reform, and Pro-censorship Activism, 1873–1933.* Urbana: University of Illinois Press.
Ruth, Rosen. 2000. "Epilogue: Backlash." In *The World Split Open: How the Modern Women's Movement Changed America,* 331–44. New York: Viking.
Schwartz, Maralee, and Kenneth J. Cooper. 1992. "Equal Rights Initiative in Iowa Attacked." *Washington Post,* August 23, A15.
Valenti, Jessica. 2007. *Full Frontal Feminism: A Young Woman's Guide to Why Feminism Matters.* Berkeley, CA: Seal Press.

Web Sources

Trixie Films. 2006. "Feminism Survey: Men on the Street." Accessed November 6, 2010. http://www.youtube.com/watch?v=3pdbnzFUsXI.

Chapter 2 What's Feminism Done (For Me) Lately? Feminist Contributions

Andersen, Ellen Ann. 2006. *Out of the Closets & Into the Courts: Legal Opportunity Structure and Gay Rights Litigation*. Ann Arbor: University of Michigan Press.

Backhouse, Constance. 1999. *Colour-Coded: A Legal History of Racism in Canada, 1900–1950*. Toronto: University of Toronto Press.

Backhouse, Constance. 2001. *The Historical Construction of Racial Identity and Implications for Reconciliation*. Halifax, NS: Department of Canadian Heritage.

Baumgardener, Jennifer, and Amy Richards. 2010. *Manifesta: Young Women, Feminism, and the Future*. New York: Farrar, Straus and Giroux.

Bear, Shirley. 1991. "You Can't Change the Indian Act?" In *Women and Social Change*, ed. Jerri Wine and Janice Ristock, 198–220. Toronto: James Lorimer and Company Publishers.

Bérubé, Allan. 2003. "The History of Gay Bathhouses." *Journal of Homosexuality* 44 (3): 33–53. http://dx.doi.org/10.1300/J082v44n03_03.

Brownmiller, Susan. 1999. *In Our Time: Memoir of a Revolution*. New York: Dial Press.

Burke, Carol. 2004. *Camp All-American, Hanoi Jane, and the High-and-Tight: Gender, Folklore, and Changing Military Culture*. Boston: Beacon Press.

Burkman, Ronald, et al. 2004. "Safety Concerns and Health Benefits Associated with Oral Contraception." *American Journal of Obstetrics and Gynecology* 4:S4–22.

Canada. Parliament of Canada. 2010. *Debates of the Senate*. 3rd Session, 40th Parliament. 147 No. 8, October 21.

Cates Jr, Williard, et al. 2003. "The Public Health Impact of Legal Abortion: 30 Years Later." *Perspectives on Sexual and Reproductive Health* 35 (1): 25–8. http://dx.doi.org/10.1363/3502503.

C.B.C. Digital Archives. "The Toronto Bathhouse Raids." Accessed April 20, 2012. http://www.cbc.ca/archives/categories/politics/rights-freedoms/gay-and-lesbian-emergence-out-in-canada/the-toronto-bathhouse-raids.html.

The Cherokee Nation v. Georgia. 30 U.S. (5 Pet.) 9 (1831).

Chiefs in Ontario. 2010. "Bill C-3 and the Indigenous Right to Identity." Prepared for the Standing Committee on Aboriginal Affairs and Northern Development. April 20. http://64.26.129.156/misc/CIO.pdf.

Deloria, Vine, and Clifford Lytle. (Original work published 1984) 1998. *The Nations Within: The Past and the Future of American Indian Sovereignty*. Austin: University of Texas Press.

Demhinska-Lemus, Karolina. 2007. "I'm a Happy Feminist." *Off Our Backs* 37 (4): 48–49.

Deutsch, Barry. N.d. "The Male Privilege Checklist." *Alas! A Blog.* Accessed June 13, 2011. http://www.amptoons.com/blog/the-male-privilege-checklist/.

Faludi, Susan. 1991. *Backlash: The Undeclared War on Women*. New York: Crown.

Fox, Mary Jo Tippeconnic, and Sheilah E. Nicholas. 2005. "Beyond Pocahontas, Princes, and Squaw." In *Women's Studies for the Future: Foundations, Interrogations, Politics*, ed. Elizabeth Lapovsky Kennedy and Agatha Beins, 170–81. New Brunswick, NJ: Rutgers University Press.

Friedan, Betty. 1963. *The Feminine Mystique*. New York: W.W. Norton.

Gehl, Lynn. 2000. "'The Queen and I': Discrimination against Women in the Indian Act Continues." *Canadian Woman Studies* 20 (2): 64–9.

Goodman, Adam. 2008. "The Long Wait for Male Birth Control." *Time.com.* August 3. Accessed January 14, 2011. http://www.time.com/time/health/article/0,8599,1829107,00.html.

Green, Joyce. 2001. "Canaries in the Mines of Citizenship: Indian Women in Canada." *Canadian Journal of Political Science* 34 (4): 715–38. http://dx.doi.org/10.1017/S0008423901778067.

Heilbrun, Carolyn. 1995. *The Education of a Woman: Gloria Steinem*. New York: Dial Press.

Hendrick, George, and Willene Hendrick. 2010. *Black Refugees in Canada: Accounts of Escape During the Era of Slavery*. Jefferson, NC: McFarland and Co.

Hillstrom, Laurie Collier. 2008. *Roe v. Wade*. Detroit, MI: Omnigraphics.

Hodgson-Smith, Kathy. 2010. Métis National, *Standing Committee on Aboriginal Affairs and Northern Development Council Standing Committee Hearing*, April 15. http://www.parl.gc.ca/HousePublications/Publication.aspx?DocId=4436471&Language=E#T OC-TS-1700.

Huffington Post. 2011. "North America's Largest Gay Pride Parade Covers Toronto in Colour." July 3. Accessed April 22, 2012. http://www.huffingtonpost.ca/2011/07/03/north-americas-largest-ga_n_889528.html.

Hurley. Mary. 2009. "The Indian Act." PRB 09-12E. Social Affairs Division. Library of Parliament. November 23. http://publications.gc.ca/collections/collection_2009/bdp-lop/prb/prb0912-e.pdf.

Johnson, Erica. 2011. "Cancer Society Spends More on Fundraising Than Research." CBC News. July 6. Accessed April 12, 2012. http://www.cbc.ca/news/canada/story/2011/07/04/cancer-society-funding.html.

Johnson, Kenneth. 1973. "Sovereignty, Citizenship and the Indian." *Arizona Law Review* 15:973–1003.

King, Samantha. 2006. *Pink Ribbons, Inc.: Breast Cancer and the Politics of Philanthropy*. Minneapolis, MN: University of Minnesota Press.

Kinsman, Gary. 2010. "Against National Security: From the Canadian War on Queers to the War on Terror." In *Locating Global Order: American Power and Canadian Security After 9/11*, ed. Wayne S. Cox and Bruno Charbonneau, 149–166. Vancouver: UBC Press.

Kinsman, Gary. 1995. "'Character Weaknesses' and 'Fruit Machines': Towards an Analysis of the Anti-Homosexual Security Campaign in the Canadian Civil Service." *Labour/Le Travail* 35:133–61. http://dx.doi.org/10.2307/25143914.

Landman, Anne. 2008. "Pinkwashing: Can Shopping Cure Breast Cancer?" Center for Media and Democracy. http://www.prwatch.org/node/7436.

Lavell, Jeannette. 2010. *Standing Committee on Aboriginal Affairs and Northern Development Council Standing Committee Hearing*. April 13. http://www.parl.gc.ca/HousePublications/Publication.aspx?DocId=4426989&Language=E.

Lawrence, Bonita. 2003. "Gender, Race, and the Regulation of Native Identity in Canada and the United States: An Overview." *Hypatia* 18 (2): 3–31. http://dx.doi.org/10.1111/j.1527-2001.2003.tb00799.x.

Lloyd-Jones, Donald, R.J. Adams, T.M. Brown, M. Carnethon, S. Dai, G. De Simone, T.B. Ferguson, E. Ford, K. Furie, C. Gillespie, et al., and the WRITING GROUP MEMBERS, and the American Heart Association Statistics Committee and Stroke Statistics Subcommittee. 2010. "Heart Disease and Stroke Statistics—2010 Update: A Report from the American Heart Association." *Circulation* 121 (7): e46–215. http://dx.doi.org/10.1161/CIRCULATIONAHA.109.192667. Medline:20019324

Lubitow, Amy, and Mia Davis. 2011. "Pastel Injustice: The Corporate Use of Pinkwashing for Profit." *Environmental Justice* 4 (2): 139–44. http://dx.doi.org/10.1089/env.2010.0026.

Luxton, Meg. 2001. "Feminism as a Class Act: Working-Class Feminism and the Women's Movement in Canada." *Labour/Le Travail*, 48: 63–88.

Marcello, Patricia Cronin. 2004. *Gloria Steinem: A Biography*. Westport, CT: Greenwood Press.

McIvor, Sharon, and Jacob Grismer. 2010. Represented By Gwen Brodsky. "Communication Submitted For Consideration Under The First Optional Protocol To The International Covenant On Civil And Political Rights Presented before the UN Human Rights Committee in Geneva, Switzerland." November 10. http://www.socialrightscura.ca/documents/legal/mcivor/McIvorPetition.pdf.

McLaren, Angus, and Arlene Tigar McLaren. 1986. *The Bedroom and the State: The Changing Practices and Politics of Contraception and Abortion in Canada, 1880–1980*. Toronto: McClelland and Stewart.

McNeil, Daniel. 2005. "Afro(Americo)centricity in Black (American) Nova Scotia." *Canadian Review of American Studies* 35 (1): 57–85.

Mensah, Joseph. 2010. *Black Canadians: History, Experiences, Social Conditions*. Black Point, NS: Fernwood Publishing.

Morgan, Robin. 1970. *Sisterhood Is Powerful: An Anthology of Writings from the Women's Liberation Movement*. New York: Random House.

Mosca, Lori, et al. 2005. "National Study of Physician Awareness and Adherence to Cardiovascular Disease Prevention Guidelines." *Circulation* III (4): 499–510. http://dx.doi.org/10.1161/01.CIR.0000154568.43333.82. Medline:15687140

Moss, Wendy. 1990. "Indigenous Self-Government in Canada and Sexual Equality Under the Indian Act: Resolving Conflicts Between Collective and Individual Rights." *Queen's Law Journal* 15:279–306.

National Cancer Institute. "Fact Sheet: Oral Contraceptives and Cancer Risk." http://www.cancer.gov/cancertopics/factsheet/Risk/oral-contraceptives.

NWAC (Native Women's Association of Canada). 2012. "Shadow Report." United Nations Committee on the Elimination of Racial Discrimination. 80th Session. February 13 – March 9. Geneva. Accessed January 30, 2012. http://www.nwac.ca/sites/default/files/imce/CERD%20-%20NWAC%20Submission%20-%20Final_0.pdf.

Pool, Léa. 2011. *Pink Ribbons Inc*. [film] Montreal: National Film Board of Canada.

Pope, J. Hector, Tom P. Aufderheide, Robin Ruthazer, Robert H. Woolard, James A. Feldman, Joni R. Beshansky, John L. Griffith, and Harry P. Selker. 2000. "Missed Diagnoses of Acute Cardiac Ischemia in the Emergency Department." *New England Journal of Medicine* 342 (16): 1163–70. http://dx.doi.org/10.1056/NEJM200004203421603. Medline:10770981

Rebick, Judy. 2005. *Ten Thousand Roses: The Making of a Feminist Revolution*. Toronto: Penguin Canada.

Redstockings. 2005. "Redstockings Manifesto." In *Feminist Theory: A Reader*, ed. Wendy Kolmar and Frances Bartkowski, 220–21. Boston: McGraw-Hill Higher Education.

Roy, Arundhati. 2001. *Power Politics*. Cambridge, MA: South End Press.

Sethna, Christabelle, and Steve Hewitt. 2009. "Clandestine Operations: The Vancouver Women's Caucus, the Abortion Caravan, and the RCMP." *Canadian Historical Review* 90 (3): 465–95. http://dx.doi.org/10.3138/chr.90.3.463.

Smith, Malinda. 2008. "'How Long, Not Long': Local and Global Anti-racism Struggles." *Ardent* 1 (1): 8–22.

Smith, Miriam. 2009. *Political Institutions and Lesbian and Gay Rights in the United States and Canada*. New York: Routledge.

Steinem, Gloria. 1983. *Outrageous Acts and Everyday Rebellions*. New York: Holt, Rinehart, and Winston.

Steinem, Gloria. 1963. "A Bunny's Tale." Reprinted as "I Was a Playboy Bunny." Accessed April 21, 2012. http://www.gloriasteinem.com/storage/I%20Was%20a%20 Playboy%20Bunny.pdf.

Thomas, Nicki. 2011. "Thirty Years after the Bathhouse Raids." *Toronto Star*. February 4. Accessed April 20, 2012. http://www.thestar.com/news/ article/933821–thirty-years-after-the-.

Turner, Jeffrey. 2010. *Sitting In and Speaking Out: Student Movements in the American South, 1960–1970*. Athens: University of Georgia Press.

Two-Axe Early, Mary. 1994. "Indian Rights for Indian Women." In *Women, Feminism, and Development*, ed. Huguette Dagenais and Denise Piché, 429–33. Montreal: McGill-Queen's University Press.

Walker, Barrington. 2008. *The History of Immigration and Racism in Canada: Essential Readings*. Toronto: Canadian Scholars' Press.

Wallis, Maria A., Lina Sunseri, and Grace-Edward Galabuzi. 2010. *Colonialism and Racism in Canada: Historical Traces and Contemporary Issues*. Toronto: Nelson Education.

Walters, Ronald. 1996. ""The Great Plains Sit-In Movement, 1958–60." *Great Plains Quarterly*. Paper 1093:85–94.

Ward, Churchill, and Jim Vander Wall. 1988. *Agents of Repression: The FBI's Secret Wars against the Black Panther Party*. Boston: South End Press.

Winks, Robin. 1997. *The Blacks in Canada*. Montreal: McGill-Queen's University Press.

Wolfley, Jeanette. 1991. "Jim Crow, Indian Style: The Disenfranchisement of Native Americans." *American Indian Law Review* 16 (1): 167–202. http://dx.doi .org/10.2307/20068694.

Worcester v. Georgia, 31 U.S. (6 Pet.) 515, 561 (1832).

Web Sources

The National Coalition for Women with Heart Disease. http://www.womenheart.org.

Harvard Medical School. "Harvard Women's Health Watch." http://www.health .harvard.edu/newsletters/Harvard_Womens_Health_Watch.

Ms. Foundation for Women. http://ms.foundation.org/.

National Coalition for Women with Heart Disease. http://womenheart.org/.

National Organization of Women (NOW). http://www.now.org/.

Chapter 3 How Do I know What I Know? Epistemology and Theory

Alcoff, Linda, ed. 1998. *Epistemology: The Big Questions*. Malden, MA: Blackwell Publishers.

Alcoff, Linda. 1988. "Cultural Feminism versus Post-Structuralism: The Identity Crisis in Feminist Theory." *Signs* 13 (3): 405–36. http://dx.doi.org/10.1086/494426.

Dyer-Witheford, Nick, and Greig de Peuter. 2009. "Empire@Play: Virtual Games and Global Captitalism." *ctheory.net*. Accessed January 5, 2011. http://www.ctheory.net/ articles.aspx?id=608.

Fausto-Sterling, Anne. 1981. "The Myth of Neutrality: Race, Sex and Class in Science." *Radical Teacher* 19: 21–25.

Fine, Cordelia. 2010. *Delusions of Gender: How Our Minds, Society, and Neurosexism Create Difference*. New York,: W.W. Norton.

Gould, Lois. December 1978. "X: A Fabulous Child's Story." *Ms.* 1 (6).

Harding, Sandra. 2006. *Science and Social Inequality: Feminist and Postcolonial Issues*. Urbana: University of Illinois Press.

Harding, Sandra, ed. 2004. *The Feminist Standpoint Theory Reader*. New York: Routledge.

Harding, Sandra. 1987. "Conclusion: Epistemological Questions." In *Feminism & Methodology*, ed. Sandra Harding, 181–90. Bloomington: Indiana University Press.

Harding, Sandra. 1986. "The Instability of the Analytic Categories of Feminist Theory." *Signs* 11 (4): 645–64. http://dx.doi.org/10.1086/494270.

Hartsock, Nancy. 1987. "The Feminist Standpoint: Developing the Ground for a Specifically Feminist Historical Materialism." In *Feminism & Methodology*, ed. Sandra Harding, 157–80. Bloomington: Indiana University Press. http://dx.doi .org/10.1007/0-306-48017-4_15.

Howard, Ella. 2010. "Pink Truck Ads: Second-Wave Feminism and Gendered Marketing." *Journal of Women's History* 22 (4): 137–61. Medline:21174889

Naples, Nancy. 2003. "Standpoint Epistemology: Explicating Multiple Dimensions." In *Feminism and Method: Ethnography, Discourse Analysis, and Activist Research*, 67–86. New York: Routledge.

Steinem, Gloria. 1970. "'Women's Liberation' Aims to Free Men, Too." *The Washington Post*. June 7. Accessed April 15, 2012. http://library.duke.edu/rubenstein/scriptorium/ wlm/aims/.

Valenti, Jessica. 2008. *He's a Stud, She's a Slut and 49 Other Double Standards Every Woman Should Know*. Berkeley, CA: Seal Press.

Chapter 4 Making My Head Spin: Critical Intersectionality

Ahmed, Sara. 1998. *Differences That Matter*. Cambridge: Cambridge University Press. http://dx.doi.org/10.1017/CBO9780511489389.

Alcoff, Linda. 2006. *Visible Identities: Race, Gender, and the Self*. New York: Oxford University Press.

Alcoff, Linda. 1995. "The Problem of Speaking for Others." In *Who Can Speak: Authority and Critical Identity*, ed. Judith Roof and Robyn Wiegman, 97–120. Champaign: University of Illinois Press.

Alcoff, Linda. 1988. "Cultural Feminism Versus Post-Structuralism: The Identity Crisis in Feminist Theory." *Signs* 13 (3): 405–36.

Anzaldúa, Gloria. 1987. *Borderlands: La Frontera*. San Francisco: Aunt Lute Book Company.

Bacchetta, Paola, et al. 2001. "Transnational Feminist Practices Against War." *Meridians: Feminism, Race, Transnationalism* 2 (2): 302–8.

Barrett, Michèle, and Anne Phillips, eds. 1992. *Destabilizing Theory: Contemporary Feminist Debates*. Cambridge, MA: Polity Press.

Bertrand, M., and S. Mullainathan. 2004. "Are Emily and Greg More Employable than Lakisha and Jamal? A Field Experiment on Labor Market Discrimination." *American Economic Review* 94 (4): 991–1013. http://dx.doi.org/10.1257/0002828042002561.

Braidotti, Rosi. (Original work published 1994) 2011. *Nomadic Subjects: Embodiment and Sexual Difference in Contemporary Feminist Theory*. New York: Columbia University Press.

Butler, Judith. 1988. "Performative Acts and Gender Constitution: An Essay in Phenomenology and Feminist Theory." *Theatre Journal* 40 (4): 519–31. http://dx.doi .org/10.2307/3207893.

Chicago Women's Liberation Union. 1971. *How To Start Your Own Consciousness-Raising Group.* Accessed April 27, 2012. http://uic.edu/orgs/cwluherstory/CWLUArchive/crcwlu.html.

Collins, Patricia Hill. 1993. "Towards a New Vision: Race, Class, and Gender as Categories of Analysis and Connection." *Race, Sex, and Class* 1 (1): 25–45.

Collins, Patricia Hill. 1990. *Black Feminist Thought.* Boston: Unwin Hyman.

Collins, Patricia Hill. 1986. "Learning from the Outsider Within: The Sociological Significance of Black Feminist Thought." *Social Problems* 33 (6): S14–32. http://dx.doi.org/10.1525/sp.1986.33.6.03a00020.

The Combahee River Collective. (Original work published 1977) 2010. "A Black Feminist Statement." In *Feminist Theory Reader: Local and Global Perspectives*, ed. Carole McCann and Kim Seung-kyung, 106–112. New York: Routledge.

Crenshaw, Kimberlé. 1989. "Demarginalizing the Intersection of Race and Sex: A Black Feminist Critique of Antidiscrimination Doctrine, Feminist Theory and Antiracist Politics." *University of Chicago Legal Forum.* 139–67.

Cudd, Ann, and Nancy Holmstrom, eds. 2011. *Capitalism, For and Against: A Feminist Debate.* Cambridge: Cambridge University Press.

Driefus, Claudia. 1973. *Woman's Fate: Raps from a Feminist Consciousness-Raising Group.* New York: Bantam.

Fausto-Sterling, Anne. 1993. "The Five Sexes: Why Male and Female Are Not Enough." *Sciences* (March/April): 20–4. http://www.uta.edu/english/timothyr/Fausto-Sterling.pdf.

Fausto-Sterling, Anne. 1981. "The Myth of Neutrality: Race, Sex and Class in Science." *Radical Teacher* 19:21.

Firestone, Shulamith. 1970. *The Dialectic of Sex: The Case for Feminist Revolution.* New York: Morrow.

Freire, Paulo. 1970. *Pedagogy of the Oppressed.* New York: Herder and Herder.

Fulcher, James. 2004. *Capitalism: A Very Short Introduction.* New York: Oxford University Press.

Givhan, Robin. 2009. "Blond? Check. Well-dressed? Check. Right 'Look' Let Salahis into White House." *Ottawa Citizen*, December 8, C9.

Grewal, Inderpal, and Caren Kaplan, eds. 1994. *Scattered Hegemonies: Postmodernity and Transnational Feminist Practices.* Minneapolis: University of Minnesota Press.

Grosz, Elizabeth. 1987. "Feminist Theory and the Challenge to Knowledges." *Women's Studies International Forum* 10 (5): 475–80. http://dx.doi.org/10.1016/0277-5395(87)90001-X.

Haraway, Donna. 1988. "Situated Knowledges: The Science Question in Feminism and the Privilege of Partial Perspectives." *Feminist Studies* 14 (3): 575–99. http://dx.doi.org/10.2307/3178066.

Harding, Sandra. 1989. "Is There A Feminist Method?" In *Feminism & Science*, ed. Nancy Tuana, 17–32. Bloomington: Indiana University Press.

Harding, Sandra. 1986. "The Instability of the Analytic Categories of Feminist Theory." *Signs* 11 (4): 645–64.

Hernández, Daisy, and Bushra Rehman, eds. 2002. *Colonize This! Young Women of Color on Today's Feminism.* New York: Seal Press.

hooks, bell. 2000. *Feminism Is for Everybody: Passionate Politics.* Cambridge, MA: South End Press.

hooks, bell. 1984. *Feminist Theory: From Margin to Center.* Boston: South End Press.

Irigaray, Luce. 1985. *This Sex Which Is Not One.* Ithaca, NY: Cornell University Press.

Jones, Deborah. 1980. "Gossip: Notes on Women's Oral Culture." *Women's Studies International Quarterly* 3 (2–3): 193–8. http://dx.doi.org/10.1016/S0148-0685(80)92155-7.

Keller, Evelyn Fox. 1987. "The Gender/Science System: Or, Is Sex to Gender as Nature Is to Science?" *Hypatia* 2 (3): 37–49. http://dx.doi.org/10.1111/j.1527-2001.1987.tb01340.x.

Keohane, Robert. 1989. "International Relations Theory: Contributions of a Feminist Standpoint." *Millennium: Journal of International Studies* 18 (2): 245–53. http://dx.doi.org/10.1177/03058298890180021001.

Kivisto, Peter, and Elizabeth Hartung. 2007. *Intersecting Inequalities: Class, Race, Sex, and Sexualities*. Upper Saddle River, NJ: Pearson Prentice Hall.

Koedt, Anne, Ellen Levine, and Anita Rapone. 1973. *Radical Feminism*. New York: Quadrangle Books.

Krishna, Sankaran. 2009. *Globalization and Postcolonialism: Hegemony and Resistance in the Twenty-First Century*. Lanham, MD: Rowman and Littlefield Publishers.

Langston, Donna. 1988. "Tired Of Playing Monopoly?" In *Changing Our Power*, ed. Jo Whitehorse Cochran, et al. Dubuque, IA: Kendall Hunt.

Linklater, Andrew. 1992. "The Question of the Next Stage in International Relations Theory: A Critical Theoretical Point of View." *Millennium: Journal of International Studies* 21 (1): 77–98. http://dx.doi.org/10.1177/03058298920210010601.

Loomba, Ania. 2005. *Colonialism/Postcolonialism*. London: Routledge.

Lorde, Audre. 1984. "Age, Race, Class, and Sex." In *Sister Outsider: Essays and Speeches*, 114–23. Trumansburg, NY: Crossing Press.

Lorde, Audre. 1984. "The Master's Tools Will Never Dismantle the Master's House." In *Sister Outsider: Essays and Speeches*, 110–13. Trumansburg, NY: Crossing Press.

Margolis, Diane Rothbard. 1985. "Redefining the Situation: Negotiations on the Meaning of 'Woman'." *Social Problems* 32 (4): 332–47. http://dx.doi.org/10.1525/sp.1985.32.4.03a00030.

McClintock, Anne. 1995. *Imperial Leather: Race, Gender, and Sexuality in the Colonial Contest*. New York: Routledge.

McIntosh, Peggy. 1989. "White Privilege: Unpacking the Invisible Knapsack." *Peace and Freedom*, n.p. Accessed March 2012. http://www.library.wisc.edu/edvrc/docs/public/pdfs/LIReadings/InvisibleKnapsack.pdf.

Miller, Chris. 1996. *The Dissident Word*. New York: Basic Books.

Millett, Kate. 1970. *Sexual Politics*. Garden City, NY: Doubleday.

Misra, Joya. 2000. "Gender and the World System: Engaging Feminist Literature on Development." In *A World-Systems Reader: New Perspectives on Gender, Urbanism, Cultures, Indigenous Peoples and Ecology*, ed. Thomas D. Hall, 105–127. Lanham, MD: Rowman and Littlefield Publishers.

Mohanty, Chandra Talpade. 2002. "'Under Western Eyes' Revisited: Feminist Solidarity through Anticapitalist Struggles." *Signs* 28 (2): 499–535. http://dx.doi.org/10.1086/342914.

Mohanty, Chandra Talpade. 1995. "Feminist Encounters: Locating the Politics of Experience." In *Social Postmodernism: Beyond Identity Politics*, ed. Linda J. Nicholson and Steven Seidman, 68–86. New York: Cambridge University Press. http://dx.doi.org/10.1017/CBO9780511520792.004.

Mohanty, Chandra Talpade. 1984. "Under Western Eyes: Feminist Scholarship and Colonial Discourses." *Boundary 2* 12 (3): 333–58. http://dx.doi.org/10.2307/302821.

Moraga, Cherríe. 1983. "La Guerra." In *This Bridge Called My Back: Writings by Radical Women of Color*, ed. Cherríe Moraga and Gloria Anzaldúa, 27–34. New York: Kitchen Table Press.

Morgan, Robin. 1970. *Sisterhood Is Powerful: An Anthology of Writings from the Women's Liberation Movement.* New York: Random House.

NARAL. The Safety of Legal Abortion and the Hazards of Illegal Abortion. See footnote # 35. http://www.prochoiceamerica.org/media/fact-sheets/abortion-distorting-science-safety-legal-abortion.pdf.

Narayan, Uma. 2002. "Minds of Their Own: Choices, Autonomy, Cultural Practices, and Other Women." In *A Mind of One's Own: Feminist Essays on Reason and Objectivity*, ed. Louise Antony and Charlotte Witt, 418–431. Boulder, CO: Westview Press.

Narayan, Uma. 1988. "Working Together across Difference: Some Considerations on Emotions and Political Practice." *Hypatia* 3 (2): 31–47. http://dx.doi.org/10.1111/j.1527-2001.1988.tb00067.x.

O'Brien, Mary. 1981. "Feminist Theory and Dialectical Logic." *Signs* 7 (1): 144–57. http://dx.doi.org/10.1086/493866.

Oreopoulos, Philip. 2009. *Why Do Skilled Immigrants Struggle in the Labor Market? A Field Experiment with Six Thousand Résumés.* Vancouver: National Bureau of Economic Research, Canadian Institute for Advanced Research, University of British Columbia. http://dx.doi.org/10.3386/w15036.

Redstockings. (Original work published 1969) 2005. "Redstockings Manifesto." In *Feminist Theory: A Reader*, ed. Wendy Kolmar and Frances Bartkowski, 220-21. Boston: McGraw-Hill Higher Education.

Rowlands, Jo. 1995. "Empowerment Examined." *Development in Practice* 5 (2): 101–7. http://dx.doi.org/10.1080/0961452951000157074.

Sarachild, Kathie. 1978. "Consciousness-Raising: A Radical Weapon." In *Feminist Revolution*, 144–50. New York: Random House. Accessed February 10, 2011. http://library.duke.edu/rubenstein/scriptorium/wlm/fem/sarachild.html.

Shaw, Susan M., and Janet Lee, eds. 2004. "Intersecting Axes of Privilege, Domination, and Oppression." In *Women's Voices, Feminist Visions: Classic and Contemporary Readings*. 2nd ed. Oregon: Oregon State University.

Shohat, Ella. 2001. "Area Studies, Transnationalism, and the Feminist Production of Knowledge." *Signs* 26 (4): 1269–72. http://dx.doi.org/10.1086/495659.

Smith, Dorothy. 1987. *The Everyday World As Problematic: A Feminist Sociology.* Boston: Northeastern University Press.

Sowards, Stacey, and Valerie Renegar. 2004. "The Rhetorical Functions of Consciousness-Raising in Third Wave Feminism." *Communication Studies* 55 (4): 535–52. http://dx.doi.org/10.1080/10510970409388637.

Spelman, Elizabeth. 1988. *Inessential Woman: Problems of Exclusion in Feminist Thought.* Boston: Beacon Press.

Spivak, Gayatri. 1988. "Can the Subaltern Speak?" In *Marxism and the Interpretation of Culture*, ed. C. Nelson and L. Grossberg, 198–222. Urbana: University of Illinois Press.

Stacey, Judith, and Barrie Thorne. 1985. "The Missing Feminist Revolution in Sociology." *Social Problems* 32 (4): 301–16. http://dx.doi.org/10.1525/sp.1985.32.4.03a00010.

Sylvester, Christine. 1994. "Empathetic Cooperation: A Feminist Method for IR." *Millennium: Journal of International Studies* 23 (2): 315–34. http://dx.doi.org/10.1177/03058298940230021301.

Tickner, Ann. 1993. *Gender in International Relations.* New York: Columbia University Press.

Tickner, Ann. 1988. "Hans Morgenthau's Principles of Political Realism: A Feminist Reformulation." *Millennium: Journal of International Studies* 17 (3): 429–40. http://dx.doi.org/10.1177/03058298880170030801.

Walker, R.B.J. 1992. *Inside/Outside: International Relations as Political Theory*. Cambridge: Cambridge University Press. http://dx.doi.org/10.1017/CBO9780511559150.

Wendell, Susan. 1996. "The Social Construction of Disability." In *The Rejected Body: Feminist Philosophical Reflections on Disability*, 35–56. New York: Routledge.

Zinn, Maxine, and Bonnie Thornton Dill. 1996. "Theorizing Difference from Multiracial Feminism." *Feminist Studies* 22 (2): 321–31. http://dx.doi.org/10.2307/3178416.

Chapter 5 So Many Details and So Much Reading: Feminist Theories

Acker, Joan. 1990. "A Theory of Gendered Organizations." *Gender & Society* 4 (2): 139–58. http://dx.doi.org/10.1177/089124390004002002.

Alcoff, Linda. 1988. "Cultural Feminism Versus Post-Structuralism: The Identity Crisis in Feminist Theory." *Signs* 13 (3): 405–36. http://dx.doi.org/10.1086/494426.

Alcoff, Linda, and Eva Feder Kittay, eds. 2007. *The Blackwell Guide to Feminist Philosophy*. Malden, MA: Blackwell Publishing.

Amott, Teresa, and Julie Matthaei. 1996. *Race, Gender, and Work: A Multi-Cultural Economic History of Women in the United States*. Boston: South End Press.

Armstrong, Pat, and Hugh Armstrong. 1983. "Beyond Sexless Class and Classless Sex: Towards Feminist Marxism." *Studies in Political Economy* 10:7–43.

Armstrong, Pat, and Hugh Armstrong. 1978. *The Double Ghetto: Canadian Women and Their Segregated Work*. Toronto: McClelland and Stewart.

Bacchi, Carol Lee. 1983. *Liberation Deferred? The Ideas of the English-Canadian Suffragists, 1877–1918*. Toronto: University of Toronto Press.

Backhouse, Constance. 1988. "Married Women's Property Law in Nineteenth-Century Canada." *Law and History Review* 6 (2): 211–57. http://dx.doi.org/10.2307/743684.

Bannerji, Himani. 2001. *The Dark Side of the Nation: Essays on Multiculturalism, Nationalism and Gender*. Toronto: University of Toronto Press.

Bannerji, Himani. 1995. *Thinking Through: Essays on Feminism, Marxism and Anti-Racism*. Toronto: Women's Press.

Bannerji, Himani. 1993. *Returning the Gaze: Essays on Racism, Feminism and Politics*. Toronto: Sister Vision.

Bedford v. Canada. 2010. ONSC4264, 07-CV-329807 PDI, September 28, 2010. Accessed January 20, 2011. http://www.cbc.ca/news/pdf/bedford-ruling.pdf.

Benston, Margaret. (Original work published 1969) 1984. "The Political Economy of Women's Liberation." In *Feminist Frameworks: Alternative Theoretical Accounts of the Relations Between Women And Men*, ed. Alison M. Jaggar and Paula Rothenberg Struhl. New York: McGraw-Hill.

Black Women's Blueprint. 2011. "An Open Letter from Black Women to the SlutWalk." Accessed October 14, 2011. http://www.blackwomensblueprint.org/2011/09/23/an-open-letter-from-black-women-to-the-slutwalk/.

Blumberg, Rae Lesser. 1984. "A General Theory of Gender Stratification." *Sociological Theory* 2:23–101. http://dx.doi.org/10.2307/223343.

Blumberg, Rae Lesser. 1978. *Stratification: Socioeconomic and Sexual Inequality*. Dubuque, IA: William Brown.

Brand, Dionne. 1999. "The Impact of Racially Constructed Roles on the Sexual Division of Labour." In *Scratching the Surface: Canadian Anti-racist Feminist Thought*, ed. Enakshi Dua and Angela Robertson, 83–96. Toronto: Women's Press.

Bunch, Charlotte. 1979. "Not by Degrees: Feminist Theory and Education." In *Feminist Theory: A Reader*, ed. Wendy Kolmar and Frances Bartkowski, 12–15. New York: McGraw-Hill.

Calliste, Agnes, and George Dei. 2000. *Anti-Racist Feminism: Critical Race and Gender Studies*. Halifax: Fernwood.

Carby, Hazel. 2000. "White Women Listen! Black Feminism and the Boundaries of Sisterhood." In *Theories of Race and Racism: A Reader*, ed. Les Back and John Solomos, 389–403. New York: Routledge.

Chambers, Lori. 1997. *Married Women and Property Law in Victorian Ontario*. Toronto: University of Toronto Press.

Clinton, Catherine. 2004. *Harriet Tubman: The Road to Freedom*. Boston: Little, Brown.

Collins, Patricia Hill. 2004. *Black Sexual Politics: African Americans, Gender, and the New Racism*. New York: Routledge. http://dx.doi.org/10.4324/9780203309506.

Collins, Patricia Hill. 2001. "Towards a New Vision: Race, Class, and Gender as Categories of Analysis and Connection." In *Women's Voices, Feminist Visions: Classic and Contemporary Readings*, ed. Susan Shaw, 72–79. Houston, TX: Mayfield Publishing.

Collins, Patricia Hill. 2000. *Black Feminist Thought*. New York: Routledge.

Collins, Patricia Hill. 1993. "Towards a New Vision: Race, Class, and Gender as Categories of Analysis and Connection." *Race, Sex, and Class* 1 (1): 25–45.

Collins, Patricia Hill. 1990. *Black Feminist Thought: Knowledge, Consciousness, and the Politics of Empowerment*. Boston: Unwin Hyman.

Crenshaw, Kimberlé. 1989. "Demarginalizing the Intersection of Race and Sex: A Black Feminist Critique of Antidiscrimination Doctrine, Feminist Theory and Antiracist Politics." *University of Chicago Legal Forum* 1989: 139–67.

Daly, Mary. 1978. *Gyn/Ecology: the Metaethics of Radical Feminism*. Boston: Beacon.

Doe, Jane. 2005. *The Story of Jane Doe: A Book About Rape*. Toronto: Random House Canada.

Dua, Enakshi, and Angela Robertson, eds. 1999. *Scratching The Surface: Canadian Anti-Racist, Feminist Thought*. Toronto: Women's Press.

Dworkin, Andrea. 1992. "Prostitution and Male Supremacy." *Michigan Journal of Gender & Law* 2:1–12.

Dworkin, Andrea. 1981. *Pornography: Men Possessing Women*. New York: Putnam.

Eastman, Crystal. 1978. *Crystal Eastman on Women and Revolution*, ed. Blanche Wiesen Cook. New York: Oxford University Press.

Eisenstein, Zillah. 1978. *Capitalist Patriarchy and the Case for Socialist Feminism*. New York: Monthly Review Press.

Flexner, Eleanor, and Ellen Fitzpatrick. 1996. *Century of Struggle: the Woman's Rights Movement in the United States*. Cambridge, MA: Belknap Press of Harvard University Press.

Fox, Bonnie, ed. 1980. *Hidden in the Household: Women's Domestic Labour under Capitalism*. Toronto: Women's Press.

Fox, Bonnie, and John Fox. 1986. "Women in the Labour Market, 1931–81: Exclusion and Competition." *Canadian Review of Sociology* 23 (1): 1–21. http://dx.doi.org/10.1111/j.1755-618X.1986.tb00393.x.

Gilman, Charlotte Perkins. (Original work published 1898) 1966. *Women and Economics*. New York: Harper and Row.

Goldman, Emma. 1969. *Anarchism, and Other Essays*. New York: Dover Publications.

Gore, Dayo. 2011. *Radicalism at the Crossroads: African American Women Activists in the Cold War*. New York: New York University Press.

Harding, Sandra. 1986. *The Science Question in Feminism*. Ithaca, NY: Cornell University Press.

Hartmann, Heidi. 1976. "Capitalism, Patriarchy, and Job Segregation by Sex." *Signs* 1 (3): 137–69. http://dx.doi.org/10.1086/493283.

Hartmann, Heidi. (Original work published 1981) 2005. "The Unhappy Marriage of Marxism and Feminism: Towards a More Progressive Union." In *Feminist Theory: A Reader*, ed. Wendy Kolmar and Frances Bartkowski. New York: McGraw-Hill. http://dx.doi.org/10.1177/030981687900800102.

Hendrick, George, and Willene Hendrick. 2010. *Black Refugees in Canada: Accounts of Escape During the Era of Slavery*. Jefferson, NC: McFarland and Co.

Hochschild, Arlie, and Anne Machung. 1989. *The Second Shift: Working Parents and the Revolution at Home*. New York: Viking Press.

hooks, bell. 2004. *We Real Cool: Black Men and Masculinity*. New York: Routledge.

hooks, bell. 1991–1992. "Theory as Liberatory Practice." *Yale Journal of Law and Feminism* 4 (1): 1–12.

hooks, bell. 1990. *Yearning: Race, Gender, and Cultural Politics*. Toronto: Between the Lines.

hooks, bell. 1984. *Feminist Theory: From Margin to Center*. Boston: South End Press.

James, Selma, and Mariarosa Dalla Costa. 1972. *The Power of Women and the Subversion of Community*. Bristol, UK: Falling Wall Press.

Jewell, K. Sue. 1993. *From Mammy To Miss America and Beyond: Cultural Images and the Shaping of US Social Policy*. Ferris State University. Accessed May 3, 2012. Museum of Racist Memorabilia. Big Rapids, MI. http://www.ferris.edu/jimcrow/sapphire/.

Jiwani, Yasmine, et al. 2001. *Erased Realities: The Violence of Racism in the Lives of Immigrant and Refugee Girls of Colour*. Vancouver: FREDA Centre for Research on Violence Against Women & Children.

Jones, Mary. 1983. *Mother Jones Speaks: Collected Writings and Speeches*, ed. Philip Foner. New York: Monad Press.

Karaian, Lara. 2005. "Troubling the Definition of Pornography: Little Sisters, a New Defining Moment in Feminists' Engagement with the Law?" *Canadian Journal of Women and the Law* 17 (1): 117–33. http://dx.doi.org/10.1353/jwl.2006.0011.

Kolmar, Wendy, and Frances Bartkowski, eds. 2010. *Feminist Theory: A Reader*. Boston: McGraw-Hill Higher Education.

Ladd-Taylor, Molly, and Lauri Umansky. 1998. *"Bad" Mothers: The Politics of Blame in Twentieth-Century America*. New York: New York University Press.

Lee, Taeku. 2002. *Mobilizing Public Opinion: Black Insurgency and Racial Attitudes in the Civil Rights Era*. Chicago: University of Chicago Press.

Lorde, Audre. 1984. *Sister Outsider: Essays and Speeches*. Trumansburg, NY: Crossing Press.

MacKinnon, Catharine. 1993. "Prostitution and Civil Rights." *Michigan Journal of Gender & Law* 1:13–31. http://www.prostitutionresearch.com/mackinnon1.html.

MacKinnon, Catharine. 1989. *Toward a Feminist Theory of the State*. Cambridge, MA: Harvard University Press.

MacKinnon, Catharine, and Andrea Dworkin, eds. 1997. *In Harm's Way: The Pornography Civil Rights Hearings*. Cambridge, MA: Harvard University Press.

MacKinnon, Catharine, and Andrea Dworkin. 1988. *Pornography and Civil Rights: A New Day for Women's Equality*. Minneapolis, MN: Organizing Against Pornography.

Mann, Susan. 2012. *Doing Feminist Theory: From Modernity to Postmodernity*. New York: Oxford University Press.

Massaquoi, Notisha, and Njoki Wane, eds. 2007. *Theorizing Empowerment: Canadian Perspectives on Black Feminist Thought*. Toronto: Inanna Publications and Education.

Millar, Sarah. 2011. "Police Officer's Remarks at York Inspire 'SlutWalk.'" Accessed March 30, 2011. http://www.thestar.com/news/article/955682–police-officer-s-remarks-at-york-inspire-slutwalk.

Mohanty, Chandra Talpade. 2002. "'Under Western Eyes' Revisited: Feminist Solidarity through Anticapitalist Struggles." *Signs* 28 (2): 499–535. http://dx.doi.org/10.1086/342914.

Mohanty, Chandra Talpade. 1984. "Under Western Eyes: Feminist Scholarship and Colonial Discourses." *Boundary* 2 12 (3): 333–58. http://dx.doi.org/10.2307/302821.

Moraga, Cherríe. 1981. "La Guera." In *This Bridge Called My Back: Writings by Radical Women of Color*, ed. Cherríe Moraga and Gloria Anzaldúa, 27–34. New York: Kitchen Table, Women of Color Press.

Moraga, Cherríe, and Gloria Anzaldúa. (Original work published 1981) 1983. *This Bridge Called My Back: Writings by Radical Women of Color*. New York: Kitchen Table, Women of Color Press.

Morgan, Robin. 1970. *Sisterhood Is Powerful: An Anthology of Writings from the Women's Liberation Movement*. New York: Random House.

Morgan, Sue, ed. 2006. *The Feminist History Reader*. New York: Routledge.

Murphy, Megan. 2011. "We're Sluts Not Feminists. Wherein My Relationship with SlutWalk Gets Rocky." *Feminista.org*. May 7. Accessed June 12, 2011. http://www.feminisms.org/2585/were- sluts-not-feminists-wherein-my-relationship-with-slutwalk-gets-rocky/.

Nash, Terre. 1995. Who's Counting? Marilyn Waring on Sex, Lies and Global Economics. National Film Board of Canada. http://www.nfb.ca/film/whos_counting.

Phillips, Anne, and Barbara Taylor. 1980. "Sex and Skill: Notes Towards a Feminist Economics." *Feminist Review* 6 (1): 79–88. http://dx.doi.org/10.1057/fr.1980.20.

Pietsch, Nicole. 2010. "'I'm Not That Kind of Girl': White Femininity, the Other, and the Legal/Social Sanctioning of Sexual Violence Against Racialized Women." *Canadian Woman Studies* 28 (1): 136–40.

Poisson, Jayme. 2011. "Parents Keep Child's Gender Secret." *Toronto Star*, May 21.

Razack, Sherene, ed. 2002. *Race, Space, and the Law: Unmapping a White Settler Society*. Toronto: Between the Lines.

Redstockings. 2001. Excerpts from Redstockings' Press Release. December 5. Accessed May 3, 2012. http://www.redstockings.org/index.php?option=com_content&view=article&id=55:excerpts-from-redstockings-press-release&catid=36:myth-pages.

Reed, Evelyn. (Original work published 1970) 1980. *Problems of Women's Liberation: A Marxist Approach*. 2nd ed. New York: Pathfinder Press.

Reed, Evelyn. 1984. "Women: Cast, Class or Oppressed Sex." In *Feminist Frameworks: Alternative Theoretical Accounts of the Relations between Women and Men*, ed. Alison M. Jaggar and Paula Rothenberg Struhl. New York: McGraw-Hill.

Rich, Adrienne. 2001. "Claiming an Education." In *Women's Voices, Feminist Visions: Classic and Contemporary Readings*, ed. Susan Shaw, 28–29. Houston, TX: Mayfield Publishing.

Rich, Adrienne. 1980. "Compulsory Heterosexuality and Lesbian Existence." *Signs* 5 (4): 631–60. http://dx.doi.org/10.1086/493756.

Roberts, Dorothy. 1995–96. "Unshackling Black Motherhood." *Michigan Law Review* 95 (4): 938–64. http://dx.doi.org/10.2307/1290050.

Royster, Jacqueline Jones. 1997. *Southern Horrors and Other Writings: The Anti-lynching Campaign of Ida B. Wells, 1892–1900*. Boston: Bedford Books.

Scholz, Sally. 2010. *Feminism: A Beginner's Guide*. Oxford: One World Publications.

Thobani, Sunera. 2007. *Exalted Subjects: Studies in the Making of Race and Nation in Canada*. Toronto: University of Toronto Press.

Thobani, Sunera, Sherene Razack, and Malinda Smith, eds. 2010. *States of Race: Critical Race Feminism for the 21st Century*. Toronto: Between the Lines.

Tomaselli, Sylvana. 2012. "Mary Wollstonecraft." In *The Stanford Encyclopedia of Philosophy*, ed. Edward N. Zalta. Accessed May 1, 2012. http://plato.stanford.edu/archives/spr2012/entries/wollstonecraft/.

Tong, Rosemarie. 2009. *Feminist Thought: A More Comprehensive Introduction*. Boulder, CO: Westview Press.

Truth, Sojourner. (Original work published 1867) 2005. "Ain't I a Woman." In *Feminist Theory: A Reader*, ed. Wendy Kolmar and Frances Bartkowski. Boston: McGraw-Hill.

Tyree, Tia. 2009. "Lovin' Momma and Hatin' on Baby Mama: A Comparison of Misogynistic and Stereotypical Representations in Songs about Rappers' Mothers and Baby Mamas." *Women & Language* 32 (2): 50–8.

Walby, Sylvia. 1989. "Theorising Patriarchy." *Sociology* 23 (2): 213–34. http://dx.doi.org/10.1177/0038038589023002004.

Walker, Alice. 1983. *In Search Of Our Mothers' Gardens: Womanist Prose*. San Diego: Harcourt, Brace and Jovanovich.

Wane, Njoki, Katerina Deliovsky, and Erica Lawson. 2002. *Back to the Drawing Board: African-Canadian Feminisms*. Toronto: Sumach Press.

Washington, Margaret. 2009. *Sojourner Truth's America*. Urbana: University of Illinois Press.

Wells, Ida B. (Original work published 1892) 1997. "Southern Horrors: Lynch Law in All Its Phases." In *Southern Horrors and Other Writings: The Anti-Lynching Campaign Of Ida B. Wells, 1892–1900*, ed. Jacqueline Jones Royster, 49–72. Boston: Bedford Books.

Wollstonecraft, Mary. 1796. *A Vindication of the Rights of Woman*. 3rd ed. London: J. Johnson, St. Paul's Church Yard.

Chapter 6 From Universalizing to Queering and Globalizing Theories

Alcoff, Linda. 1988. "Cultural Feminism Versus Post-Structuralism: The Identity Crisis in Feminist Theory." *Signs* 13 (3): 405–36.

Alexander, Jacqui, and Chandra Mohanty. 2010. "Cartographies of Knowledge and Power: Transnational Feminism as Transnational Praxis." In *Critical Transnational Feminist Praxis*, ed. Richa Nagar and Amanda Lock Swarr. Albany: State University of New York Press.

Anthias, Floya, and Nira Yuval-Davis. 2005. *Racialized Boundaries: Race, Nation, Gender, Colour and Class and the Anti-Racist Struggle*. New York: Routledge.

Bartky, Sandra. (Original work published 1990) 2010. "Foucault, Femininity, and the Modernization of Patriarchal Power." In *Feminist Theory Reader*, ed. Carole McCann and Seung-Kyung Kim, 404–418. New York: Routledge.

Beauvoir, Simone de. 1952. *The Second Sex*. New York: Knopf.

Benería, Lourdes. 2003. *Gender, Development, and Globalization: Economics as If All People Mattered*. New York: Routledge.

Benería, Lourdes, and Shelley Feldman, eds. 1992. *Unequal Burden: Economic Crises, Persistent Poverty, and Women's Work*. Boulder: Westview Press.

Blommaert, Jan. 2005. *Discourse: A Critical Introduction*. New York: Cambridge University Press. http://dx.doi.org/10.1017/CBO9780511610295.

Braziel, Jana. 2008. "Queer Diasporas." In *Diaspora: An Introduction*. 105–27. Malden, MA: Blackwell Publishing.

Brodribb, Somer. 1993. *Nothing Mat(t)Ers: A Feminist Critique of Postmodernism*. Toronto: James Lorimer.

Butler, Judith. 1993. *Bodies That Matter: On the Discursive Limits of "Sex."* New York: Routledge.

Butler, Judith. [1990] 2006. *Gender Trouble: Feminism and the Subversion of Identity*. New York: Routledge.

Cardoso, Fernando Henrique, and Enzo Faletto. 1979. *Dependency and Development in Latin America*. Berkeley: University of California Press.

Cheldelin, Sandra, and Maneshka Eliatamby. 2011. *Women Waging War and Peace: International Perspectives of Women's Roles in Conflict and Post-Conflict Reconstruction*. New York: Continuum International Publishing Group.

Christenson, Marcus, and Paul Kelso. 2004. "Soccer Chief's Plan to Boost Women's Game? Hotpants." *The Guardian*, 16 January. Accessed June 7, 2011. http://www.guardian.co.uk/uk/2004/jan/16/football.gender.

Collins, Patricia Hill. 2000. *Black Feminist Thought: Knowledge, Consciousness, and the Politics of Empowerment*. New York: Routledge.

Collins, Patricia Hill. 1998. *Fighting Words: Black Women and the Search for Justice*. Minneapolis: University of Minnesota Press.

Conrad, Peter, and S. Markens. 2001. "Constructing the 'Gay Gene' in the News: Optimism and Skepticism in the US and British Press." *Health* 5 (3): 373–400. http://dx.doi.org/10.1177/136345930100500306.

Coyote, Ivan. 2011a. "Dear Lady in the Women's Washroom." *Xtra: Canada's Gay & Lesbian News*. September 22. Accessed November 2, 2011. http://www.xtra.ca/public/vancouver/dear_lady_in_the_womens_washroom-10801.aspx.

Coyote, Ivan. 2011b. "Bathroom Bullshit Redux: Gender Segregation." *Xtra: Canada's Gay & Lesbian News*. November 17. Accessed February 3, 2012. http://www.xtra.ca/public/Vancouver/Bathroom_bullshit_redux-11107.aspx.

Davis, Simone Weil. 2002. "Loose Lips Sink Ships." *Feminist Studies* 28 (1): 7–36. http://dx.doi.org/10.2307/3178492.

Derrida, Jacques. 1976. *Of Grammatology*. Baltimore, MD: Johns Hopkins University Press.

Dreby, Joanna. 2006. "Honor and Virtue: Mexican Parenting in the Transnational Context." *Gender & Society* 20 (1): 32–59. http://dx.doi.org/10.1177/0891243205282660.

Duggan, Lisa. 1992. "Making It Perfectly Queer." *Socialist Review* 21 (1): 11–32.

Ehrenreich, Barbara, and Arlie Russell Hochschild, eds. 2003. *Global Woman: Nannies, Maids, and Sex Workers in the New Economy*. New York: Metropolitan Books/Henry Holt.

Enloe, Cynthia. 2007. *Globalization and Militarism: Feminists Make the Link*. Lanham, MD: Rowman and Littlefield Publishers.

Enloe, Cynthia. 2010. *Nimo's War, Emma's War: Making Feminist Sense of the Iraq War*. Berkeley: University of California Press.

Erdbrink, Thomas. 2011. "Olympics 2012: FIFA Bans Headscarves for Iranian Women's Soccer Team." *Washington Post*, June 6. Accessed June 7, 2011. http://

www.washingtonpost.com/sports/united/olympics-2012-fifa-bans-headscarves-for-irans-women-soccer-team/2011/06/06/AGzT1JKH_story.html.

Flax, Jane. 1987. "Postmodernism and Gender Relations in Feminist Theory." *Signs* 12 (4): 621–43. http://dx.doi.org/10.1086/494359.

Foucault, Michel. 1980. *Power/Knowledge: Selected Interviews and Other Writings, 1972–1977*. New York: Pantheon Books.

Fraser, Arvonne, and Irene Tinker, eds. 2004. *Developing Power: How Women Transformed International Development*. New York: Feminist Press at the City University of New York.

Girshick, Lori. 2008. "Gender Policing." In *Transgender Voices: Beyond Women and Men*. 133–53. Lebanon, NH: University Press of New England.

Goodman, Michael. 2011. "Female Genital Cosmetic and Plastic Surgery: A Review." *Journal of Sexual Medicine* 8 (6): 1813–25. http://dx.doi.org/10.1111/j.1743-6109.2011.02254.x. Medline:21492397

Gopinath, Gayatri. 2008. *Impossible Desires: Queer Diasporas and South Asian Public Cultures*. Durham, NC: Duke University Press.

Graves, Nicola. 1996. "Third World and Third World Women." Accessed May 9, 2012. http://www.english.emory.edu/Bahri/ThirdWorld.html.

Grewal, Inderpal. 2005. *Transnational America: Feminisms, Diasporas, Neoliberalisms*. Durham, NC: Duke University Press.

Grewal, Inderpal, and Caren Kaplan, eds. 1994. *Scattered Hegemonies: Postmodernity and Transnational Feminist Practices*. Minneapolis: University of Minnesota Press.

Halberstam, Judith. 2005. *In a Queer Time and Place: Transgender Bodies, Subcultural Lives*. New York: New York University Press.

Halberstam, Judith. 2002. "An Introduction to Female Masculinity." In *The Masculinity Studies Reader*, ed. Rachel Adams and David Savran, 355–74. Malden, MA: Blackwell Publishing.

Halberstam, Judith. 1998. *Female Masculinity*. Durham, NC: Duke University Press.

Hall, Stuart. 2001. "Power, Knowledge and Discourse." In *Discourse Theory and Practice: A Reader*, ed. Margaret Wetherell, 72–81. London: The Open University Press.

Hamer, Dean, and Peter Copeland. 1994. *Science of Desire: The Gay Gene and the Biology of Behavior*. New York: Simon and Schuster.

Haraway, Donna. (Original work published 1985) 2005. "A Cyborg Manifesto: Science, Technology, and Socialist Feminism in the Late Twentieth Century." In *Feminist Theory: A Reader*, ed. Wendy Kolmar and Frances Bartkowski. Boston: McGraw-Hill.

Harcourt, Wendy, ed. 2009. *Body Politics in Development: Critical Debates in Gender and Development*. New York: Zed Books.

Harcourt, Wendy, ed. 1994. *Feminist Perspectives on Sustainable Development*. Atlantic Highlands, NJ: Zed Books.

Hawley, John. 2001. *Postcolonial, Queer: Theoretical Intersections*. Albany: State University of New York Press.

Hesse-Biber, Sharlene Nagy, ed. 2012. *Handbook of Feminist Research: Theory and Praxis*. 2nd ed. Thousand Oaks, CA: SAGE Publications.

Hoodfar, Homa. 1993. "The Veil in Their Own Minds and on Our Heads: The Persistence of Colonial Images of Muslim Women." *Resources for Feminist Research* 22 (3/4): 5–18.

Irigaray, Luce. (Original work published 1977) 1985. *This Sex Which Is Not One*. Ithaca, NY: Cornell University Press.

Jiwani, Yasmin. 2009. "Helpless Maidens and Chivalrous Knights: Afghan Women in the Canadian Press." *University of Toronto Quarterly* 78 (2): 728–44. http://dx.doi.org/10.3138/utq.78.2.728.

Jónasdóttir, Anna, Valerie Bryson, and Kathleen Jones, eds. 2011. *Sexuality, Gender and Power: Intersectional and Transnational Perspectives*. New York: Routledge.

Karaian, Lara, Lisa Bryn Rundel, and Allyson Mitchell, eds. 2001. *Turbo Chicks: Talking Young Feminisms*. Toronto: Sumach Press.

Kinsman, Gary. 1996. *The Regulation of Desire: Homo and Hetero Sexualities*. Montreal: Black Rose Books.

Kulpa, Robert, and Joanna Mizielinska, eds. 2011. *De-Centring Western Sexualities: Central and Eastern European Perspectives*. Farnham, UK: Ashgate.

Lewis, Reina, and Sara Mills, eds. 2003. *Feminist Postcolonial Theory: A Reader*. Edinburgh: Edinburgh University Press.

Lorber, Judith. 2010. *Gender Inequality: Feminist Theory and Politics*. New York: Oxford University Press.

Lyotard, Jean-François. 1984. *The Postmodern Condition: A Report on Knowledge*. Minneapolis: University of Minnesota Press.

Mackie, Vera. 2012. "The 'Afghan Girls': Media Representations and Frames of War." *Continuum: Journal of Media & Cultural Studies* 26 (1): 115–31.

Mann, Susan. 2012. *Doing Feminist Theory: From Modernity to Postmodernity*. New York: Oxford University Press.

Marchand, Marianne, and Jane Parpart, eds. 1995. *Feminism/Postmodernism/Development*. New York: Routledge.

McClintock, Anne. 1995. *Imperial Leather: Race, Gender, and Sexuality in the Colonial Contest*. New York: Routledge.

McClintock, Anne, Aamir Mufti, and Ella Shohat, eds. 1997. *Dangerous Liaisons: Gender, Nation, and Postcolonial Perspectives*. Minneapolis: University of Minnesota Press.

Micheletti, Michele, Andreas Føllesdal, and Dietlind Stolle, eds. 2006. *Politics, Products, and Markets: Exploring Political Consumerism Past and Present*. New Brunswick, NJ: Transaction Publishers.

Miles, Angela. 1996. *Integrative Feminisms: Building Global Visions 1960s–1990s*. New York: Routledge.

Moghadam, Valentine M. 2005. *Globalizing Women: Transnational Feminist Networks*. Baltimore, MD: Johns Hopkins University Press.

Mohanty, Chandra Talpade. 2003. *Feminism Without Borders: Decolonizing Theory, Practicing Solidarity*. Durham, NC: Duke University Press.

Mohanty, Chandra Talpade. 1995. "Feminist Encounters: Locating the Politics of Experience." In *Social Postmodernism: Beyond Identity Politics*, ed. Linda J. Nicholson and Steven Seidman, 68–86. New York: Cambridge University Press. http://dx.doi.org/10.1017/CBO9780511520792.004

Mohanty, Chandra. 1984. "Under Western Eyes: Feminist Scholarship and Colonial Discourses." *Boundary 2* 12/13 (1): 333–58. http://dx.doi.org/10.2307/302821.

Mohanty, Chandra, and Sarah Miraglia. 2012. "Gendering Justice, Building Alternative Futures." In *Alternatives to Privatization: Public Options for Essential Services in the Global South*, ed. David A. McDonald and Greg Ruiters, 99–132. New York: Routledge/Taylor and Francis.

Mohanty, Chandra, Ann Russo, and Lourdes Torres, eds. 1991. *Third World Women and the Politics of Feminism*. Bloomington: Indiana University Press.

Momsen, Janet, ed. 2008. *Gender and Development: Critical Concepts in Development Studies*. New York: Routledge.

Mottet, Lisa. 2002–03. "Access to Gender-Appropriate Bathrooms: A Frustrating Diversion on the Path to Transgender Equality." *Georgetown Journal of Gender and the Law* 4:739–46.

Myrick Stocker, Heather. 2004. "Labial Lifts and Vaginal Rejuvenation: The New Hunt for a Youthful Look." *Expository Magazine* 4 (2).

Nagar, Richa, and Amanda Lock Swarr. 2010. *Critical Transnational Feminist Praxis.* Albany: State University of New York Press.

Namaste, Viviane. 2000. *Invisible Lives: The Erasure of Transsexual and Transgendered People.* Chicago: University of Chicago Press.

Namaste, Viviane. 2005. *Sex Change, Social Change: Reflections on Identity, Institutions, and Imperialism.* Toronto: Women's Press.

Narayan, Uma. 1997. *DisLocating Cultures: Identities, Traditions, and Third World Feminism.* New York: Routledge.

Narayan, Uma. 1998. "Essence of Culture and Sense of History: A Feminist Critique of Cultural Essentialism." *Hypatia* 13 (2): 86–106. http://dx.doi.org/10.1111/j.1527-2001.1998.tb01227.x.

Narayan, Uma, and Sandra Harding, eds. 2000. *Decentering the Center: Philosophy for a Multicultural, Postcolonial, and Feminist World.* Bloomington: Indiana University Press.

Parker, Emma. 2011. "Introduction: Queer, There and Everywhere." *Textual Practice* 25 (4): 639–47. http://dx.doi.org/10.1080/0950236X.2011.586773.

Patton, Cindy, and Benigno Sánchez-Eppler. 2000. *Queer Diasporas.* Durham, NC: Duke University Press.

Poisson, Jayme. 2011. "Parents Keep Child's Gender Secret." *Toronto Star*, May 21.

Rich, Adrienne. 1980. "Compulsory Heterosexuality and Lesbian Existence." *Signs* 5 (4): 631–60. http://dx.doi.org/10.1086/493756.

Riley, Robin, Chandra Mohanty, and Minnie Bruce Pratt, eds. 2008. *Feminism and War: Confronting US Imperialism.* New York: Zed Books.

Rostow, Walter. 1960. *The Stages of Economic Growth: A Non-Communist Manifesto.* Cambridge: Cambridge University Press.

Rubin, Gayle. 1984. "Thinking Sex: Notes for a Radical Theory of the Politics of Sexuality." In *The Lesbian and Gay Studies Reader*, ed. Henry Abelove, Michèle Aina Barale, and David M. Halperin, 3–44. New York: Routledge.

Saadallah, Sherin. 2007. "Muslim Feminism in the Third Wave: A Reflective Inquiry." In *Third Wave Feminism: A Critical Exploration*, ed. Stacy Gillis, Gillian Howie, and Rebecca Munford, 216–26. New York: Palgrave Macmillan.

Samuels, J. 1999. "Dangerous Liaisons: Queer Subjectivity, Liberalism and Race." *Cultural Studies* 13 (1): 91–109. http://dx.doi.org/10.1080/095023899335383.

Schilt, Kristen, and Laurel Westbrook. 2009. "Doing Gender, Doing Heteronormativity: 'Gender Normals,' Transgender People, and the Social Maintenance of Heterosexuality." *Gender & Society* 23 (4): 440–64. http://dx.doi.org/10.1177/0891243209340034.

Scott, Catherine V. 1995. *Gender and Development: Rethinking Modernization and Dependency Theory.* Boulder: Lynne Rienner Publishers.

Sedgwick, Eve. 1990. *Epistemology of the Close.* Berkeley: University of California Press.

Sen, Gita, Asha George, and Piroska Ostlin, eds. 2002. *Engendering International Health: The Challenge of Equity.* Cambridge, MA: MIT Press.

Sen, Gita, and Caren Grown. 1987. *Development, Crises, and Alternative Visions: Third World Women's Perspectives.* New York: Monthly Review Press.

Shaffer, Nancy. Aug 2005. "Transgender Patients: Implications for Emergency Department Policy and Practice." *Journal of Emergency Nursing: JEN* 31 (4): 405–7. http://dx.doi.org/10.1016/j.jen.2005.06.017. Medline:16126113

Spivak, Gayatri Chakravorty. 1988. "Can the Subaltern Speak?" In *Marxism and the Interpretation of Culture*, ed. Cary Nelson and Lawrence Grossberg, 271–313. Urbana: University of Illinois Press.

Spurlin, William. 2010. "Sexual/Cultural Hybridity in the New South Africa: Emergent Sites of Transnational Queer Politics." In *Gendering Border Studies*, ed. Jane Aaron, Henrice Altink, and Chris Weedon. Cardiff: University of Wales Press.

Stasiulis, Daiva, and Abigail Bakan. 2005. *Negotiating Citizenship: Migrant Women in Canada and the Global System*. Toronto: University of Toronto Press.

Turnbull, Lornet. 2007. "Mall-Restroom Evictions Raise Transgender Ire." *The Seattle Times*. September 15, 2007. Accessed June 3, 2011. http://seattletimes.nwsource.com/html/localnews/2003872953_transbath07m.html.

Warner, Michael, ed. 1992. *Fear of a Queer Planet: Queer Politics and Social Theory*. Minneapolis: University of Minnesota Press.

West, Cornel. 1993. "Black Culture and Postmodernism." In *A Postmodern Reader*, ed. Joseph Natoli and Linda Hutcheon, 390–397. Albany: State University of New York Press.

Wetherell, Margaret, and Chandra Talpade Mohanty, eds. 2010. *The Sage Handbook of Identities*. Thousand Oaks, CA: Sage Publications.

Wibben, Annick. 2011. *Feminist Security Studies: A Narrative Approach*. New York: Routledge.

Wilchins, Riki. 2004. *Queer Theory, Gender Theory*. Los Angeles: Alyson Books.

Young, Iris Marion. 2005. *On Female Body Experience: "Throwing Like a Girl" and Other Essays*. New York: Oxford University Press.

Zarkov, Dubravka. 2006. "Towards a New Theorizing of Women, Gender, and War." In *Handbook of Gender and Women's Studies*, ed. Kathy Davis, Mary Evans, and Judith Lorber, 214–233. London: Sage Publishing. http://dx.doi.org/10.4135/9781848608023.n13.

Zinn, Maxine, Pierrette Hondagneu-Sotelo, and Michael Messner, eds. 2011. *Gender through the Prism of Difference*. New York: Oxford University Press.

Web Sources

UNIFEM. United Nations Entity for Gender Equality and Women's Empowerment, http://www.unifem.org/gender_issues/women_poverty_economics/facts_figures.php.

Chapter 7 Taking Feminism on the Road: Feminist Methods

Bromley, Victoria. 2002. "Human Security, Gendered Violence, and Women's Rights: Lives on the Line in the US-Mexican Borderlands." PhD diss., Carlton University.

Burt, Sandra, and Lorraine Code, eds. 1995. *Changing Methods: Feminists Transforming Practice*. Peterborough, ON: Broadview Press.

Collins, Patricia Hill. 1991. "Learning from the Outsider Within: The Sociological Significance of Black Feminist Thought." In *Beyond Methodology: Feminist Scholarship As Lived Research*, ed. Mary Fonow and Judith Cook. Bloomington: Indiana University Press. http://dx.doi.org/10.1525/sp.1986.33.6.03a00020.

Denzin, Norman, and Yvonna Lincoln, eds. 2003. *The Landscape of Qualitative Research Theories and Issues*. Los Angeles: Sage Publications.

Denzin, Norman, Yvonna Lincoln, and Linda Tuhiwai Smith, eds. 2003. *Handbook of Critical and Indigenous Methodologies*. Thousand Oaks, CA: Sage Publications.

Fonow, Mary, and Judith Cook, eds. 1991. *Beyond Methodology: Feminist Scholarship As Lived Research*. Bloomington: Indiana University Press.

Haraway, Donna. 1988. "Situated Knowledges: The Science Question in Feminism and the Privilege of Partial Perspectives." *Feminist Studies* 14 (3): 575–99. http://dx.doi .org/10.2307/3178066.

Haraway, Donna. 1981. "In the Beginning Was the Word: The Genesis of Biological Theory." *Signs* 6 (3): 469–81. http://dx.doi.org/10.1086/493819.

Harding, Sandra. 2006. *Science and Social Inequality: Feminist and Postcolonial Issues*. Urbana: University of Illinois Press.

Harding, Sandra. 1993. "Rethinking Standpoint Epistemology: What is 'Strong Objectivity'." In *Feminist Epistemologies*, ed. Linda Alcoff and Elizabeth Potter, 49–82. New York: Routledge.

Harding, Sandra. 1989. "Is There a Feminist Method?" In *Feminism & Science*, ed. Nancy Tuana, 17–32. Bloomington: Indiana University Press.

Harding, Sandra, ed. 1987. *Feminism & Methodology*. Bloomington: Indiana University Press.

Harding, Sandra. 1986. "The Instability of the Analytic Categories of Feminist Theory." *Signs* 11 (4): 645–64.

Hawkesworth, Mary. 1989. "Knowers, Knowing, Known: Feminist Theory and Claims of Truth." *Signs* 14 (3): 533–57. http://dx.doi.org/10.1086/494523.

Hesse-Biber, Sharlene Nagy, and Patricia Leavy. 2011. *The Practice of Qualitative Research*. Thousand Oaks, CA: SAGE Publications.

Hesse-Biber, Sharlene Nagy, and Patricia Lina Leavy, eds. 2007. *Feminist Research Practice: A Primer*. Thousand Oaks, CA: Sage Publications.

hooks, bell. 1984. *Feminist Theory: From Margin to Center*. Boston: South End Press.

Kirby, Sandra, et al., eds. 2006. *Experience Research Social Change: Methods beyond the Mainstream*. Peterborough, ON: Broadview Press.

Kindon, Sara, Rachel Pain, and Mike Kesby, eds. 2007. *Participatory Action Research Approaches and Methods: Connecting People, Participation and Place*. New York: Routledge.

Longino, Helen. 2002. "Subjects, Power, and Knowledge: Descriptions and Prescriptions in Feminist Philosophies of Science." In *Knowledge and Inquiry: Readings in Epistemology*, ed. K. Brad Wray. Orchard Park, NY: Broadview Press.

Lloyd, Genevieve. 2002. "Maleness, Metaphor, and the 'Crisis' of Reason." In *A Mind of One's Own: Feminist Essays on Reason and Objectivity*, ed. Louise Antony and Charlotte Witt. Cambridge, MA: Westview Press.

Meezan, William, and James Martin, eds. 2009. *Handbook of Research with Lesbian, Gay, Bisexual, and Transgender Populations*. New York: Routledge.

Narayan, Uma, and Sandra Harding. 2000. *Decentering the Center: Philosophy for a Multicultural, Postcolonial, and Feminist World*. Bloomington, IN: Indiana University Press.

Nelson, Lynn Hankinson. 1990. *Who Knows: From Quine to a Feminist Empiricism*. Philadelphia: Temple University Press.

Tuana, Nancy. 1992. "The Radical Future of Feminist Empiricism." *Hypatia* 7 (1): 100–14. http://dx.doi.org/10.1111/j.1527-2001.1992.tb00700.x.

Tuana, Nancy. 1989. *Feminism & Science*. Bloomington: Indiana University Press.

Wong, Yut-Lin. 2009. "Review Paper: Gender Competencies in the Medical Curriculum: Addressing Gender Bias in Medicine." *Asia-Pacific Journal of Public Health* 21 (4): 359–76. http://dx.doi.org/10.1177/1010539509337730. Medline:19661102

Chapter 8 It's Not Dead? Connecting the Dots across the Waves of Feminisms

Bacchi, Carol Lee. 1983. *Liberation Deferred? The Ideas of the English-Canadian Suffragists, 1877–1918*. Toronto: University of Toronto Press.

Backhouse, Constance, and David Flaherty, eds. 1992. *Challenging Times: The Women's Movement in Canada and the United States*. Montreal: McGill-Queen's University Press.

Bannerman, Jean. 1977. *Leading Ladies Canada*. Belleville, ON: Mika Publishing Company.

Braithwaite, Ann. 2002. "The Personal, the Political, Third-Wave and Postfeminisms." *Feminist Theory* 3 (3): 335–44. http://dx.doi.org/10.1177/146470002762492033.

Bromley, Victoria, and Aalya Ahmad. 2006. "Wa(i)ving Solidarity: Feminist Activists Confronting Backlash." *Canadian Woman Studies* 25 (3/4): 61–71.

Brooks, Ann. 1997. *Postfeminisms: Feminism, Cultural Theory, and Cultural Forms*. New York: Routledge.

Chakraborty, Mridula Nath. 2004. "Wa(i)ving it All Away: Producing Subject and Knowledge in Feminisms of Colour." In *Third Wave Feminism: A Critical Exploration*, ed. Stacy Gillis, Gillian Howie, and Rebecca Munford, 205–215. New York: Palgrave Macmillan.

Chouinard, Vera. 2011. "Connecting Our Lives With Yours: Why Disability is Every Woman's Issue." In *Gendered Intersections: An Introduction to Women's and Gender Studies*, ed. C. Lesley Biggs, Susan Gingell, and Pamela J. Downe. Halifax, NS: Fernwood Publishing.

Dicker, Rory, and Alison Piepmeier. 2003. *Catching a Wave: Reclaiming Feminism for the 21st Century*. Boston: Northeastern University Press.

DiFranco, Ani. 1994. *"Overlap." Out of Range. Out of Range Records*. Righteous Babe.

Douglass, Frederick. (Original work published 1845) 1963. *Narrative of the Life of Frederick Douglass: An American Slave*. Garden City, NY: Doubleday.

Douglass, Frederick. (Original work published 1882) 2005. "Why I Became A 'Women's-Rights Man." In *Feminist Theory: A Reader*, ed. Wendy Kolmar and Frances Bartkowski, 98–99. Boston: McGraw-Hill.

Fawcett, Barbara. 2000. *Feminist Perspectives on Disability*. New York: Pearson Education.

Fixmer, Natalie, and Julia T. Wood. 2005. "The *Personal* is *Still* Political: Embodied Politics in Third Wave Feminism." *Women's Studies in Communication* 28 (2): 235–57. http://dx.doi.org/10.1080/07491409.2005.10162493.

Fugitive Slave Act. 1850. http://avalon.law.yale.edu/19th_century/fugitive.asp.

Fuss, Diana, ed. 1989. *Essentially Speaking: Feminism, Nature and Difference*. New York: Routledge.

Friedman, Jaclyn, and Jessica Valenti, eds. 2008. *Yes Means Yes! Visions of Female Sexual Power and a World Without Rape*. Berkeley: Seal Press.

Garland-Thomson, Rosemarie. 2002. "Integrating Disability, Transforming Feminist Theory." *NWSA Journal* 14 (3): 1–32. http://dx.doi.org/10.2979/NWS.2002.14.3.1.

Gillis, Stacy, Gillian Howie, and Rebecca Munford, eds. 2004. *Third Wave Feminism: A Critical Exploration*. New York: Palgrave Macmillan. http://dx.doi.org/10.1057/9780230523173.

Gilmore, Stephanie, ed. 2008. *Feminist Coalitions: Historical Perspectives on Second-Wave Feminism in the United States*. Urbana: University of Illinois Press.

Glick, Elisa. 2000. "Sex Positive: Feminism, Queer Theory, and the Politics of Transgression." *Feminist Review* 64 (1): 19–45. http://dx.doi.org/10.1080/014177800338936.

Goldin, Claudia, and Lawrence Katz. 2002. "The Power of the Pill: Oral Contraceptives and Women's Career and Marriage Decisions." *Journal of Political Economy* 110 (4): 730–70. http://dx.doi.org/10.1086/340778.

Green, Eli. 2006. "Debating Trans Inclusion in the Feminist Movement: A Trans-Positive Analysis." *Journal of Lesbian Studies* 10 (1/2): 231–48. http://dx.doi.org/10.1300/J155v10n01_12.

Greenberg, Julia. 2012. "Janet Howell, Virginia State Senator, Adds Rectal Exam to Anti-Abortion Bill in Amendment." *International Business Times*, January 31. Accessed February 2, 2012. http://www.ibtimes.com/articles/290523/20120131/janet-howell-rectal-exam-anti-abortion-bill.htm.

Grimm, Ray. 2011. "Democratic Congresswoman Jackie Speier Talks About Her Terminated Pregnancy." *Huffington Post*. February 18. Accessed March 9, 2011. http://www.huffingtonpost.com/2011/02/18/jackie-speier-abortion-planned-parenthood_n_824978.html.

Hernandez, Daisy, and Bushra Rehman. 2002. *Colonize This! Young Women of Color, On Today's Feminism*. New York: Seal Press.

Heywood, Leslie, and Jennifer Drake, eds. 1997. *Third Wave Agenda: Being Feminist, Doing Feminism*. Minneapolis: University of Minnesota Press.

Keetley, Dawn, and John Pettegrew, eds. 1997. *Public Women, Public Words: A Documentary History of American Feminism*. Madison: Madison House.

Kinahan, Anne-Marie. 2004. "Women Who Run from the Wolves: Feminist Critique as Post-Feminism." In *Feminisms and Womanisms*, ed. Althea Prince and Susan Silva-Wayne, 119–130. Toronto: Women's Press. http://dx.doi.org/10.3138/CRAS-s031-02-03.

Kinser, Amber. 2004. "Negotiating Spaces For/Through Third-Wave Feminism." *Feminist Formations* 16 (3): 124–53.

Lind, JoEllen. 1994. "Dominance and Democracy: The Legacy of Woman Suffrage for the Voting Right." *UCLA Women's Law Journal* 5: 103–26.

Lorber, Judith. 2010. *Gender Inequality: Feminist Theories and Politics*. New York: Oxford University Press.

Lorde, Audre. [1984] 2007. *Sister Outsider: Essays and Speeches*. Berkeley: Crossing Press.

Mann, Susan. 2012. *Doing Feminist Theory: From Modernity to Postmodernity*. New York: Oxford University Press.

McRobbie, Angela. 2004. "Post-Feminism and Popular Culture." *Feminist Media Studies* 4 (3): 255–64. http://dx.doi.org/10.1080/1468077042000309937.

Mitchell, Allyson. 2001. "The Writing's on the Wall: Feminist and Lesbian Graffiti as Cultural Production." In *Turbo Chicks: Talking Young Feminisms*, ed. Allyson Mitchell, Lisa Bryn Rundle, and Lara Karaian, 221–231. Toronto: Sumach Press.

Mitchell, Allyson, Lisa Bryn Rundle, and Lara Karaian, eds. 2001. *Turbo Chicks: Talking Young Feminisms*. Toronto: Sumach Press.

Moynagh, Maureen, and Nancy Forestell. 2012. *Documenting First Wave Feminisms: Transnational Collaborations and Crosscurrents*. Toronto: University of Toronto Press.

Pankhurst, Christabel. 1913. *Plain Facts About a Great Evil (The Great Scourge and How To End It)*. London: Women's Social and Political Union.

Renegar, Valerie, and Stacey Sowards. 2009. "Contradiction As Agency: Self-Determination, Transcendence, and Counter-Imagination in Third Wave Feminism." *Hypatia* 24 (2): 1–20. http://dx.doi.org/10.1111/j.1527-2001.2009.01029.x.

Rosen, Ruth. 2000. *The World Split Open: How The Modern Women's Movement Changed America*. New York: Viking.

Sanders, Lise Shapiro. 2004. "'Feminists Love a Utopia': Collaboration, Conflict, and the Futures of Feminism." In *Third Wave Feminism: A Critical Exploration*, ed. Stacy Gillis, Gillian Howie, and Rebecca Munford, 49–59. New York: Palgrave Macmillan.

Sethna, Christabelle. 2005. "The University of Toronto Health Service, Oral Contraception, and Student Demand for Birth Control, 1960–1970." *Historical Studies in Education/Revue d'histoire de l'éducation* 17 (2): 265–92.

Sharpe, Robert, and Patricia McMahon. 2007. *The Persons Case: The Origins and Legacy of the Fight for Legal Personhood*. Toronto: University of Toronto Press.

Showden, Clarisa. 2012. "Theorising Maybe: A Feminist/Queer Theory Convergence." *Feminist Theory* 13 (1): 3–25. http://dx.doi.org/10.1177/1464700111429898.

Showden, Clarisa. 2009. "What's Political about the New Feminisms?" *Frontiers* 30 (2): 166–98.

Snyder-Hall, Claire. 2010. "Third-Wave Feminism and the Defense of 'Choice.'" *Perspectives on Politics* 8 (1): 255–61. http://dx.doi.org/10.1017/S1537592709992842.

Snyder, Claire R. 2008. "What Is Third-Wave Feminism? A New Directions Essay." *Signs* 34 (1): 175–96.

Sorisio, Carolyn. 1997. "A Tale of Two Feminisms: Power and Victimization in Contemporary Feminist Debate." In *Third Wave Agenda: Being Feminist, Doing Feminism*, ed. Leslie Heywood and Jennifer Drake, 134–154. Minneapolis: University of Minnesota Press.

Springer, Kimberly. 2002. "Third Wave Black Feminism?" *Signs* 27 (4): 1059–82. http://dx.doi.org/10.1086/339636.

Staggenborg, Suzanne, and Verta Taylor. 2005. "Whatever Happened to the Women's Movement?" *Mobilization: An International Journal* 10 (1): 37–52.

Stanton, Elizabeth Cady. (Original work published 1848) 2005. "Declaration of Sentiments from *The History of Women's Suffrage* (1848)." In *Feminist Theory: A Reader*, ed. Wendy Kolmar and Frances Bartkowski, 71–73. Boston: McGraw-Hill.

Stryker, Susan. 2004. "Transgender Feminism: Queering the Woman Question." In *Third Wave Feminism: A Critical Exploration*, ed. Stacy Gillis, Gillian Howie, and Rebecca Munford, 59–70. New York: Palgrave Macmillan.

Terborg-Penn, Rosalyn. 1998. *African American Women in the Struggle for the Vote, 1850–1920*. Bloomington: Indiana University Press.

Tone, Andrea. 2001. *Devices & Desires: A History of Contraceptives in America*. New York: Hill and Wang.

Truth, Sojourner. (Original work published 1851) 2005. "Ain't I A Women." In *Feminist Theory: A Reader*, ed. Wendy Kolmar and Frances Bartkowski, 79. Boston: McGraw-Hill.

Truth, Sojourner. (Original work published 1867) 2005. "Keep the Thing Going While Things Are Stirring." In *Feminist Theory: A Reader*, ed. Wendy Kolmar and Frances Bartkowski, 79–80. Boston: McGraw-Hill.

Washington, Margaret. 2009. *Sojourner Truth's America*. Urbana, IL: University of Illinois Press.

Wendell, Susan. 1996. *The Rejected Body: Feminist Philosophical Reflections on Disability*. New York: Routledge.

Wendell, Susan. 1989. "Toward a Feminist Theory of Disability." *Hypatia* 4 (2): 104–24.

Whitfield, Gina. 2006. "From Riot Grrrl to Radical: Reflections from a Working-Class Feminist." *Canadian Woman Studies* 25 (3/4): 185–87.

Woodhull, Victoria. (Original work published 1873) 2005. "The Elixir of Life: or, Why Do We Die?" In *Feminist Theory: A Reader*, ed. Wendy Kolmar and Frances Bartkowski, 95–98. Boston: McGraw-Hill.

Woodhull, Winifred. 2004. "Global Feminisms, Transnational Political Economies, Third World Cultural Production." In *Third Wave Feminism: A Critical Exploration*, ed. Stacy Gillis, Gillian Howie, and Rebecca Munford, 252–262. New York: Palgrave Macmillan.

Yee, Shirley. 1997. "Finding a Place: Mary Ann Shadd Cary and the Dilemmas of Black Migration to Canada, 1850–1870." *Frontiers: A Journal of Women Studies* 18 (3): 1–16. http://dx.doi.org/10.2307/3347171.

Zobl, Elke. 2009. "Cultural Production, Transnational Networking, and Critical Reflection in Feminist Zines." *Signs* 35 (1): 1–12. http://dx.doi.org/10.1086/599256.

Web Sources

Disabled Women's Network (DAWN). http://www.dawncanada.net/.

Feminists with Disabilities (FWD).

INCITE! Women of Color Against Violence. http://www.incite-national.org/.

Third Wave Foundation. http://www.thirdwavefoundation.org/.

Chapter 9 Don't Men Count, Too? Feminisms and Masculinities

Anderson, Eric. 2009. "The Maintenance of Masculinity among the Stakeholders of Sport." *Sport Management Review* 12 (1): 3–14. http://dx.doi.org/10.1016/j.smr.2008.09.003.

Balaji, Murali. 2011. "Beyond Jackie Chan." In *Global Masculinities and Manhood*, eds. Ronald L Jackson and Murali Balaji, 186–201. Urbana: University of Illinois Press.

CNN. 2003. "Kobe Bryant Charged with Sexual Assault." July 22, 2003. Accessed May 15, 2011. http://articles.cnn.com/2003-07-18/justice/kobe.bryant_1_paul-pastoor-sexual-penetration-or-intrusion-actual-physical-force?_s=PM:LAW.

Cohen, Marcia. 2009. *The Sisterhood: The Inside Story of the Women's Movement and the Leaders Who Made It Happen*. Santa Fe, NM: Sunstone Press.

Collins, Patricia Hill. 2004. *Black Sexual Politics: African Americans, Gender, and the New Racism*. New York: Routledge. http://dx.doi.org/10.4324/9780203309506.

Connell, R.W. (Original work published 1995) 2005. *Masculinities*. Berkeley: University of California Press.

Connell, R.W. 2002. "Studying Men and Masculinity." *Resources for Feminist Research* 29 (1/2): 43–55.

Connell, R.W. 1997. "Men, Masculinities and Feminism." *Social Alternatives*. 16 (3): 7–10.

Connell, R.W. 1992. "A Very Straight Gay: Masculinity, Homosexual Experience, and the Dynamics of Gender." *American Sociological Review* 57 (6): 735–51. http://dx.doi.org/10.2307/2096120.

Connell, R.W., and James Messerschmidt. 2005. "Hegemonic Masculinity: Rethinking the Concept." *Gender & Society* 19 (6): 829–59. http://dx.doi.org/10.1177/0891243205278639.

Correctional Services Canada (CSC). 2010. "Aboriginal Corrections: Quick Facts." Accessed August 12, 2012. http://www.csc-scc.gc.ca/text/pblct/qf/pdf/01-eng.pdf.

Davis, Nickolas, and Margaret Duncan. 2006. "Sports Knowledge is Power Reinforcing Masculine Privilege through Fantasy Sport League Participation." *Journal of Sport and Social Issues* 30 (3): 244–64. http://dx.doi.org/10.1177/0193723506290324.

Fausto-Sterling, Anne. 1981. "The Myth of Neutrality: Race, Sex and Class in Science." *Radical Teacher* 19:21–25.

Ferber, Abby. 2007. "The Construction of Black Masculinity: White Supremacy Now and Then." *Journal of Sport and Social Issues* 31 (1): 11–24. http://dx.doi.org/10.1177/0193723506296829.

Gerami, Shahin. 2005. "Islamic Masculinity and Muslim Masculinities." In *Handbook of Studies on Men and Masculinities*, ed. Michael S. Kimmel, Jeff Hearn, and R.W. Connell, 448–457. Thousand Oaks, CA: Sage Publications. http://dx.doi.org/10.4135/9781452233833.n26.

Goldin, Claudia, and Cecilia Rouse. 2000. "Orchestrating Impartiality: The Impact of 'Blind' Auditions of Female Musicians." *American Economic Review* 90 (4): 715–41. http://dx.doi.org/10.1257/aer.90.4.715.

Gutmann, Matthew. 2007. *The Meanings of Macho*. Berkeley: University of California Press.

Gutmann, Matthew, and Mara Vigoya. 2005. "Masculinities in Latin America." In *Handbook of Studies on Men and Masculinities*, ed. Michael S. Kimmel, Jeff Hearn, and R.W. Connell, 114–128. Thousand Oaks, CA: Sage Publications. http://dx.doi.org/10.4135/9781452233833.n7.

Hearn, Jeff. 2004. "From Hegemonic Masculinity to the Hegemony of Men." *Feminist Theory* 5 (1): 49–72. http://dx.doi.org/10.1177/1464700104040813.

Hearn, Jeff, and Michael Kimmel. 2006. "Changing Studies on Men and Masculinity." In *Handbook of Gender and Women's Studies*, ed. Kathy Davis, Mary Evans, and Judith Lorber, 53–70. London: Sage Publications. http://dx.doi.org/10.4135/9781848608023.n4.

hooks, bell. 2004. *We Real Cool: Black Men and Masculinity*. New York: Routledge.

Holmgrena, Linn Egeberg, and Jeff Hearn. 2009. "Framing 'Men in Feminism': Theoretical Locations, Local Contexts and Practical Passings in Men's Gender-Conscious Positionings on Gender Equality and Feminism." *Journal of Gender Studies* 18 (4): 403–18. http://dx.doi.org/10.1080/09589230903260076.

Hunter, Andrea G., and James Earl Davis Idden. 1994. "The Hidden Voices of Black Men: The Meaning, Structure, and Complexity of Manhood." *Journal of Black Studies* 25 (1): 20–40. http://dx.doi.org/10.1177/002193479402500102.

Hurtado, Aída, and Mrinal Sinha. 2008. "More than Men: Latino Feminist Masculinities and Intersectionality." *Sex Roles* 59 (5–6): 337–49. http://dx.doi.org/10.1007/s11199-008-9405-7.

Jiwa, Fazeela. 2010. "Death Does Not Become Her: The Second Night." *Vancouver Media Co-op*. April 22, 2010. Accessed May 15, 2011. http://vancouver.mediacoop.ca/story/3280.

Kaufman, Michael. 2008. "The White Ribbon Campaign: Involving Men and Boys in Ending Global Violence Against Women." In *The Gendered Society Reader: Canadian Edition*, ed. Michael Kimmel, Amy Aronson, and Amy Kaler, 436–444. Toronto: Oxford University Press.

Kimmel, Michael. 2008. *Guyland: The Perilous World Where Boys Become Men*. New York: Harper.

Kimmel, Michael. 1997. "Masculinity as Homophobia: Fear, Shame, and Silence in the Construction of Gender Identity." In *Toward a New Psychology of Gender*, ed. Mary Gergen and Sarah Davis, 223–42. New York: Routledge. http://dx.doi.org/10.4135/9781452243627.n7.

Kimmel, Michael, Jeff Hearn, and R.W. Connell. 2005. *Handbook of Studies on Men and Masculinities*. Thousand Oaks: SAGE Publications.

King, L.J., and Karen Hunter. 2004. *On the Down Low: A Journey Into the Lives of "Straight" Black Men Who Sleep with Men*. New York: Harlem Moon, Random House.

Kleinman, Sherryl. 2007. "Why Sexist Language Matters." *Alternet.com*. March 12. Accessed November 18, 2010. http://www.alternet.org/story/48856/?page=entire.

Lease, Suzanne H., Ashley B. Hampton, Kristie M. Fleming, Linda R. Baggett, Sarah H. Montes, and R. John Sawyer. 2010. "Masculinity and Interpersonal Competencies: Contrasting White and African American Men." *Psychology of Men & Masculinity* 11 (3): 195–207. http://dx.doi.org/10.1037/a0018092.

Liang, Christopher T.H., Jime Salcedo, and Holly A. Miller. 2011. "Perceived Racism, Masculinity Ideologies, and Gender Role Conflict Among Latino Men." *Psychology of Men & Masculinity* 12 (3): 201–15. http://dx.doi.org/10.1037/a0020479.

Martin, Emily. 1991. "The Egg and the Sperm: How Science Has Constructed a Romance Based on Stereotypical Male-Female Roles." *Signs: Journal of Women in Culture & Society* 16 (3): 485–501. http://dx.doi.org/10.1086/494680.

McDowell, Linda. 2005. "Men and the Boys: Bankers, Burger Makers and Barmen." In *Spaces of Masculinities*, ed. Bettina van Hoven and Kathrin Hörschelmann, 19–30. New York: Routledge.

Meuser, Michael. 2004. "Homosociality." In *Men and Masculinities: A Social, Cultural and Historical Encyclopedia*, ed. Michael Kimmel and Amy Aronson, 396–98. Santa Barbara, CA: ABC-CLIO.

Mutluer, Nil. 2011. "Disposable Masculinities in Istanbul." In *Global Masculinities and Manhood*, ed. Ronald L Jackson and Murali Balaji, 75–105. Urbana: University of Illinois Press.

Nandy, Ashis. 1983. *The Intimate Enemy: Loss and Recovery of Self under Colonialism*. Delhi: Oxford University Press.

NHTSA. 2000. *Aggressive Driving: Enforcement Strategies for Implementing Best Practices*. National Highway Traffic Safety Administration, United States. Accessed May 15, 2011. http://www.nhtsa.gov/people/injury/enforce/aggressdrivers/aggenforce/define.html.

Sánchez, Francisco J., Stefanie T. Greenberg, William Ming Liu, and Eric Vilain. 2009. "Reported Effects of Masculine Ideals on Gay Men." *Psychology of Men & Masculinity* 10 (1): 73–87. http://dx.doi.org/10.1037/a0013513. Medline:20628534.

Shipp, E.R. 1992. "Tyson Gets 6-Year Prison Term For Rape Conviction in Indiana." *New York Times*. March 27, 1992. Accessed May 15, 2011. http://www.nytimes.com/1992/03/27/sports/tyson-gets-6-year-prison-term-for-rape-conviction-in-indiana.html?pagewanted=all&src=pm.

Taga, Futoshi. 2005. "East Asian Masculinities." In *Handbook of Studies on Men and Masculinities*, ed. Michael S. Kimmel, Jeff Hearn, and R.W. Connell, 129–140. Thousand Oaks, CA: Sage Publications. http://dx.doi.org/10.4135/9781452233833.n8.

Tager, David, and Glenn Good. 2005. "Italian and American Masculinities: A Comparison of Masculine Gender Role Norms." *Psychology of Men & Masculinity* 6 (4): 264–74. http://dx.doi.org/10.1037/1524-9220.6.4.264.

Tarrant, Shira. 2009. *Men and Feminism*. Berkeley: Seal Press.

The Pew Charitable Trusts. 2010. *Collateral Costs: Incarceration's Effect on Economic Mobility*. Washington, DC: The Pew Charitable Trusts.

Warner, Carolyn. 2010. *The Words of Extraordinary Women*. New York: Newmarket Press.

Wolff, Michael. "Disorder in the Court." *New York Magazine*. October 27, 2003. Accessed May 15, 2011. http://nymag.com/nymetro/news/media/columns/medialife/n_9383/.

Woodward, Kath. 2011. "Body Politics: Masculinities in Sport." In *Global Masculinities and Manhood*, ed. Ronald L Jackson and Murali Balaji, 202–22. Urbana: University of Illinois Press.

Zinner, Lynn, and Nate Schweber. 2010. "Lawrence Taylor Charged With Rape." *New York Times*. May 6, 2010. Accessed May 15, 2011. http://www.nytimes.com/2010/05/07/sports/football/07taylor.html.

Web Sources

Correctional Services Canada. 2006. "Aboriginal Corrections Fact Sheet." Accessed May 12, 2011. http://www.csc-scc.gc.ca/text/pblct/qf/01-eng.pdf.

Chapter 10 The Strategies that Empower Us: Feminist Activism

Acker, Alison, and Betty Brightwell. 2004. *Off Our Rockers and Into Trouble: The Raging Grannies*. Victoria: Touch Wood Editions.

Ambinder, Marc. 2011. "Obama Won't Go to Court Over Defense of Marriage Act." *National Journal* (February): 23. http://www.nationaljournal.com/obama-won-t-go-to-court-over-defense-of-marriage-act-20110223. Accessed March 1, 2011.

Bobel, Chris. 2006. "'Our Revolution Has Style': Contemporary Menstrual Product Activists 'Doing Feminism' in the Third Wave." *Sex Roles* 54 (5–6): 331–45. http://dx.doi.org/10.1007/s11199-006-9001-7.

Borowy, Jan, Shelly Gordon, and Gayle Lebans. 2004. "Are These Clothes Clean? The Campaign for Fair Wages and Working Conditions for Home Workers." In *Feminisms and Womanisms: A Women's Studies reader*, ed. Althea Prince and Susan Silva Wayne, 301–317. Toronto: Women's Press.

Bromley, Victoria, and Aalya Ahmad. 2006. "Wa(i)ving Solidarity: Feminist Activists Confronting Backlash." *Canadian Woman Studies* 25 (3/4): 61–71.

Brownmiller, Susan. 1999. *In Our Time: Memoir of a Revolution*. New York: Dial Press.

Carlson, Marvin. 2004. *Performance: A Critical Introduction*. New York: Routledge.

Davis, Angela. 1981. *Women, Race and Class*. New York: Random House.

Demo, Anne Teresa. 2000. "The Guerrilla Girls' Comic Politics of Subversion." *Women's Studies in Communication* 23 (2): 133–56. http://dx.doi.org/10.1080/07491409.2000.10162566.

Dery, Mark. [1993] 2010. "Culture Jamming: Hacking, Slashing, and Sniping in the Empire of Signs." http://markdery.com/?page_id=154.

Diamond, Diana. 2009. "The Fourth Wave of Feminism: Psychoanalytic Perspectives." *Studies in Gender and Sexuality* 10 (4): 213–23. http://dx.doi.org/10.1080/15240650903228187.

Farrar, Margaret, and Jamie L. Warner. 2006. "Rah-Rah-Radical: The Radical Cheerleaders' Challenge to the Public Sphere." *Politics & Gender* 2 (3): 281–302. http://dx.doi.org/10.1017/S1743923X06060090.

Garrison, Ednie. 2000. "U.S. Feminism-Grrrl Style! Youth (Sub)Cultures and the Technologics of the Third Wave." *Feminist Studies* 26 (1): 141–70. http://dx.doi.org/10.2307/3178596.

Gillis, Stacy. 2007. "Neither Cyborg Nor Goddess: The (Im)Possibilities of Cyberfeminism." In *Third Wave Feminism: A Critical Exploration*, ed. Stacy Gillis, Gillian Howie, and Rebecca Munford, 185–198. New York: Palgrave Macmillan.

Gillis, Stacy, Gillian Howie and Rebecca Munford. 2007. *Third Wave Feminism: A Critical Exploration*. New York: Palgrave Macmillan.

Gillis, Stacy, and Rebecca Munford. 2004. "Genealogies and Generations: The Politics and Praxis of Third Wave Feminism." *Women's History Review* 13 (2): 165–82. http://dx.doi.org/10.1080/09612020400200767.

Granny Pat. 2011. Personal communication. Ottawa Chapter, Raging Grannies, March 3.

Gregory, Jill, April Lewton, Stephanie Schmidt, Diane "Dani" Smith, and Mark Mattern. 2002. "Body Politics with Feeling: The Power of the Clothesline Project." *New Political Science* 24 (3): 433–48. http://dx.doi.org/10.1080/0739314022000005455.

Hannah, Kathleen. 1991. "Riot Grrrl Manifesto." *Bikini Kill, Zine 2*. Republished: http://onewarart.org/riot_grrrl_manifesto.htm http://rebelgrrrl.wordpress.com/2010/02/24/the-riot-grrrl-manifesto/.

Henry, Astrid. 2004. *Not My Mother's Sister: Generational Conflict and Third-Wave Feminism*. Bloomington: Indiana University Press.

Hesse-Biber, Sharlene Nagy. 2012. *The Handbook of Emergent Technologies in Social Research*. Thousand Oaks, CA: SAGE Publications.

Kelly, Liz. 1988. *Surviving Sexual Violence*. Cambridge: Polity Press.

Kennedy, Florence. 1976. *Color Me Flo: My Hard Life And Good Times*. New York: Prentice-Hall.

Kinser, Amber. 2004. "Negotiating Spaces for/through Third-Wave Feminism." *Feminist Formations* 16(3): 124–53.

Mann, Susan, and Douglas Huffman. 2005. "The Decentering of Second Wave Feminism and the Rise of the Third Wave." *Science and Society* 69 (1): 56–91. http://dx.doi.org/10.1521/siso.69.1.56.56799.

Moraga, Cherríe, and Gloria Anzaldúa. (Original work published 1981) 1983. *This Bridge Called My Back: Writings by Radical Women of Color.* New York: Kitchen Table, Women of Color Press.

Narushima, Miya. 2004. "A Gaggle of Raging Grannies: The Empowerment of Older Canadian Women through Social Activism." *International Journal of Lifelong Education* 23(1): 23–42.

Orbach, Susie. (Original work published 1978) 1997. *Fat Is a Feminist Issue*. New York: BBS Publishing Corp.

Orr, Catherine. 1997. "Charting the Currents of the Third Wave." *Hypatia* 12 (3): 29–45. http://dx.doi.org/10.1111/j.1527-2001.1997.tb00004.x.

Purvis, Jennifer. 2004. "Grrrls and Women Together in the Third Wave: Embracing the Challenges of Intergenerational Feminism(s)." *NWSA Journal* 16 (3): 93–123. http://dx.doi.org/10.2979/NWS.2004.16.3.93.

Roy, Carole. 2007. "When Wisdom Speaks Sparks Fly: Raging Grannies Perform Humor as Protest." *Women's Studies Quarterly* 35 (3/4): 150–64.

Roy, Carole. 2004. *The Raging Grannies: Wild Hats, Cheeky Songs and Witty Actions for a Better World*. Montreal: Black Rose Books.

Roy, Carole. 2002. "The Transformative Power of Creative Dissent: The Raging Grannies' Legacy." In *Expanding the Boundaries of Transformative Learning: Essays on Theory and Praxis*, ed. Edmund O'Sullivan, Amish Morrell, and Mary Ann O'Connor, 257–272. New York: Palgrave.

Sawchuk, Dana. 2009. "The Raging Grannies: Defying Stereotypes and Embracing Aging Through Activism." *Journal of Women & Aging* 21 (3): 171–85. http://dx.doi.org/10.1080/08952840903054898.

Seely, Megan. 2007. *Fight Like a Girl: How to Be a Fearless Feminist*. New York: New York University Press.

Siegel, Deborah. 1997. "The Legacy of the Personal: Generating Theory in Feminism's Third Wave." *Hypatia* 12 (3): 46–75. http://dx.doi.org/10.1111/j.1527-2001.1997.tb00005.x.

Showden, Carisa R. 2009. "What's Political about the New Feminisms?" *Frontiers* 30 (2): 166–98. http://dx.doi.org/10.1353/fro.0.0056.

Snyder, Claire R. 2008. "What Is Third-Wave Feminism? A New Directions Essay." *Signs* 34 (1): 175–96.

Springer, Kimberly. 2002. "Third Wave Black Feminism?" *Signs* 27(4): 1059–82.

Swarr, Amanda Lock, and Richa Nagar, eds. 2010. *Critical Transnational Feminist Praxis.* Albany: State University of New York Press.

Thompson, Rachel. 2003. "Pom Poms, Not Bombs." *Herizons* 17 (1).

Turner, Chérie. 2001. *Everything You Need to Know About the Riot Grrrl Movement: The Feminism of a New Generation.* New York: Rosen Publishing Group.

Vaccaro, Jeanne. 2005. "Give Me An F: Radical Cheerleading and Feminist Performance." *Women & Performance: A Journal of Feminist Theory* 14 (2): 43–50. http://dx.doi.org/10.1080/07407700508571464.

Whittier, Nancy. 2006. "From the Second to the Third Wave: Continuity and Change in Grassroots Feminism." In *The U.S. Women's Movement in Global Perspective*, ed. Lee Ann Banaszak. Lanham, MD: Rowman, Littlefield Publishers.

Wrye, Harriet. 2009. "The Fourth Wave of Feminism: Psychoanalytic Perspectives Introductory Remarks." *Studies in Gender and Sexuality* 10 (4): 185–9. http://dx.doi .org/10.1080/15240650903227999.

Activism on the Web

Antidote: Multiracial and Indigenous Girls and Women's Network. http://www .antidotenetwork.org/.

Antigone Foundation. http://antigonefoundation.wordpress.com/.

Girls Action Foundation. http://girlsactionfoundation.ca/.

Feministing: Young Feminists Blogging, Organizing and Kicking Ass. Feministing. com.

Food Not, Bombs. http://www.foodnotbombs.net/.

Guerrilla Girls. 1989. http://www.guerrillagirls.com/posters/getnaked.shtml (accessed: February 7, 2012).

Guerrilla Girls, 2006. http://www.guerrillagirls.com/posters/unchained.shtml (accessed: February 7, 2012).

Miss G. Project. http://www.themissgproject.wix.com/index_new (accessed: February 7, 2012).

Pink Code. http://www.codepink.org/.

RebELLEs. http://www.rebelles.org/ (accessed: February 7, 2012).

Chapter 11 Still Struggling: Making Change

Amnesty International. 2004. *Stolen Sisters: Discrimination and Violence Against Indigenous Women in Canada.* AMR 20/001/2004. Accessed January 4, 2005. http:// www.amnesty.ca/stolensisters/amr2000304.pdf.

Arat-Koc, Sedef. 2006. "Whose Social Reproduction? Transnational Motherhood and Challenges to Feminist Political Economy." In *Social Reproduction: Feminist Political Economy Challenges Neo-Liberalism*, ed. Kate Bezanson and Meg Luxton, 75–92. Montreal: McGill-Queen's University Press.

Arthur, Joyce. 2009. "Women's Rights Are Not Up for Debate." Abortion Rights Coalition of Canada (ARCC). Accessed June 13, 2011. http://www.arcc-cdac.ca/ action/nodebate.html.

Arthur, Joyce. 2008. "Expect a Bill C-484 Clone Soon." Abortion Rights Coalition of Canada. December 2. Accessed November 3, 2011. http://www.arcc-cdac.ca/action/c484-clone.html.

Ayling, Russel, and Avril Mewse. 2011. "'It Kills Me To Be Too Safe': Gay Men's Experience of Internet Sex-Seeking and Barebacking." *Gay and Lesbian Issues and Psychology Review* 7 (2): 102–16.

Bailey, Alison. 2011. "Reconceiving Surrogacy: Toward a Reproductive Justice Account of Indian Surrogacy." *Hypatia* 26 (4): 715–41. http://dx.doi.org/10.1111/j.1527-2001.2011.01168.x.

Bakst, Dina, and Gary Phelem. 2010. "Happy Mother's Day: You're Fired!" Accessed June 12, 2010. http://www.ctpost.com/opinion/article/Happy-Mother-s-Day-You-re-fired-478425.php.

Banerjee, Swapnendu, and Sanjay Basu. 2009. "Rent a Womb: Surrogate Selection, Investment Incentives and Contracting." *Journal of Economic Behavior & Organization* 69 (3): 260–73. http://dx.doi.org/10.1016/j.jebo.2008.10.003.

Barndt, Deborah. 2002. *Tangled Routes: Women, Work, and Globalization on the Tomato Trail*. Lanham, MD: Rowman and Littlefield Publishers.

Beckman, Linda, and S. Marie Harvey. 2005. "Current Reproductive Technologies: Increased Access and Choice?" *Journal of Social Issues* 61 (1): 1–20. http://dx.doi.org/10.1111/j.0022-4537.2005.00391.x.

Benería, Lourdes. 2003. *Gender, Development, and Globalization: Economics as if all People Mattered*. New York,: Routledge.

Bernhard, Judith, Patricia Landolt, and Luin Goldring. 2005. "Transnational, Multi-Local Motherhood: Experiences of Separation and Reunification among Latin American Families in Canada." Early Childhood Education Publications and Research. Paper 6. Accessed April 2, 2010. http://digitalcommons.ryerson.ca/ece/6.

Binion, Gayle. 1995. "Human Rights: A Feminist Perspective." *Human Rights Quarterly* 17 (3): 509–26. http://dx.doi.org/10.1353/hrq.1995.0022.

Blount, Jackie M. 2000. "Spinsters, Bachelors, and Other Gender Transgressors in School Employment, 1850–1990." *Review of Educational Research* 70 (1): 83–101.

Borowy, Jan, Shelly Gordon, and Gayle Lebans. 2004. "Are These Clothes Clean? The Campaign for Fair Wages and Working Conditions for Homemakers." In *Feminisms and Womanisms: A Women's Studies Reader*, ed. Althea Prince and Susan Silva-Wayne, 303–316. Toronto: Women's Press.

Cavanagh, Sheila L. 2005. "Female-Teacher Gender and Sexuality in Twentieth-Century Ontario, Canada." *History of Education Quarterly* 45 (2): 247–73. http://dx.doi.org/10.1111/j.1748-5959.2005.tb00036.x.

Center for Reproductive Rights. 2011. "Reimposing the Global Gag Rule Threatens Women's Health and Lives, and Undermines Democracy." Center for Reproductive Rights. Accessed May 21, 2012. http://reproductiverights.org/sites/crr.civicactions.net/files/documents/fac_GGR_7.18.pdf.

Center for Reproductive Rights. 2003. *Breaking the Silence: The Global Gag Rule's Impact on Unsafe Abortion*. New York: Center for Reproductive Rights. http://reproductiverights.org/.

Chollet, Derek, and Robert Orr. 2001. "Carpe Diem: Reclaiming Success at the United Nations." *Washington Quarterly* 24 (4): 7–18. http://dx.doi.org/10.1162/016366001317149147.

Chuck, Anderson, and Charles Yan. 2009. "Assisted Reproductive Technologies: Economic Evaluation." Institute of Health Economics. Edmonton, Alberta.

Accessed: June 2, 2011. http://www.ihe.ca/documents/Assistive_Reproductive_Technologies.pdf.

CLC. 2006. Working Women: Still a Long Way from Equality. Canadian Labour Congress. http://www.canadianlabour.ca/sites/default/files/pdfs/EN-wage-gap-in-general_0.pdf.

CNN. 2011. "Annual Ranking of Fortune 500 Companies, Women CEOs." *CNNMoney.* May 23, 2011. Accessed June 10, 2011. http://money.cnn.com/magazines/fortune/fortune500/2011/womenceos/.

Collin, Chantal, and Hilary Jensen. 2009. "A Statistical Profile of Poverty in Canada." Social Services Division: Parliamentary Information and Research Service. September 28, 2009. Accessed May 3, 2011. http://www.parl.gc.ca/Content/LOP/ResearchPublications/prb0917-e.htm.

Correll, Shelley J., Stephen Benard, and In Paik. 2007. "Getting a Job: Is There a Motherhood Penalty?" *American Journal of Sociology* 112 (5): 1297–339. http://dx.doi.org/10.1086/511799.

Crane, Barbara, and Jennifer Dusenberry. 2004. "Power and Politics in International Funding for Reproductive Health: The US Global Gag Rule." *Reproductive Health Matters* 12 (24): 128–37. http://dx.doi.org/10.1016/S0968-8080(04)24140-4.

CRIAW (Canadian Research Institute for the Advancement of Women). 2011. "Violence against Women and Girls." Accessed May 23, 2011. http://criaw-icref.ca/ViolenceagainstWomenandGirls#_edn8.

Dana, Leo, Robert Hamilton, and Brooke Pauwels. 2007. "Evaluating Offshore and Domestic Production in the Apparel Industry." *Journal of International Entrepreneurship* 5 (3-4): 47–63. http://dx.doi.org/10.1007/s10843-007-0015-1.

Dean, Tim. 2011. *Unlimited Intimacy: Reflections on the Subculture of Barebacking.* Chicago: University of Chicago Press.

Deeb-Sossa, Natalia, and Heather Kane. 2009. "Not Avoiding a 'Sensitive Topic': Strategies to Teach about Women's Reproductive Rights." *NWSA Journal* 21 (1): 151–77.

Di Nicola, Kathi. 2011. "Planned Parenthood Files Suit to Protect Women's Health and Safety." Minnesota: Planned Parenthood Advocate. 27 May 2011. Accessed June 5, 2011. http://www.plannedparenthoodadvocate.org/2011/05/planned-parenthood-files-suit-to-protect-womens-health-and-safety-.html#more.

Eckholm, Eric. 2011. "Planned Parenthood Financing Is Caught in Budget Feud." *The New York Times.* February 17, 2011. Accessed March 3, 2011. http://www.nytimes.com/2011/02/18/us/politics/18parenthood.html.

Ehrenreich, Barbara, and Arlie Russell Hochschild, eds. 2003. *Global Woman: Nannies, Maids, and Sex Workers in the New Economy.* New York: Metropolitan Books/Henry Holt.

Enloe, Cynthia. 2004. *The Curious Feminist: Searching for Women in a New Age of Empire.* Berkeley: University of California Press.

Enloe, Cynthia. 2000. *Bananas, Beaches and Bases: Making Feminist Sense of International Politics.* Berkeley: University of California Press.

Gandy, Kim. 2007. "Ancient Laws, Current Consequences." Below the Belt, NOW. Accessed March 6, 2007. http://www.now.org/news/note/030607.html.

Gertzog, Irwin. 2004. *Women and Power on Capitol Hill: Reconstructing the Congressional Women's Caucus.* Boulder: Lynne Rienner Publishers.

Goldin, Claudia. 1988. "Marriage Bars: Discrimination Against Married Women Workers, 1920s to 1950s." National Bureau of Economic Research. Cambridge, MA. Accessed May 17, 2012. http://www.nber.org/papers/w2747.pdf?new_window=1.

Goldman, Russel. 2010. "Teacher Fired for Becoming Pregnant out of Wedlock." abcnews.go.com, June 11. Accessed June 15, 2010. http://abcnews.go.com/Business/Media/teacher-fired-pregnant-wedlock/story?id=10878802.

Government of Canada. 2011. "Backgrounder—New Maternal, Newborn and Child Health Initiatives." Office of the Prime Minister, Government of Canada. Accessed May 22, 2012. http://news.gc.ca/web/article-eng.do?nid=603569.

Greenberg, Judith. 1998. "The Pregnancy Discrimination Act: Legitimating Discrimination Against Pregnant Women in the Workforce." *Maine Law Review* 50 (2): 225–54.

Grinberg, Emanuella. 2012. "The Highs and Lows of Foreign Surrogacy." Accessed May 22, 2012. http://www.cnn.com/2012/03/29/living/sacred-thread-foreign-surrogacy/index.html.

Harper, Anita Olsen. 2006. "Is Canada Peaceful and Safe for Aboriginal Women?" *Canadian Woman Studies/Les Cahiers De La Femme* 25 (1–2): 33–38.

Harris, Lynn. 2010. "Female Heads of State: The Chosen Ones." *Glamour Magazine*. November 1, 2010. Accessed June 10, 2011. http://www.glamour.com/inspired/women-of-the-year/2010/female-heads-of-state.

Hartmann, Betsy. 1995. *Reproductive Rights and Wrongs: The Global Politics of Population Control*. Boston: South End Press.

Hodge, David, and Cynthia Lietz. 2007. "The International Sexual Trafficking of Women and Children." *Affilia: Journal of Women and Social Work* 22 (2): 163–74. http://dx.doi.org/10.1177/0886109907299055.

Hondagneu-Sotelo, Pierrette, and Ernestine Avila. 1997. "'I'm Here, but I'm There': The Meanings of Latina Transnational Motherhood." *Gender & Society* 11 (5): 548–71. http://dx.doi.org/10.1177/089124397011005003.

Israel, Betsy. 2002. *Bachelor Girl: The Secret History of Single Women in the Twentieth Century*. New York: William Morrow.

Jaiswal, Sreeja. 2012. "Commercial Surrogacy in India: An Ethical Assessment of Existing Legal Scenario from the Perspective of Women's Autonomy and Reproductive Rights." *Gender, Technology and Development* 16 (1): 1–28. http://dx.doi.org/10.1177/097185241101600101.

Jiwani, Yasmin, and Mary Young. 2006. "Missing and Murdered Women: Reproducing Marginality in News Discourse." *Canadian Journal of Communication* 31 (4): 895–917.

Kapel, Claudine. 2011. "Gender Wage Gap a Complex Issue." *HR Reporter*. May 2, 2011. Accessed May 18, 2012 http://www.hrreporter.com/blog/compensation-rewards/archive/2011/05/02/gender-wage-gap-a-complex-issue.

Kelly, Liz. 1988. *Surviving Sexual Violence*. Cambridge: Polity Press.

King, Samantha. 2007. "Designer Babies, Stem Cells, and the Market for Genetics: The Limits of the Assisted Human Reproduction Act." *Canadian Journal of Communication* 32 (3/4): 613–20.

Kirby, Jane. 2010. "Canada: Confronting the Rise of Anti-Choice Activities on University Campuses." *Briarpatch*. Accessed July 12, 2011. http://briarpatchmagazine.com/articles/view/freedom-of-hate-speech.

Kristof, Nicholas. 2007. "Birth without the Bother?" *The New York Times*. July 23. Accessed March 9, 2011. http://www.nytimes.com/2007/07/23/opinion/23kristof.html?th&emc=th.

Locin, Mitchell. 1991. "House Backs Bush Veto of Abortion Gag Rule." *Chicago Tribune*. November 20, 1991. Accessed March 12, 2011. http://articles.chicagotribune.com/1991-11-20/news/9104150131_1_veto-victories-override-gag-rule.

Lorde, Audre. 1997. *The Cancer Journals*. San Francisco: Aunt Lute Books.

McMullen, Kathryn, et al. 2010. "Women in Non-traditional Occupations and Fields of Study." Statistics Canada. Accessed June 20, 2011. http://www.statcan.gc.ca/pub/81-004-x/2010001/article/11151-eng.htm.

Mohammad, Shoaib. 2011. "The Legal Status of Surrogacy: A Global Scenario." *Pragyaan: Journal of Law* 1 (1): 6–16.

Morris, Mike, and Justin Barnes. 2009. *Globalization, the Changed Global Dynamics of the Clothing and Textile Value Chains and the Impact on Sub-Saharan Africa.* United Nations Industrial Development Organization (UNIDO). Accessed June 13, 2011. https://www.unido.org/fileadmin/user_media/Publications/Pub_free/Globalization_changed_global_dynamics_of_clothing_and_textile_value_chains_and_impact_on_subSaharan_Africa.pdf.

Mukhopadhyay, Maitrayee, and Navsharan Singh. 2007. *Gender Justice, Citizenship and Development.* Ottawa: International Development Research Centre.

Native Women's Association of Canada (NWAC). 2011. *Sisters in Spirit.* Accessed June 5, 2011. http://www.nwac.ca/programs/sisters-spirit.

Nicholson, Melanie. 2006. "Without Their Children: Rethinking Motherhood among Transnational Migrant Women." *Social Text* 24 (3 88): 13–33. http://dx.doi.org/10.1215/01642472-2006-002.

NOW. "Women Deserve Equal Pay." Accessed May 18, 2011. http://www.now.org/issues/economic/factsheet.html#endref1.

Pande, Amrita. 2010. "Commercial Surrogacy in India: Manufacturing a Perfect Mother-Worker." *Signs* 35 (4): 969–92. http://dx.doi.org/10.1086/651043.

Pilkington, Ed. 2011. "Outcry in America as Pregnant Women Who Lose Babies Face Murder Charges." *The Guardian.* 24 June 2011. Accessed June 27, 2011. http://www.guardian.co.uk/world/2011/jun/24/america-pregnant-women-murder-charges.

QMI Agency. 2010. "Canada Gender Pay Gap among Worst In OECD." Monday, March 08, 2010. Accessed March 15, 2011. http://www.torontosun.com/money/2010/03/08/13155136.html.

Rennison, Callie Marie. 2002. *Rape and Sexual Assault: Reporting to Police and Medical Attention, 1992–2000.* Washington, DC: U.S. Bureau of Justice Statistics, U.S. Department of Justice, NCJ 194530.

Schumacher, Rob. 2005. "Pregnant Workers Report Growing Discrimination." *USA Today*, February 16. Accessed June 12, 2010. http://www.usatoday.com/money/workplace/2005-02-16-pregnancy-bias-usat_x.htm.

Sen, Gita, Piroska Östlin, and Asha George. 2007. *Unequal, Unfair, Ineffective and Inefficient: Gender Inequity in Health: Why It Exists and How We Can Change It.* Antigonish, NS: WHO Women and Gender Equity Knowledge Network, National Collaborating Centre for Determinants of Health. Accessed March 2012. http://www.who.int/social_determinants/themes/womenandgender/en/index.html.

Shepherd, Laura. 2010. *Gender Matters in Global Politics: A Feminist Introduction to International Relations.* New York: Routledge.

Smith, Andrea. 2005. "Beyond Pro-Choice Versus Pro-Life: Women of Color and Reproductive Justice." *NWSA Journal* 17 (1): 119–40. http://dx.doi.org/10.2979/NWS.2005.17.1.119.

Sweetman, Caroline, ed. 2005. *Gender and the Millennium Development Goals.* Oxford: Oxfam Great Britain.

Tjaden, Patricia, and Nancy Thoennes. 2006. *Extent, Nature, and Consequences of Rape Victimization: Findings from the National Violence Against Women Survey.* Washington, DC: Bureau of Justice Statistics, U.S. Department of Justice, NCJ 210346.

Triunfol, Marcia. 2003. "Barebacking and Bug Chasers: Expressions of an HIV Subculture." *AIDScience* 3 (4). Accessed June 4, 2011. http://aidscience.org/Articles/aidscience030.asp.

UNAIDS. 2010. *Global Report: UNAIDS Report on the Global AIDS Epidemic, 2010. Joint United Nations Programme on HIV/AIDS*. UNAIDS.

United Nations. 1979. *Convention on the Elimination of All Forms of Discrimination Against Women (CEDAW)*. United Nations. http://www.un.org/womenwatch/daw/cedaw/text/econvention.htm.

United Nations. 1995. *Beijing Declaration and Platform for Action*. The United Nations Fourth World Conference on Women. Beijing, China. http://www.un.org/womenwatch/daw/beijing/platform/plat1.htm.

U.S. Department of Labor. 2010. "Leading Occupations of Employed Women 2010." U.S. Department of Labor, Bureau of Labor Statistics. Accessed June 20, 2011. http://www.dol.gov/wb/factsheets/20lead2010.htm.

U.S. District Court of South Dakota. 2011. *PPMNS v. State of South Dakota*. Case 4: CIV. 11–4071-KES, document 39, filed 06/30/11. Accessed August 30, 2011. http://msnbcmedia.msn.com/i/MSNBC/Sections/NEWS/AbortionOrder.pdf.

Walby, Sylvia. 2009. *Globalization and Inequalities: Complexity and Contested Modernities*. Los Angeles,: Sage Publications.

Walker, Rebecca. 2009. *One Big Happy Family*. New York: Riverhead Books.

WHO. 2008. *Unsafe Abortion: Global and Regional Estimates of the Incidence of Unsafe Abortion and Associated Mortality in 2008*. New York: World Health Organization.

WHO. 2012. *Trends in Maternal Mortality: 1990 to 2010, WHO, UNICEF, UNFPA and the World Bank Estimates*. New York: World Health Organization.

Web Sources

G(irls)20 Summit. http://www.girlsandwomen.com/.

Global Exchange. http://www.globalexchange.com/.

Maquila Solidarity Network. http://en.maquilasolidarity.org/.

UNIFEM. 2010. "Violence Against Women Fact Sheet." Accessed May 23, 2011. http://www.unifem.org/campaigns/sayno/docs/SayNOunite_FactSheet_VAWworldwide.pdf.

INDEX